Nobody
Left Behind

Nobody
Left Behind

Insight into
"End-Time" Prophecies

David Vaughn Elliott

Methuen, Massachusetts

Nobody Left Behind: Insight into "End-Time" Prophecies

ISBN 0-9754596-0-0
Library of Congress Control Number: 2004094742

Cover design by Jeffrey Johnson

Published in Methuen, Massachusetts
Requests for information should be addressed to:
David Vaughn Elliott
36 Oakland Ave # 8
Methuen, MA 01844-3783
email: insight2bp@earthlink.net

On the Internet, visit:
http://www.nobodyleftbehind.net
http://insight2bp.homestead.com

Printed in the United States of America

Contents

Illustrations

Preface

Nobody Left Behind: Insight into "End-Time" Prophecies is much more than a reaction to the popular "Left Behind" novels by Tim LaHaye and Jerry Jenkins. *Nobody Left Behind* offers a detailed study of some of the most exciting prophecies of Scripture: the destruction of Jerusalem in A.D. 70, the rise of the Antichrist, and the arrival of God's kingdom on earth, among others. These prophecies are examined with an open Bible and open history books. In view of such evidence, a critique of the "Left Behind" series is also offered.

The origins of *Nobody Left Behind* can be traced to the 1960's when I began to teach and preach on prophecy, especially Daniel and Revelation. I have preached series of sermons and taught advanced classes on prophecy in New York, Massachusetts, North Carolina, Puerto Rico, El Salvador, Guatemala, and Belarus. The written form of this book began in 1996, when I wrote an article entitled "Why Study Prophecy?" This article was the first in a series of articles involving the Bible and prophecy that appeared in the quarterly publication *The Sword and Staff*. The series ran through 2002.

In the fall of 1998, I began *Insight into Bible Prophecy*, a semimonthly e-mail newsletter utilizing old writings as well as new material. Within a year of initiating *Insight*, I set up my own Internet web site on which all *Insights* to date are archived.

During these years, my articles have found their way into various other periodicals, pamphlets, and websites. Several times I have received requests to put my articles into book form. The present work is the result. In writing the book, I have revised much of the older material and added whole chapters that have not previously appeared in print.

To the extent that *Nobody Left Behind* is a critique of the popular "Left Behind" novels, it is based on several sources. I have examined the authors' fold-out chart, "A Visual Guide to the Left Behind Series." It gives their brief outline of Revelation, showing where each novel of the series fits in. More importantly, I have carefully considered Tim LaHaye's newest Revelation commentary, *Revelation Unveiled*. This updated edition appeared in 1999, and it is offered, as expressed on the back cover, as "The biblical foundation for the best-selling Left Behind series." In addition, I have digested novel #1 of the series, *Left Behind, A Novel of the Earth's Last Days,* which introduces most of the leading characters and issues. I have also read #2 of the series, *Tribulation Force.* Reading the remaining novels is unnecessary. Since I am not examining the novels as literature but rather as they relate to Bible truth, Tim LaHaye's Revelation commentary is a more important source for critiquing than the novels themselves.

Nobody Left Behind will guide the reader in an examination of the "biblical foundation" for the "Left Behind" series. This "foundation" is a view of Bible prophecy called *futurism,* a term defined in Chapter 1, "Prophecy via Fiction." In this book, I also examine other popular sources of futuristic teaching. The important consideration is not one set of novels, but rather the popular view of biblical prophecy underlying these novels.

My hope is that *Nobody Left Behind* will provide the reader with compelling biblical and historical evidence that various "end-time" prophecies have already been wonderfully fulfilled. This view, commonly called the *historical view* or *historicism,* was the most popular view among believers for centuries before the twentieth century. A study of God's fulfilled prophecy can be a very enriching experience. It is my desire to aid the reader in his or her own quest for greater insight into Bible prophecy while striving to reach a better understanding of it myself.

David Vaughn Elliott
Methuen, Massachusetts
July 2004

Acknowledgments

In the process of seeking to better understand God's prophetic Word, I am much indebted to the early Christian writers—from the second century onward—for their confirmation of the teachings in the Bible and for their insight into many of the Bible's predictions. Among other things, many of them recognized they were actually living during the fourth empire predicted by Daniel. As for authors of more recent times, I have gained much insight and information from Thomas Newton, E. B. Elliott, Albert Barnes, B. W. Johnson, John T. Hinds, Henry H. Halley, and Ralph Woodrow among others.

Regarding the motivating factors that resulted in the writing of this book, I am indebted to James Gibbons, editor of *The Sword and Staff,* for graciously inviting me to write a series of articles on Bible prophecy for his quarterly paper. The response of his readers was quite favorable; several requested that my articles be put into book form. Similar requests have come from readers of my email *Insights* and from brethren who have heard my teaching and preaching on prophecy. All this interest and encouragement strongly motivated me to publish this present work.

I am much indebted to those who with patience and care went over the entire manuscript once or twice or whatever time it took. They located typographical errors, corrected grammar, told me how to say what I wanted to say, pointed out inconsistencies, improved arguments, improved the flow of thought, improved my tone in dealing with those I disagree with, suggested additional points to include, and suggested items to leave out. They are Margaret Elliott, my beloved wife, Lois Elliott, our daughter-in-law, David L. Elliott, our son, and John McDonald. Some may think family members could not objectively criticize, correct, and improve my writing; however, they proved to be keen editors. They offered insightful corrections and suggestions in abundance, each according to their individual expertise. I

9

am most grateful to each one of them for their input and aid, as well as their time, care, and encouragement.

In addition to those who worked over the entire manuscript, I also received the gracious help of a number of brethren in the Northboro, Mass., church: Dennis Steward, Donna LaLiberty, Jesse Jakubiak, Jim Drake, Joel Jansson, Laura Frick, Paul and Barbara Gorham, and Paul Barber. They each worked on several different chapters during the two months I preached a prophecy series there on Wednesday evenings. They offered many helpful corrections and improvements as well as strong support. I enjoyed working with them.

Numerous brethren, all of whom I could not name now, aided with many helpful ideas for both the title of the book and the design of the front cover. My thanks go to Jeffrey Johnson for using well his professional graphics skills in the development of the cover design. I appreciate all the work of my son David in making my rough charts and other illustrated pages far more attractive and understandable. In addition, I am thankful for Rafael Moreno and Bill and Sandy McLaughlin. When the work on the book seemed endless, they kindly urged me to continue with my original plan to include the indexes, knowing that many readers would expect them and benefit from them. Besides her work on the manuscript already mentioned, Margaret was a constant help in countless ways, not the least of which was the laborious task of manually keyboarding all the index entries. Computer indexing software was a great help, but software without human input can do nothing.

My greatest debt of all is to Almighty God, His Son Jesus Christ, and His Holy Scriptures. Whatever merit may be in this work, it is above all due to the great themes that the Ruler of the universe has presented in His Word coupled with the amazing fulfillments that He has brought about throughout history. To the extent that my message faithfully reflects His message, the glory and credit are His.

Section One

Getting Started in Prophecy

Chapter 1

Prophecy via Fiction

The "Left Behind" novels captured the imagination of the nation, shattering all-time best-seller records. These are not ordinary novels. Whereas historical novels are built on the past, these "prophecy novels" are built on the future. Whereas science fiction is built on confidence in how science will shape the future, "prophecy fiction" is built on confidence in how God will shape the future. The authors of the "Left Behind" series, Tim LaHaye and Jerry Jenkins, believe their novels are true to biblical end-time prophecies that are soon to be fulfilled.

There is much to be commended in the "Left Behind" series. The authors uphold the Bible as the inspired Word of God. They present Jesus of Nazareth as the only one who can save us from our sins. They strongly urge all people to be ready for the return of Christ. They clearly believe spiritual matters take precedence over material concerns. They are opposed to marital infidelity—even in the mind. They are opposed to superficial religion. In a pleasure-loving, materialistic age, we need strong reminders of our spiritual nature and spiritual needs. We need a call to the Bible, a call to Jesus, a call to prepare for the next life. In many ways, that is the call given in this series of novels.

Good Fiction?

There are those who believe the "Left Behind" novels are terrific. They rapidly read each one and could hardly wait for the sequel to come off the press. Indeed, there are those who tell of their lives being changed by these novels. They tell of Bible prophecy becoming more real to them. They tell of "accepting Christ" because of reading them.

Others take a dim view of the literary value of the "Left Behind" series. They consider the novels to be unimpressive, more fantasy than true-to-life fiction. They consider them to be poorly written with unrealistic scenarios, even if they accept the miraculous elements and the underlying view of prophecy. Be that as it may, the question of how these novels rank as literature can be left to the literary critics.

The Real Issue

The important matter is not the literary merits of the "Left Behind" series. What does matter is the biblical foundation of the novels. What does matter is whether the prophetic view behind these novels is fact or fiction. Are these novels based on God's truth? Are they true to the Bible?

While the "Left Behind" series is relatively new with the first novel appearing in 1995, the underlying concepts of the series are not new. Before the "Left Behind" series, Hal Lindsey held the spotlight as the number-one popular advocate of Bible prophecy. His fame began with the success of *The Late Great Planet Earth* published in 1970. Before Hal Lindsey, the most popular voice was the *Scofield Reference Bible*. Today, prophecy novels and videos of end times are "hot," including three dozen volumes in the "Left Behind: The Kids" series.

All these works have one thing in common: *futurism*. Futurism is a prophetic point of view that says the fulfillment of a vast array of Bible prophecies is yet in our future. Futurism says most of the book of Revelation foretells events yet in our future. Futurism says the Antichrist, the Great Tribulation, and the Millennium are yet in our future.

Nobody Left Behind is not only a critique of the "Left Behind" series, it is a critique of futurism in general. In addition to examining futurism, it aims to present the historical interpretation of several great prophecies of Scripture—prophecies which are often thought to be end-time prophecies, but which upon examination can be seen to have already been wonderfully and powerfully fulfilled. The fulfillments are a part of history, not something to anticipate in the future.

This immediately removes the excitement for many people. While many of us find history boring, we may be easily captivated by the frightening predictions of secular and religious doom prophets. We may eat up their predictions like a "good" horror movie. It is this type of excitement that makes the futurist approach irresistible to many believers.

Scripture posts an alert concerning the things we enjoy listening to:

> For the time will come when they will not endure sound doctrine, but according to their own desires, because they have itching ears, they will heap up for themselves teachers; and they will turn their ears away from the truth, and be turned aside to fables (2 Tim. 4:3-4).

As captivating as the "Left Behind" series may be, Scripture exhorts us to examine whether the prophetic view of the series is "truth" or "fable."

Many believers are unaware that futurism is only one of several ways to look at Bible prophecy. In fact, in centuries gone by, the popular viewpoint of Bible believers was very different from what it is today. It is the aim of *Nobody Left Behind* to deepen the believer's understanding of some of these great prophecies of the Word of God—or at least to open searching eyes to alternative interpretations.

Methods of Interpreting Prophecy

Nobody Left Behind is written with the average person in mind. It is not filled with technical "theological" terms, nor does it attempt to dissect and evaluate the multitude of varying views on prophecy that exist in today's world. A few paragraphs will be sufficient to simply name and identify the major prophetic views that a person may encounter.

The main term used throughout *Nobody Left Behind* to express the prophetic view of the "Left Behind" series is *futurism*. The *futurist* view says that great quantities of Bible prophecy, in both the Old and New Testaments, have yet to be fulfilled.

The opposite of the futurist view is the *preterist* view. *Preterism,* in its fullest expression, claims that all Bible prophecy was fulfilled by A.D. 70, with the destruction of Jerusalem. Other preterist views believe that most Bible prophecy was fulfilled by the time of the fall of the Roman Empire in A.D. 476. These moderate preterist views, like non-preterist views, believe Jesus' return, the general resurrection, and the final judgment are yet to be fulfilled in our future.

Between the two extremes of futurism and preterism is *historicism*. The *historical* view holds that fulfillment of Bible prophecy has been taking place throughout the history of the world. Historicism agrees with preterism that much Bible prophecy was fulfilled in ancient times. Historicism agrees with futurism that there are important prophecies yet to be fulfilled. Yet historicism differs from both preterism and futurism because it maintains that there is a considerable body of Bible prophecy that has been and is being fulfilled during the present Church Age, from the time John wrote Revelation until Jesus returns.

Of these three views, the most popular one in evangelical circles is futurism. Most of the radio preaching on prophecy and most of the prophecy books for sale today expound the futurist view. The "Left Behind" series is simply the most recent and most popular expression of what has been the popular view among evangelicals for perhaps a century.

There are also three views concerning the one thousand years (millennium) mentioned in Revelation 20. The first, *premillennialism*, which literally means before the Millennium, expresses a belief in a future literal thousand-year reign of Christ on earth. The *before* (pre-) refers to the belief that Christ will return before that thousand-year reign. The most popular premillennialist view today is called *dispensationalism*. In addition to a future literal thousand-year reign of Christ, dispensationalism believes that the Rapture will take place seven years before the Millennium and that the events of the Millennium will be centered around the Jews, Jerusalem, and a rebuilt temple.

An opposite view is called *postmillennialism*, which holds that Christ will return *after* (post-) the Millennium. Postmillennialism believes that the entire world will gradually be Christianized through the work of the church in preaching God's Word. It is believed this process will bring about a glorious period of peace that will culminate in the return of Christ.

A third view is commonly called *amillennialism* because it believes that there will *not* (a-) be any millennium— literally or physically, that is. This view holds that the "thousand years" of Revelation 20 is a figurative expression for an unspecified, long period of time. Amillennialism says we are now living in the figurative "thousand years" predicted. To express it another way, this view equates the kingdom of God with the church of Jesus Christ. It does *not* look forward to a literal physical reign of Christ upon the earth. Rather, it places emphasis on the present spiritual reign of King Jesus as Head of His church.

The prophetic view that is by far the most popular today is at the same time futuristic and dispensational. This is the only view that large numbers of church members have ever heard of, even if they are not acquainted with those terms. When you read the term *futurism* in this book, you can interpret it as *"futuristic-premillennial-pretribulational-dispensationalism."*

Nobody Left Behind will not belabor the multitude of technical terms and variations of views that exist today. To the extent that this book is a critique, it will deal with today's most widespread popular view of prophecy in evangelical circles. In striving for simplicity for the average person, the terms *futurism* and *futurist* seem to be the most logical, inclusive, comprehensible, and acceptable terms to use in referring to that popular view.

The Issue and the Issues

The issue is whether futurism is true to the Bible. The issue is whether the "Left Behind" series presents a possible scenario of what the Bible teaches about end times. The issue is whether many prophecies that the novels assume are end-time have already been fulfilled.

This basic issue may be broken down into numerous sub-issues. Those sub-issues are the theme of Chapter 2, "Introducing the Issues," which will give an overview of what to expect in the remainder of *Nobody Left Behind: Insight into "End-Time" Prophecies*.

Chapter 2

Introducing the Issues

What if "end-time" prophecies are not end time at all? What if many of these significant prophecies have already been fulfilled—and we missed them? What if we are vainly looking into the future for what is already in the past?

It may be more exciting to imagine future scenarios than to dust off the history books and read about events of yesteryear. We may choose to enjoy an adrenaline surge from being alarmed about the future rather than suffer the boredom of studying history.

Society today is attracted to instantaneous coverage of news around the globe. We are even more attracted to predicting what the news will be tomorrow. Did you ever notice how much "news analysis" is not an analysis of the news at all? Rather, the time is spent trying to second-guess coming events. If bad times are being predicted, it is even more provocative. We seem to take pleasure in worrying about the future.

It is time to divest ourselves of the excitement generated by conjuring up future scenarios. More specifically, it is time to resist the thrill of imagining startling future fulfillments of Bible prophecies when those prophecies have already been fulfilled. It is time to look at Bible prophecy in its context. It is time to seriously consider that, inasmuch as the last book of the Bible was written nearly two millennia ago, it is quite possible that many of its prophecies have already been fulfilled.

When studying Bible prophecy, we need to look at the context in which individual prophecies were given. In search of the fulfillment of any particular prophecy, we need to *begin* looking in the days when the prediction was made. From there, we move forward in time until we find the fulfillment. It makes no sense whatsoever to ignore two thousand years of history and to begin our search for fulfillment in today's newspapers. By carefully examining the last two millennia, it quickly becomes clear that many so-called, end-time prophecies already have been gloriously fulfilled.

What follows is an overview of the major issues to be discussed in *Nobody Left Behind.* Each issue is briefly presented and reference is made to the chapter that deals in depth with that particular issue. We begin now where the "Left Behind" series begins—with the Rapture.

The Rapture

Most would agree that the return of Jesus is an end-time topic. However, does the Word of God give any hint of the futurist concept—airplanes without pilots, cars without drivers, and trains without engineers causing eerie fatal accidents all over the globe? So begins the plot of the "Left Behind" series. This Rapture theory captivates the imagination of many people. I have heard real-life cases in which someone did not find family members where and when they fully expected to find them. Their immediate reaction was to panic—imagining that the Rapture had taken their family away and left them behind. The fact that anyone in real life would react this way shows how strongly many believe in the Rapture doctrine.

However, the scene of crashing planes and cars (or ships and chariots) is found nowhere in the Bible. The major unproven premise of the Rapture doctrine is that after Jesus secretly snatches away the believers, life will continue on earth more or less as we know it. This doctrine says that there will be multitudes of people left behind who will be totally ignorant of what caused the disappearances. Can such ideas be found anywhere in the Bible? Or are such ideas fiction? The issue is not simply that the "Left Behind" series is written and sold as fiction. The issue is whether the supposed biblical basis for the series is an accurate one.

Will Jesus return? Absolutely! Will believers be caught up to meet Him in the air? Absolutely! Will the dead arise from their graves? Absolutely! Will there be a separation of the saved from the lost? Absolutely! Will the world continue on when all this happens? No! The Bible paints no such picture.

In no place does the Word of God depict a "left behind" scene. Nowhere in Scripture does it teach that life on earth will continue after Jesus returns. In no text of the Bible can anyone find a hint of people in the world trying to deal with the problem of multitudes having disappeared. Nowhere in the Bible do we find driverless cars crashing into guardrails, driverless chariots crashing into walls, husbands frantically searching for wives who have mysteriously disappeared, or unborn babies evaporating from their mothers' wombs. Such scenarios are neither mentioned nor hinted at in any verse in the Bible.

Someone might quote Matt. 24:40: "Then two men will be in the field: one will be taken and the other left." However, what happens then? Look at the context by reading the two preceding verses: "Marrying and giving in marriage, until the day that Noah entered the ark, and did not know until the *flood came and took them all away,* so also will the coming of the Son of Man be" (24:38-39, italics mine). The flood took away the wicked! Righteous Noah and his family were left behind! "So also will the coming of the Son of Man be." Nobody left behind but God's saints!

That sounds like the very opposite of the Rapture doctrine.

To delve more deeply into Bible teaching that relates to the Rapture, study Chapter 15, "The Rapture."

Seven-year Tribulation

The plot of the entire "Left Behind" series takes place during a supposed seven-year Tribulation in the future. This seven-year period is a major element of today's futurist doctrine. It is seen as the period of time between the Rapture (the starting point of the novels) and Jesus' return to earth, which ushers in the Millennium (the ending point of the novels). It is believed that the seven-year Tribulation will be broken into two parts, with the second half being the Great Tribulation.

What is the biblical basis for this widely accepted view? Although many texts are involved, the claimed foundation of this view is located in the seventy-weeks prophecy of Daniel 9. This is made clear in Chapter 13 of Tim LaHaye's *Revelation Unveiled,*[1] as well as in most futurist works that deal with the topic. LaHaye initiates each chapter of his commentary with a topical title and a mention of the verses of Revelation he will discuss in that chapter. The title of his Chapter 13 is "The Tribulation Period," and the text given is Dan. 9:24-27.

The seventy-weeks prophecy is one of the most awesome prophecies regarding the *first* coming and great work of our Messiah, Jesus Christ. Futurism admits that Daniel 9 provides the date for the Messiah's coming. Daniel 9 prophesies that the Messiah will come before the destruction of Jerusalem (which happened in A.D. 70), thereby putting all Israel on notice today—if they would have ears to hear—that the Messiah has already come. Daniel 9 outlines the redemptive work of the Messiah in cleansing us from our sins. It teaches that God has put an end to the sacrificial system of the Jerusalem temple, replacing it with the sacrifice of Jesus on Calvary. It teaches that with the arrival of the Messiah and the destruction of Jerusalem, God would be finished dealing with Israel as His holy people; God would be finished dealing with Jerusalem as His holy city.

Chapter 5, "The Jews' Time Has Run Out," and Chapter 6, "Jesus Fulfilled God's Timetable," offer comprehensive studies of these remarkable themes.

Did God's Clock Stop?

The chronology of the seventy-weeks prophecy is so outstanding that the prophecy usually is identified by reference to that time period. Literally, seventy weeks is 490 days. A literal 490 days offers no fulfillment of anything. This is fine for those who reject the Bible as the inspired Word of God. In contrast, all believers of every category accept the reality that we must regard these 490 days as symbolic. Some consider them symbolic in a general non-numerical sense emptying them of all chronological value. However, the futurist and historical views agree that the key in Ezek. 4:6 is to be applied to this prophecy: "I have laid on you a day for each year"—a day for a year. Using this key, 490 days is understood as symbolic of 490 years.

Thus, futurism accepts a non-literal interpretation of one of the leading elements of this prophecy. Futurism agrees with the historical view that the 490 years is roughly the historical span of time between the rebuilding of Jerusalem and the first coming of the Messiah.

If that were the whole story, there would be no problem. However, what futurism actually does is transform the accepted 490 years into nearly 2,500 years! How does futurism do this? By placing a two thousand year gap between the first sixty-nine weeks and the final week of the prophecy. Consequently, even though the futurist method claims to be the literal method of interpretation, in this key text futurism transforms seventy weeks into more than 350 weeks!

Of course, futurism does not explain it that way. Futurism says, "God stopped the prophetic clock"—never mind the fact that "prophetic clock" itself is not a literal expression. More importantly, Scripture nowhere mentions such a clock.

Did God really have to change His plans? Was the fulfillment of outstanding prophecies put on hold? This whole issue is worthy of the extensive study found in Chapter 9, "Did God Stop the Prophetic Clock?"

Literal or Figurative?

What the futurist view does with the seventy weeks offers insight into their claim that futurism interprets the Bible in general, and prophecy in particular, in its literal sense. The claim of literal interpretation is expressed by Tim LaHaye this way: "For the most part, all who believe the Bible to be literal are premillennialists ... Only in taking the Bible other than literally can a person be anything but a premillennialist."[2] This is the uniform claim of futuristic premillennialism. However, futurism's interpretation of the seventy weeks shows that it does not live up to its own claim of literalism.

Not taking the prophecy literally is fine; however, by not doing so, futurism negates its claim that literal interpretation is the basis of the futuristic-premillennial viewpoint. In fact, if students read enough, they will come across many examples of futurism explaining symbolic elements in prophecy. It is true that futurism takes more elements literally than do many other prophetic views. However, the implication that the trouble with these other views is that they spiritualize prophecy is not in accord with reality. All methods of Bible interpretation take some parts literally and other parts figuratively, symbolically, or spiritually.

The question for futurism and all views is this: How do you decide which elements to take literally and which to take figuratively? Chapter 3, "Prophecy: Literal or Figurative?" documents many elements which the "literalists" take figuratively. More importantly, this chapter offers guidelines to help us determine which way we should interpret individual Scriptures, prophecy included.

The Tribulation

Will Christians go through the Tribulation? Today's

common reply is the one given in the "Left Behind" series: "No." For many believers, the principal hope involved in the Rapture is escaping the Tribulation. Indeed, the thrill of the "Left Behind" novels is not the Rapture itself but rather the contemplation of what happens to those unfortunate people who missed the Rapture. Those people enter the Tribulation. According to the initial novel of the series, some of those left behind are quickly converted, and they form themselves into a "Tribulation force" to fight the evil expected during the Tribulation. *Tribulation Force* then becomes the title of the second book in the series.

There is much misunderstanding today regarding what Scripture teaches about tribulation. Many believers assume "tribulation" refers to a time yet in our future. They do not question it. They only have questions about its nature and timing. Tribulation becomes mainly a curiosity to those who fully expect to be raptured away before the Tribulation begins.

Is this a correct view of Bible teaching on tribulation? Jesus prophesied and promised, "In the world you will have tribulation" (John 16:33). Jesus suffered for us, and He declares here in John that we will suffer—have tribulation—for Him. When the apostle John wrote the book of Revelation, which is claimed to be the basis of the "Left Behind" series, John said, "I, John, both your brother and companion *in the tribulation*" (1:9, italics mine). John was already "in the tribulation"! "The tribulation" was not two thousand years in the future. The Scriptural teaching on tribulation will be explored in much detail in Chapter 4, "Which Tribulation?"

"Great Tribulation"

The futurist viewpoint would respond to the above by saying: Yes, we have tribulation now, but we are speaking of "the Great Tribulation." The common belief is that the Great Tribulation is the second half of the Tribulation. However, Scripture teaches *three* "great" tribulations—not just one—

and they are all in our past, not our future. To gain greater insight into this interesting topic, study Chapter 8, "Three Great Tribulations."

As will be seen in Chapter 8, one of the "great" tribulations is that which transpired in A.D. 70 when the Roman armies devastated Jerusalem and its temple. Today's popular prophetic viewpoint gives scant attention to the earth-shaking events of A.D. 70. Nevertheless, this is one of the most significant fulfillments of Bible prophecy. To miss this is to miss not just a fulfillment of prophecy, but some vital truths regarding God's relationship to Israel and Jerusalem. To push Daniel 9 and Matthew 24 almost totally into our future completely changes the prophetic and doctrinal land-scape of much of the Word of God. In addition to most of the chapters already mentioned, see Chapter 7, "Not One Stone upon Another," for further study of the events of A.D. 70.

Rebuilt Temple

There is much talk today about rebuilding the temple in Jerusalem. Conservative evangelicals talk about it as much as orthodox Jews do, if not more. Many evangelicals today join with elements of the Jewish population in a fervent desire and expectation of seeing Israel gain full control of the Temple Mount so this dream may become a reality. Since a rebuilt temple in Jerusalem is a major factor in futurist doctrine, it naturally finds its way into the "Left Behind" series, even being mentioned several times in the first book of the series.

What does Scripture say about the rebuilding of the temple in Jerusalem in modern times? Nothing! No Scrip-ture predicts a rebuilding of the temple in our day. The temple was destroyed in A.D. 70, and there is no text that predicts a rebuilding after that date.

Since there is no such Scripture, where does the idea originate? Among other things, it comes from two New Testament prophecies of a temple—one in 2 Thessalonians 2 and the other in Revelation 11. Futurism claims that since these two prophecies speak of a temple, the Jewish Jerusalem temple must be rebuilt so these predictions can be fulfilled.

This claim, however, ignores a very important fact. When Messiah Jesus died on Calvary, the God of heaven tore in two the veil of the temple, which separated the Holy Place from the Holy of Holies. In this way, God boldly declared that He was finished with that temple. Forty years later Almighty God sent the Romans to totally obliterate that temple from the face of the earth; God was finished with it. The perfect sacrifice for sin had replaced it.

Following Jesus' death, the New Testament speaks of another temple, which is now the temple of God. Study this issue more thoroughly in Chapter 11, "Man of Sin—the Prophecy." In particular, see the section, "Which 'Temple of God'?"

"The Antichrist"

Most students of Scripture, both past and present, see a connection between the man of sin of 2 Thessalonians 2, the little horn of Daniel 7, and the beasts in Revelation 13 and 17. From ancient times, these outstanding prophecies have usually been lumped together under a common title—"the Antichrist."

Some believers object to applying the term "antichrist" to the texts mentioned. They point out that the term "antichrist" is found only in John's epistles, and that antichrist has no connection to the beasts of Daniel and Revelation or to the man of sin of Thessalonians. They further notice that John says, "Even now many antichrists have come" (1 John 2:18). This causes them to believe it is improper to speak of "the" Antichrist.

Indeed, John does refer to many antichrists. However, upon careful reading of John's three epistles, there is no verse where John denies the coming of "the" Antichrist. The complete text of 1 John 2:18 reads: "Little children, it is the last hour; and as you have heard that the Antichrist is coming, even now many antichrists have come, by which we know that it is the last hour." John explains that there are already many antichrists. However, he does *not* deny "the Antichrist is coming." He simply explains that there are more than one, and that many are already present. He does *not* dispute the concept that one particular outstanding Antichrist is yet in *their* future. Consider this issue at length in Chapter 13, "Man of Sin—the Reality," in the section, "Antichrist?"

Although there are indeed many antichrists, the descriptions of the enemy of God in the texts previously mentioned definitely describe the major Antichrist of all time. Whenever the Antichrist is mentioned in commentaries or in fiction, the authors generally have in mind a composite view of the enemy of God predicted in Daniel 7, Revelation 13 and 17, and 2 Thessalonians 2. Therefore, as Bible students, we must ask ourselves if what the commentaries and novels say about the Antichrist is in agreement with these texts. Some of the initial questions to investigate are these:

1. Is the Antichrist past, present, or future?

2. Is the Antichrist one individual or a group of individuals?

3. What is the relationship between the Antichrist and "the temple of God"?

4. Is the Antichrist primarily a political or a religious figure?

The "Left Behind" series in particular and futurism in general maintain that the Antichrist is one man in *our* future who will have important connections to a rebuilt Jewish temple in Jerusalem. With 2 Thessalonians 2 as the basis, these questions and more are explored extensively in the three chapters dealing with the man of sin: Chapters 11, 12, and 13.

Antichrist's Seven-year Pact with Israel

Another important element of the futurist doctrine is the idea that the Antichrist will make a seven-year pact with

Israel. The very first volume of the "Left Behind" series mentions this idea several times. There seems to be only one text in the Bible that is claimed as the source for this idea. As LaHaye says in his *Revelation Unveiled*: "Daniel 9:27 indicates that the Antichrist will make a covenant with Israel for seven years."[3]

However, note what Dan. 9:27 and the context do *not* say:

1. No antichrist is mentioned. Verse 27 speaks only of "he." Who is this "he"? Futurism looks back to verse 26 where it says that the city of Jerusalem will be destroyed by "the people of the prince who is to come." Futurism agrees that verse 26 is predicting the destruction in A.D. 70 by the Romans under Titus. The disagreement is about "the prince who is to come." In the context, it would be Titus. Futurism, however, with no warrant from the context, says this refers to the future Antichrist. On the contrary, Daniel 9 has nothing whatsoever to do with any antichrist. It first has to do with the real Christ. It secondly has to do with the punishment that God would bring upon the Jewish nation because of their rejection of the real Christ.

2. Verse 27 says nothing about *making* a covenant. It says, "he shall *confirm* a covenant with many for one week" (italics mine). This contradicts futurism's own teaching. Futurism teaches that the Antichrist will *break* the covenant in the middle of the week, whereas the prophecy says that he (whoever) will "confirm" the covenant for one complete week.

3. Daniel 9 says nothing about a *second* rebuilding of the temple to take place after the prophesied destruction. The futurist interpretation holds that the destruction mentioned in verse 26 took place in A.D. 70, whereas the destruction in verse 27 is still in the future. In order to get such a future destruction, futurism invents a two thousand year gap between verses 26 and 27. In addition, it envisions a rebuilding of the temple sometime during that gap. However, Daniel 9 says nothing about such a gap and nothing about a second rebuilding.

Futurism reads many things into Daniel 9 that simply

are not there. This turns the prophecy into something that it is not. This approach misses wonderful truths that God revealed to Daniel. For a clearer understanding of the seventy-weeks prophecy of Daniel 9, consult the entire "Section Two: The Great Tribulation of A.D. 70."

The Roman Connection

Most Bible believers agree that Daniel, Thessalonians, and Revelation make predictions about Rome. A major reason for this agreement is the interpretation of Nebuchadnezzar's dream in Daniel 2. The awesome image he saw forms the basis for several prophecies that follow, especially in Daniel 7 and Revelation 13 and 17. According to Scripture and history, the succession of empires predicted is unquestionably Babylon, Medo-Persia, Greece, and Rome.

LaHaye refers to various details of the Roman connection in his *Revelation Unveiled*. However, in *Left Behind, A Novel of the Earth's Last Days,* #1 of the "Left Behind" series, LaHaye barely acknowledges the Roman connection. He gives Nicolae Carpathia, the future Antichrist in the novels, Roman ancestry—that is all. Any connection to the Roman Empire is totally lost.

In the last half of the twentieth century as the European Union was emerging, futurists followed the news closely and claimed the rebirth of the Roman Empire was imminent. It was said that the ten horns of Daniel 7 and Revelation 13 and 17 would be realized in the ten nations that would make up the European Union. For example, Hal Lindsey wrote in his best-selling *The Late Great Planet Earth*:

> We are beginning to see the Ancient Roman Empire draw together, just as predicted . . . We believe that the Common Market and the trend toward unification of Europe may well be the beginning of the ten-nation confederacy predicted by Daniel and the Book of Revelation.[4]

What is now the European Union began in 1950 with six

countries. In 1973, three years after Lindsey wrote, the number increased to nine. In 1981, the tenth member was added—just right for the futurist theory. However, the process did not stop there. In 1986, two more members were added. By 1995, there were fifteen members. More recently, after years of preparation and anticipation, the largest increase ever made became history. Ten more countries were added on May 1, 2004, making a total of twenty-five member countries.

Therefore, it comes as no surprise that in Tim LaHaye's *Revelation Unveiled* we find no mention of a "revived Roman Empire." LaHaye clearly identifies the first beast in Revelation 13 with the Roman Empire, and then he explains regarding the seven heads: "They represent five kings up to the time of John; the sixth, Domitian, was the Roman king at the time of John, who then skips forward to the end time for the seventh head, the Antichrist."[5] "Skips forward to . . . the Antichrist." With this fictitious break of more than nineteen hundred years, only lip service is paid to Rome. Any meaningful connection to Rome is totally obliterated.

What a difference it would make if people would close their novels and open their history books. For more insight into the historical fulfillment of the Roman connection, read Chapter 10, "Why Rome?" and Chapter 12, "Man of Sin—the History."

The Mark of the Beast

People in general give free rein to their imaginations when conjuring up scenarios involving "the mark of the beast." Most assume this mark relates to end times. Once again, the excitement of predicting the future takes precedence over the drudgery of studying history. Consider the thoughts presented in Chapter 14, "666: the Mark of the Beast," and keep in mind that since the beast is related to Rome, the mark of the beast must also somehow be related to Rome.

The Kingdom and the Church

Another major issue involved in the futurist method of interpretation is the nature of Jesus' church and the nature of the kingdom of God. Although this issue does not have a major place in the plot of the "Left Behind" series, the underlying concept is always there—after the Rapture and the Tribulation, Jesus will return to earth to establish the Millennium, a thousand-year physical kingdom. The issue is not simply that futuristic premillennialism affirms Jesus will come before the Millennium. The issue is whether there will be a literal millennium at all. The issue is whether God's kingdom is still in the future *or* if the kingdom of God is a present reality.

What does the Bible teach about the nature of the kingdom? What does the Bible teach about when the kingdom is supposed to arrive? Is the kingdom here now? Is the church the kingdom? Is the "thousand years" of Revelation 20 to be understood literally or figuratively? To investigate these issues, read Chapter 16, "The Millennium is *Not . . .*," and Chapter 17, "Jesus Revealed the Nature of the Kingdom."

Nobody Left Behind?

What exactly is meant by the title of *this* book: *Nobody Left Behind*? The entire "Left Behind" series is built on the unproven assumption that when Jesus comes, saints will be taken away and sinners will be left behind. The term "left behind" carries the idea that life here on this planet will continue its normal course. Yes, people will be greatly disturbed. Yes, the Tribulation will be around the corner. However, those left behind will continue to eat, sleep, work, marry, divorce, give birth, die, shop, fly in airplanes, and watch TV. That is the underlying assumption of the whole Rapture theory.

The title of this book, *Nobody Left Behind*, bears witness to a very different view of end times. The view proposed in this book and accepted by many believers today is that when it is over, everything is over. It is the belief that Jesus is coming only one more time. It is the belief that when He does come, the world as we know it will be finished. It is the belief that when Jesus comes, time will be no more—no seven years, no thousand years, no time at all. Eternity will have arrived. For a Scriptural study of this vital topic, see Chapter 19, "Nobody Left Behind."

The title *Nobody Left Behind* in no way implies that everyone in the world will be raptured to be with Jesus in heaven. Neither does the title imply that all the wicked will be blotted out of existence when Jesus comes for the saints. Instead, the title is an affirmation that when Jesus comes it will be too late to make a decision to follow Him; it will be too late to reconsider. The title is an affirmation that there will be no . . .

Second Chance

One of the most important questions anyone can ask is this: After the Rapture, will unsaved people have a fresh opportunity to get right with God? Will Jesus' invitation for salvation still be open? The message of the "Left Behind" series is a resounding, "Yes!" In fact, the title of the second book in the "Left Behind: The Kids" series is exactly that: *#2: Second Chance*. In the same manner, the fourth book in the adult series announces the doctrine of second chance by its very title, *Soul Harvest*. This is no side issue. Tim La-Haye introduces his comments on Revelation 7 with this amazing declaration: "The greatest revival the world has ever known is yet to come. It will not occur within the Church Age but during the Tribulation period."[6]

The popular futurist view interprets "He who now re-strains" in 2 Thess. 2:7 as the Holy Spirit. The teaching goes somewhat like this: The influence of the Holy Spirit in the church today is what keeps the man of sin from taking over the world. It further states that after the church is taken out of the world by the Rapture of all the saints, the man of sin will be able to deceive those who remain. LaHaye, however, in his commentary on Revelation 7, openly refutes this common belief of his fellow futurists. He states that the outpouring of the Holy Spirit on Pentecost, A.D. 30, was only a small token fulfillment of Joel 2. He claims that the real fulfillment will take place during the Tribulation.[7]

Does the Rapture indeed open the way for the greatest soul harvest the world has ever seen? If I miss the Rapture, is there still a chance for me to get my life right with God? Chapter 19, "Nobody Left Behind," will examine the biblical perspective of how we should view the return of Christ in relationship to our personal salvation.

The Salvation Prayer

Speaking of salvation brings us to the most important issue in the "Left Behind" series. Virtually all those who believe the Bible is the inspired, inerrant, final message of God to man also believe that Jesus died for our sins and that there is no salvation apart from His shed blood. Nevertheless, there is widespread debate regarding man's part in the salvation process. The ideas range from "saving oneself by good works" to "there is nothing you can do." Probably most believers position themselves somewhere between these two extremes.

Repeatedly, co-authors LaHaye and Jenkins make their view plain in the "Left Behind" series. For them, salvation involves a personal decision to receive Christ and pray for salvation. For example, consider this portion from Chapter 12 of Book #1 of the series: "If you accept God's message of salvation, his Holy Spirit will come in unto you and make you spiritually born anew . . . You can become a child of God by praying to him right now as I lead you."[8]

The hope of the authors is to lead many people to Christ before the Rapture. However, are people being led to Christ or are they unintentionally being diverted from Christ? This question is not asked lightly. Does the Word of God say, "They who receive Christ and pray the sinner's prayer shall be saved"? Chapter 18, "The 'Salvation Prayer,'" offers a Scriptural answer to this life and death question.

How This Book is Organized

Nobody Left Behind: Insight into "End-Time" Prophecies is divided into four sections:

"Section One: Getting Started in Prophecy,"
"Section Two: The Great Tribulation of A.D. 70,"
"Section Three: The Roman Connection,"
"Section Four: From Here to Eternity."

Section One contains general introductory material. The aim of the other sections is to study selected Bible prophecies at length—first and foremost to present my understanding of the correct interpretation of these prophecies, and secondly to examine the claims of today's popular futurist viewpoint, of which the "Left Behind" series is a major example.

Open Mind and Open Bible

If the views presented in this book are new to you, I ask that you give them honest consideration. May the good Lord help us all to have the attitude of the Jews of Berea when they heard the teaching of the apostle Paul: "These were more fair-minded than those in Thessalonica, in that they received the word with all readiness, and searched the Scriptures daily to find out whether these things were so" (Acts 17:11). My desire is to exalt, understand, and correctly explain the Holy Word of God. I urge you to accept whatever you find in this book that agrees with Scripture. On the other hand, I urge you to reject as the teaching of a fallible man whatever you find in this book that is not in harmony with God's revealed Word. Let God's Word have the last word.

Caution:

"The simple believes every word, but the prudent considers well his steps."   (Prov. 14:15)

"Test all things; hold fast what is good."   (1 Thess. 5:21)

They "searched the Scriptures daily to find out whether these things were so."   (Acts 17:11)

Do not believe this book or any book unless you test it with Scripture.

Chapter 3

Prophecy: Literal or Figurative?

Does the Bible mean what it says? Should we take it at face value? Should we interpret it literally, or should we understand it figuratively (symbolically, spiritually)? Few questions are more important in the study of Bible prophecy.

NOT "EITHER-OR"

Is the Bible history or poetry? Both! Do Bible laws apply to us today or not? Both! Does the Bible contain the word of God or the word of the devil? Both! (If that does not sound right, see Luke 4:6.) Is the Bible easy or hard to understand? Both!

There are many things in life that cannot be forced into an "either-or" situation. So it is with Bible interpretation. Should we understand Bible prophecy literally or figuratively? The answer can be given in one word: both!

Much of the Bible is Literal

The Bible is a book of real people. Many of them are known in secular history: Ahab, Jehu, Hezekiah, Nebuchadnezzar, Pontius Pilate, the Herods, Caesar Augustus, John the Baptist, James the Lord's brother, to name a few.

The Bible is a book of real places. It tells of Babylon, Egypt, Samaria, Syria, Edom, Rome, and more. It takes us to the Euphrates and Jordan Rivers, to the Red Sea and the Sea of Galilee.

Real people in real places: a true, literal history of God's dealings with mankind. Since the Bible is solidly set in history, Bible interpretation should *begin* with the literal meaning.

Many prophecies of the Bible are likewise to be understood literally. When Abraham's visitors told him that Sarah would shortly have a son, Sarah laughed. Why? It was impossible; she was past menopause. However, with God all things are possible. He fulfilled it literally (Gen. 18:9-15; 21:1-7).

God foretold that if the children of Israel disobeyed him, they would experience miserable sieges of their cities. They would be driven to the extreme of eating their own children! That was literally fulfilled (Deut. 28:45-57; 2 Kings 6:24-29).

Centuries before Christ, Isaiah prophesied that a voice would one day cry out in the wilderness. Such was the unusual literal location of John the Baptist's ministry (Isa. 40:3; Matt. 3:1-5). Zechariah prophesied that the King of the Jews would enter Jerusalem on a donkey. It was literally fulfilled (Zech. 9:9; John 12:12-16).

We should start reading the Bible like a book of history with a literal meaning. The Bible tells us that God created Adam and Eve, that they sinned by eating the forbidden fruit, that God destroyed the world with a flood, that Jesus died on the cross, and that He arose again. Once God is seen as the Creator of the universe, miraculous events make as much sense as ordinary events. We take both types of events literally.

Bible prophecy, like other portions of the Bible, should often be understood literally.

Much of the Bible is Figurative

The problem among Bible believers today is not whether

we should understand much of the Bible literally. Believers accept that, but some talk as if *all* the Bible should be taken literally.

Tim LaHaye, in *Revelation Unveiled,* claims: "For the most part, all who believe the Bible to be literal are premillennialists."[1] Such a statement is misleading. Nobody believes all the Bible to be literal as the statement appears to imply. Neither is a literal interpretation of much of the Bible the determining factor in the decision of a person to adopt futuristic premillennialism. The issue is not as clear-cut as the statement seems to indicate.

The reality is that, like Tim LaHaye, many of us believe much of the Bible to be literal. No question. The question is whether the Bible is also filled with much figurative language. Elsewhere, LaHaye himself recognizes this. The following is only a partial list of items for which LaHaye gives figurative interpretations in the early pages of his Revelation commentary (page numbers given):

- "Seven denotes perfection" (29)
- Seven churches represent "divisions of church history" (35)
- Jesus' golden sash "refers to a symbol of strength" (38)
- "A key is a symbol of release" (41)
- "He who has an ear" "could not refer to physical ears" (49)
- "Ten days" refers to "ten periods of persecution" (52)
- The double-edged sword "refers to the Word of God" (60)
- The white stone is a "symbol of the eternal acquittal" (64)
- Woman is "used symbolically to convey a religious teaching" (70)
- Fornication is "a symbol of the idolatry brought in" (70)
- Key of David is a "reference to the authority of Christ" (80)
- John's "elevation to heaven is a picture of the Rapture" (99)
- "John obviously represents the Church" (100)[2]

This sampling is most enlightening. First, it demonstrates that futuristic premillennialism does not interpret all of prophecy literally. Secondly, several of the things that futuristic premillennialism views figuratively, historicism views as literal! For example, the historical view says the seven churches of Revelation are seven literal churches, not seven divisions of church history. The historical view affirms that John is John, not the church. The historical view holds that John going to heaven at the time of the vision is actually John going to heaven, not in any way a symbol of the Rapture of the church. These examples are the very opposite of futurism's claim to literalism. Historicism interprets literally many things futurism interprets figuratively! Futurism does not interpret all the book of Revelation literally. Nobody does! Neither does futurism interpret all of the Bible literally. Nobody does! Everybody interprets some expressions literally and others figuratively.

It is very instructive to look at Tim LaHaye's excellent "golden rule of interpretation": "When the plain sense of Scripture makes common sense, seek no other sense." Excellent. He continues: "Take every word at its primary . . . literal meaning unless . . ." Then he gives various situations that require a non-literal meaning.[3] The essence of his helpful, though complicated, rule is this: take the literal meaning unless the situation calls for a non-literal meaning. Excellent.

We start Bible interpretation with the literal meaning, but not even the "literalists" remain there. Mr. LaHaye's rule includes the words "when" and "unless" precisely because it is not always true that "the plain sense of Scripture makes common sense."

The "golden rule of interpretation" highlights an important fact: Despite seeming claims to the contrary, futurism admits it does not interpret the Bible literally. Similar to other views, futurism interprets some of it literally and some of it figuratively.

It does not require much Bible reading for anybody to discover figurative language. For instance, consider Jesus' parables: the sower, the net, the ten virgins, the vineyard, and the pearl of great price. Who can doubt that they must all be interpreted figuratively? Examine, for example, Jesus' claim, "I am the vine." Taken literally, this makes no sense at all. It must be understood figuratively or spiritually. Likewise, to say that a four-legged mammal could overcome God's saints in war does not make sense literally. Thus, the beast in Revelation 13 must be a figure of a great power. The Bible is full of such language.

The Psalms declare that God is our rock, our shield, and our fortress. Who does not understand that these are figures of speech? Paul said: "I fed you with milk and not with solid food"; "I planted, Apollos watered." No one believes that Paul was literally a nursemaid or a farmer.

The question is not whether the Bible—and its prophecy—should be taken literally or figuratively. The real question is this: What parts are literal and what parts are figurative? The question for the believer is not whether we should start with the literal understanding. Certainly we should! The question is this: How can we tell when certain words, phrases, or verses are to be understood figuratively?

COMMON SENSE

Why not start with everyday common sense? Daily conversation is filled with figurative language. Dad says, "You kids quit raising the roof." What do you think would happen to the youngster who replied, "Dad, come take a look; the roof hasn't been raised one inch"?

"I'm up to my neck in debt." "Don't be a pig." "We were flying down the highway." "I had butterflies in my stomach." Common sense. No one has to explain these figures to anyone—except to a child. Did you ever notice how often small children are confused because grown-ups speak figuratively, and the child takes it literally? However, as children grow up, they catch on.

What is *common sense,* anyway? It is the sense you would expect an ordinary person to have. A person of normal intelligence. A person with a reasonable amount of knowledge about life.

Exactly how is common sense applied to determine if a

statement is literal or figurative? Take "raising the roof" for example. A person of common intelligence and experience knows that kids cannot lift a roof by yelling; it is impossible. Therefore, the expression must be figurative. When words taken literally involve self-contradiction, absurdity, or unreality, then it is time to consider a figurative meaning.

Common Sense and the Bible

Jesus spoke of two men—one with a speck in his eye, the other with a plank in his eye. However, it is not physically possible to have a plank in one's eye. Conclusion? Jesus was speaking figuratively; He was revealing spiritual truth. On another occasion He said, "If your right eye causes you to sin, pluck it out" (Matt. 5:29). Jesus did not mention two eyes, just one; but did you ever hear of anybody who sinned with just one eye? "I'll cover my left eye and lust after this woman with just my right eye." Absurd? Yes. Therefore, it must be figurative or symbolic language.

The Gospel of John contains the famous "I am's" of Jesus: "I am the bread" (6:35), "I am the light" (8:12), "I am the door" (10:9), "I am the vine" (15:5). Have you ever heard of anyone who has a problem with these assertions? Yes, we may dispute the precise meanings Jesus was trying to express, but nobody would claim that Jesus meant He was a literal door or vine. That is totally unreal. Whenever we first heard these statements, our common sense immediately told us Jesus was speaking figuratively or spiritually.

On the other hand, unbelievers often use the common-sense rule to argue against miracles. They say it does not make sense that someone could walk on water; it goes against common sense to record that a touch of the hand could give sight to a man born blind; and it is absurd to say that a virgin could give birth to a child. However, it must be understood that these arguments are based on the supposition that there is no God who is intervening in the affairs of this world. That is a very different topic—a worthy one—but completely outside the realm of this book.

The Bible is full of figurative language.

"Hypocrite! First remove the plank from your own eye, and then you will see clearly..."
– Jesus

It is not a question of whether we should interpret the Bible literally or figuratively.

THE QUESTION IS:

1 - Which parts are literal, and
2 - Which parts are figurative?

Nobody Left Behind is written with the assumption that God exists and that He is the real Author of the Bible. Once we accept God in the picture, miracles are entirely possible.

Using common sense, therefore, in the interpretation of the Bible should not be confused with having a materialistic mind-set. Using common sense does not mean that we humans know more than God does. Using common sense means to approach the Bible with the minds God has given us. God does not ask us to serve Him with a blind faith. God does not expect us to close our minds when approaching Him. On the contrary, God invites us: "Come now, and let us reason together" (Isa. 1:18).

Common Sense and Prophecy

Turning to prophecy, it is important to note that no one interprets all prophecy literally, not even the very people who sometimes appear to claim it is all literal. Common sense is part of the reason.

Everyone agrees that the beasts of Revelation 13 and 17 are symbolic. With a wild imagination, someone might think a literal beast could have seven heads (13:1) and maybe even talk (13:5). However, no adult imagination is wild enough to accept13:7 as referring to a literal beast: "It was granted to him to make war with the saints and to overcome them. And authority was given him over every tribe, tongue, and nation." Imagination fails. Common sense says the beasts represent some human powers.

Prophecies often mention stars. For example, Rev. 6:13 says: "And the stars of heaven fell to the earth, as a fig tree drops its late figs when it is shaken by a mighty wind." Yet, in verses 15 and 16, the earth and its people still exist. This is literally impossible. Stars are huge. If just one star collided with the earth, the earth would be obliterated but the star hardly affected. Thus, the student must look for a figurative explanation.

Common sense tells us the beasts of Revelation represent some human powers, but what powers? Common sense tells us the stars in Revelation 6 cannot be literal heavenly bodies. In the same way that we speak of movie stars, maybe the stars of Revelation 6 are notable people, but what people? Common sense can help us see that we must look for a figurative or spiritual interpretation to a prophecy. It may even give an initial idea of what is meant. A beast seems to represent some power. A star seems to represent someone important. However, this is not to suggest that common sense alone will provide the interpretation of a prophecy. We will usually need considerably more information to determine the exact interpretation of the figures in prophecy.

THE BIBLE TELLS ME SO

"Jesus loves me, this I know; For the Bible tells me so." In like manner, many times we can say, "The text is figurative, this I know; for the Bible tells me so." What surer ground than to let the Bible interpret itself!

Simile: "like," "as"

Formal classes in language arts sometimes explore *figures of speech*. Some of the examples already given are called metaphors. In a metaphor, something is said to *be* something else. It was more forceful for Jesus to say, "I am the door" (a *metaphor*), than to say, "I am like a door" (a *simile*). To recognize a metaphor, one must use common sense. On the other hand, a simile uses *like* and *as* to make comparisons, plainly declaring itself a figure of speech

Ps. 44:22 says: "We are accounted as sheep for the slaughter." *As* sheep. Matt. 23:27 reads: "Woe to you, scribes and Pharisees, hypocrites! For you are like whitewashed tombs which indeed appear beautiful outwardly, but inside are full of dead men's bones." *Like* whitewashed tombs. These are similes.

Another figure of speech, the parable, may be defined as an extended simile. "The kingdom of heaven is like . . ." The entire account that follows "like" is figurative language.

Interpretation Given

Often the Bible does more than simply say that certain language is figurative; it often interprets the figure. Parables are an example. In some cases, an account is identified as a parable but no meaning is given. In other cases, the meanings of the various figures in the parable are explained: "He answered and said to them: 'He who sows the good seed is the Son of Man. The field is the world, the good seeds are the sons of the kingdom, but the tares are the sons of the wicked one'" (Matt. 13:37-38).

The book of Revelation opens with a vision of Christ. He is standing in the midst of seven lampstands and has seven stars in his hand. Are the stars literal or figurative? He himself answers in 1:20: "The seven stars are the angels of the seven churches, and the seven lampstands which you saw are the seven churches." The identity of these angels is not clear, but there is no question about the seven churches. They are named in 1:11; the Bible has explained the figure.

Prophetic Figures Explained

Figurative prophecy did not begin in Revelation. It began in Genesis! Pharaoh had a dream that he did not understand. He summoned Joseph, who explained:

> God has shown Pharaoh what He is about to do: The seven good cows are seven years . . . And the seven thin and ugly cows which came up after them are seven years, and the seven empty heads blighted by the east wind are seven years of famine (Gen. 41:25-27).

Prophecy utilized figurative language—and explained it—in the very first book of the Bible.

As we have seen, common sense says that beasts in prophecy are figurative, but figures of what? An example is found in Dan. 8:20-21: "The ram which you saw, having the two horns—they are the kings of Media and Persia. And the male goat is the kingdom of Greece." The Bible itself identifies the beasts in these verses as nations or empires.

One time in the temple Jesus foretold his resurrection. The Jews totally misunderstood Him because they thought He was speaking literally. John 2:19-21 explains:

> Jesus answered and said to them, 'Destroy this temple, and in three days I will raise it up.' Then the Jews said, 'It has taken forty-six years to build this temple, and will You raise it up in three days?' But He was speaking of the temple of His body.

This prophecy was *not* about the literal temple where they were standing, even though a person would logically think that. In this case, Jesus spoke of "this temple" in a figurative sense referring to His own body. How do we know? The Bible says so.

On the day of Pentecost, Peter explains a prophecy that in part is figurative. He quotes Psalm 16 where David is speaking: "I . . . my . . . me." To be literally fulfilled, it must refer to David himself. Rather, Peter carefully shows that David was not speaking of himself but of Jesus, his physical descendent (Acts 2:25-32). This prophecy seems to be literally speaking of David; however, it is figuratively speaking of Jesus. Peter explains and proves this figurative interpretation of this Psalm.

"Stars" as Important People

Common sense has shown that stars in prophecy are sometimes figurative. Figures of what? In any ordinary English dictionary, at least one meaning of "star" has to do with people. Outstanding people are stars: football stars, movie stars, and the star of the show. One dictionary explains: "Anyone who shines prominently in a calling or profession."[4] Stars shine. They stand out.

Thus, in the English language, "star" does not necessarily mean a heavenly body that twinkles at night. Nor in the Bible. In fact, as early as Genesis, the sun, moon, and eleven stars are used in Joseph's prophetic dream to represent people (Gen. 37). His father Jacob understood the sun represented himself and the stars represented his other eleven sons.

The prophecy in Dan. 8:8-10 says a little horn of the goat became so great that it threw stars down to the ground. Since Gabriel tells us the goat and ram represent two nations (8:20-21), the obvious conclusion is that these stars represent important people in some enemy nation.

The stars in Rev. 1:16, 20 have already been seen to be angels (messengers). Whether they are heavenly angels or human messengers, these stars are living beings as in Genesis. In Rev. 6:13, it says, "the stars of heaven fell." As we have seen previously, this cannot be interpreted literally. We must accept that this prophecy deals with the fall of prominent leaders.

To make a proper interpretation of star prophecies, we must always take into account the possibility that the prophecy is dealing with important people and not with the stars that twinkle at night. This figurative use of stars in the Bible agrees with our modern English usage. The ancient Bible is not as strange as we sometimes make it out to be.

FULFILLED PROPHECY

The Bible contains clear examples of prophecies that were literally fulfilled. For example, Jeremiah predicted that the desolation of Jerusalem would be seventy years. This was literally fulfilled (Jer. 29:4-10; 2 Chron. 36:19-23).

The Bible likewise contains prophecies that were clearly fulfilled in a figurative sense. Long after He was literally baptized by John, Jesus said, "I have a baptism to be baptized with, and how distressed I am till it is accomplished!" (Luke 12:50). This never happened literally. However, in Mark 10:38-39 Jesus connected this baptism with a cup He had to drink. What cup? Later in Gethsemane, Jesus pled with the Father, "Take this cup away from Me; nevertheless, not what I will, but what You will" (Mark 14:36). This cup and baptism were symbolically or spiritually fulfilled in Jesus' overwhelming suffering from Gethsemane to Calvary. It was a "cup" like drinking medicine. It was a "baptism" because He was overwhelmed, immersed in suffering.

How can we tell beforehand if a prophecy will be fulfilled literally or figuratively? That may be very difficult, and we need to exercise extreme caution not presuming to know what we do not know. Unless the Word of God itself gives us some clear indications, how can we know? In the past, God has fulfilled some prophecies literally and some figuratively. God certainly has the prerogative to fulfill them either way in the present and in the future. Therefore, we should exercise great caution when dealing with prophecies yet unfulfilled.

God's first command to man serves as an example. God said of the tree of the knowledge of good and evil, "In the day that you eat of it you shall surely die" (Gen. 2:17). A literal, common-sense approach would dictate that the punishment would be literal, physical death during that literal day of twenty-four hours. However, Adam and Eve did not physically die on the literal day they ate. Since God does not lie, we are forced to recognize some figurative or spiritual fulfillment. Was God speaking of spiritual death? Was God using the word "day" in some broad sense? Did God mean they would become mortal—capable of dying—the day they ate? Whichever explanation a person prefers, a literal, physical interpretation of both "day" and "die" simply did not happen. Thus, the very first prophetic warning in the Bible at least partially had a figurative or spiritual fulfillment. It becomes clear that before a prophecy is fulfilled, we must not presumptuously teach that it will be fulfilled literally or that it will be fulfilled figuratively or spiritually.

On the other hand, once a prophecy has been fulfilled—albeit figuratively—there is no Scriptural justification for expecting a future literal fulfillment as well. To do so puts one in the position of denying the fulfillment that has already taken place. This is of utmost importance in the study of many New Testament teachings relating to prophecy. There are numerous examples of Old Testament prophecies that are explained in a figurative or spiritual sense in the New Testament. The New Testament declaration of the fulfillment of an Old Testament prophecy is an inspired interpretation of that prophecy. How can we reject that inspired interpretation with a claim that it must still be literally fulfilled? The following examples of Elijah, John the Baptist, and God's kingdom are more than examples—they are a study of inspired interpretations of some very significant Old Testament prophecies.

The Prophecy Concerning Elijah

Four hundred years before Christ, the Old Testament closes thus:

> Behold, I will send you Elijah the prophet
> Before the coming of the great and dreadful day of the LORD.
> And he will turn
> The hearts of the fathers to the children,
> And the hearts of the children to their fathers,
> Lest I come and strike the earth with a curse (Mal. 4:5-6).

Elijah is coming! Is this supposed to have a literal fulfillment—Elijah himself is coming, even though he had long since departed this world? Or, is this to be understood figuratively (symbolically, spiritually)—someone like Elijah is coming? There is nothing in the context to indicate one way or the other. Therefore, we might assume it is literal, unless God clearly tells us otherwise.

Matt. 17:10-13 is a key text:

> And His disciples asked Him, saying, "Why then do the scribes say that Elijah must come first?" Jesus answered and said to them, "Indeed, Elijah is coming first and will restore all things. But I say to you that Elijah has come already, and they did not know him but did to him whatever they wished" . . . Then the disciples understood that He spoke to them of John the Baptist.

John himself, however, proclaimed the opposite: "This is the testimony of John, when the Jews sent priests and Levites from Jerusalem to ask him, 'Who are you?' . . . 'Are you Elijah?' He said, 'I am not'" (John 1:19, 21).

Who was right? Jesus or John? The angel Gabriel had already solved the problem before John was born: "Elizabeth will bear you a son, and you shall call his name John . . . He will also go before Him in the spirit and power of Elijah, 'to turn the hearts of the fathers to the children'" (Luke 1:13, 17). The last expression is a direct quotation of the prophecy in Malachi. Therefore, Gabriel is saying that John the Baptist is the fulfillment of this prophecy about Elijah.

Gabriel said that John came "in the spirit and power of Elijah." With this insight, we can harmonize the statements of Jesus and John. Jesus was saying that, yes, John was the fulfillment of the Elijah prophecy. John was saying that, no, he was not Elijah—physically. We can only surmise why John answered this way. On the other hand, it is unnecessary to guess about Jesus' and Gabriel's statements. Gabriel and Jesus agree: The prophecy was not intended to be fulfilled literally; it was intended to be fulfilled figuratively or spiritually. Gabriel gives the key: "in the spirit and power of Elijah."

Many prophecies of the Messiah and His kingdom can only be correctly understood by applying this God-given key: "in the spirit." Gabriel said in effect: Do not look for a physical fulfillment; rather look for a spiritual fulfillment. Only in this way can many Old Testament prophecies be harmonized with New Testament reality.

John the Bulldozer

John is often called "John the Baptist" or "John the Immerser" to distinguish him from John the apostle. He could also be called "John the bulldozer." Here is the work Isaiah pictured for him:

Prepare the way of the LORD,
Make his paths straight.

Every valley shall be filled
And every mountain and hill brought low;
The crooked places shall be made straight
And the rough ways smooth;
And all flesh shall see the salvation of God (Luke 3:4-6).

Level the mountains, fill the valleys, straighten the wind-
ing roads, and smooth out the entire terrain—the work of a
bulldozer. It is surely obvious to anyone that spiritual work
was envisioned, not physical. The section begins with "Prepare the way of the LORD," and it ends with "all flesh shall
see the salvation of God."

Malachi spoke more directly when he prophesied of John:

And he will turn
The hearts of the fathers to the children,
And the hearts of the children to their fathers (Mal. 4:6).

John smoothed the way. He worked on crooked hearts. He
brought low the conceited. He removed spiritual obstacles.
He called all Israel to repentance saying, "Repent, for the
kingdom of heaven is at hand!" (Matt. 3:2). John paved the
road for Jesus to start His ministry.

Keep this obvious interpretation in mind the next time
you hear or read that prophecies of Israel and the kingdom
must be fulfilled literally and physically. John's work was
certainly not to be a literal or physical bulldozer. Who would
believe it? His work was to spiritually prepare Israel for a
spiritual King of a spiritual kingdom.

Jesus' Kingdom

The rule discussed earlier says that we should take the
literal meaning of Scripture unless the situation calls for a
non-literal meaning. One of the most important situations is
the manner in which the New Testament deals with an Old
Testament prophecy. Surely New Testament interpretations
supersede Old Testament impressions. Surely we must not
interpret Old Testament prophecies literally when the New

Testament interprets them spiritually.

When Jesus repeatedly said, "You have heard that it was said . . . But I say to you . . ." (Matt. 5:27-28), He was affirming His superiority over the Old Testament. When the book of Hebrews says, "the law, having a shadow of the good things to come, and not the very image" (Heb. 10:1), it is saying the Old Testament contains only a shadow of reality, while the New Testament presents the reality itself. Therefore, the New (reality) contains the clear truths and rules for interpreting the Old (shadow); not visa versa.

When the New Testament explains the nature of the kingdom promised in the Old Testament, that explanation becomes a divine rule of interpretation. Even if Old Testament texts strongly appear to predict an earthly kingdom, we are bound to accept the explanations that Jesus and His apostles gave to these prophecies.

It is a well-known fact that the Jews of Jesus' day were awaiting the fulfillment of numerous Old Testament prophecies regarding the King and His kingdom. It is also well known that they were expecting a literal, physical kingdom. We can sympathize with disciples who lamented over Jesus' death saying, "We were hoping that it was He who was going to redeem Israel" (Luke 24:21). However, now that we have recorded in the New Testament the Messiah's own explanation of the prophecies, we should understand that such materialistic interpretations were wrong. Far from impeding the establishment of God's eternal kingdom as futurism affirms, the Jews' rejection and murder of Jesus was the very basis required to make God's kingdom a possibility.

Before He was crucified, Jesus had declared to the Roman governor in no uncertain terms: "My kingdom is not of this world. If My kingdom were of this world, My servants would fight, so that I should not be delivered to the Jews" (John 18:36). Even though Jesus was the "Son of David," He would not have a kingdom like David. He would not war like David. David fought for a physical kingdom: he slaughtered

Goliath; he conquered Jerusalem from the Jebusites; he greatly extended his earthly domains. In contrast, Jesus would not take up arms either to save his own life or to evict the Romans from Jerusalem. "My kingdom is not of this world." Jesus' kingdom has nothing to do with temporal power, politics, or force of arms.

Jesus *did* come to fulfill the kingdom prophecies. Listen to His words: "The time is fulfilled, and the kingdom of God is at hand. Repent, and believe in the gospel" (Mark 1:15). Since the time was fulfilled and the kingdom was at hand, it had to be set up soon after Jesus spoke. Nobody claims that a physical kingdom of Christ was set up in the first century. However, even futurism recognizes that a spiritual kingdom was set up in the first century. Listen to Tim LaHaye: "Jesus said, 'My kingdom is not of this world' (John 18:36). He came the first time to establish a spiritual kingdom, to which one gains entrance by being born again."[5] Amen! Absolutely! How can one escape the fact that this spiritual kingdom is the kingdom promised by the prophets of old!

Because of Jesus' own teaching, the King and kingdom prophecies of the Old Testament cannot be interpreted literally. They must be interpreted figuratively, spiritually. It is a spiritual kingdom with a spiritual message, a spiritual King, and a spiritual hope. The King himself has spoken.

Looking for Figurative Keys

There is no escaping the conclusion: Many Bible prophecies must be interpreted figuratively, symbolically, spiritually. Indeed, all these examples should alert us to always investigate the possibility of a figurative interpretation to any given prophecy. When the Bible clearly declares a figure, it may be a key to open up our understanding of other prophecies.

In some prophecies, for example, stars must be interpreted figuratively either by the rule of common sense or because the Bible tells us so. In other prophecies, there may be a doubt. What then? The Bible sometimes shows stars to be important people. This can become a key. It can alert us to the possibility that unexplained stars in other prophecies may also be important people.

A word of caution must be given when using such *keys* to interpret prophecy. It is similar to keys for a literal lock: If the key fits—if it helps to make sense out of the prophecy—well and good, then use it. If the key does not fit—if it does not make sense in that particular prophecy—do not try to force it to fit, but reject it for that prophecy.

An important key to unlocking several *time* prophecies is found in Ezek. 4:6: "A day for each year." Some time prophecies, such as Jeremiah's prophecy of the seventy-years captivity, must be taken literally. The seventy-weeks prophecy of Daniel 9, on the other hand, simply was not fulfilled—if a literal interpretation is forced upon it. Most believers, including futurists, take this prophecy figuratively, applying the day-for-a-year rule. In this way Daniel 9 undoubtedly becomes one of the most powerful prophecies of Scripture. The next portion of this book, "Section Two: The Great Tribulation of A.D. 70," examines the seventy-weeks prophecy in great depth. Chapter 6, "Jesus Fulfilled God's Timetable," applies the day-for-a-year rule to determine the exact dates involved in the fulfillment of the seventy-weeks prophecy.

Both Literal and Figurative

Futurism today is looking for a future literal fulfillment of many prophecies that have already been fulfilled figuratively. The futurist view seems to be like the woman at the well who had a hard time grasping that Jesus was not talking about literal water. Futurism does not seem to comprehend that the same Jesus who is spiritually a door, spiritually a shepherd, and spiritually a lamb, is also spiritually a king. The futurist viewpoint does not seem to understand that the same people who are spiritually the body of Christ and spiritually the family of God are also spiritually the temple of God and spiritually the kingdom of God.

This does not mean that all prophecy is to be interpreted figuratively or spiritually. However, it *does* mean that figurative and spiritual fulfillments must be taken seriously. It does mean that we cannot lock ourselves into a literal-only mode, just as we cannot lock ourselves into a figurative-only mode. Clearly some prophecies should be interpreted literally, and just as clearly, other prophecies should be interpreted figuratively. When examining a specific prophecy, one should not have a prejudice for either the literal or the figurative. Throughout history, God has spoken to us in both modes.

Jesus seemed to recognize the difficulties that some people might have in accepting a figurative interpretation of a prophecy. Concerning the Elijah prophecy discussed earlier, Jesus told His disciples: "For all the prophets and the law prophesied until John. And *if you are willing to receive it*, he is Elijah who is to come" (Matt. 11:13-14, italics mine). Jesus was alerting His disciples—then and now—that accepting a non-literal interpretation calls for a certain willingness on our part. Jesus was alerting us to the fact that the literal interpretation is not always the right interpretation; it is not always what God had in mind. The student of God's Word must have an open mind and a willing heart to accept what the evidence shows in each case. Start with the literal, yes; but where the evidence calls for a figurative-symbolic-spiritual interpretation, accept it.

Section Two

The Great Tribulation of A.D. 70

Chapter 4

Which Tribulation?

Will Christians live through "the Tribulation"? Will the Tribulation begin less than ten years from now? Such popular questions pose a problem. The problem is not that someone might receive wrong answers. The problem is that the questions themselves could be wrong. The Tribulation? Which tribulation?

The Popular View of Tribulation

Today's popular futurist belief is that the Tribulation will take place in the near future for a period of seven years. It is foreseen as the worst period of suffering the world will ever know. It is widely thought that the church will not suffer through the Tribulation because the Rapture will occur first.

The common claim of futurism is that large portions of Bible prophecy will be fulfilled in the coming Tribulation. It equates that period with the final week of Daniel's seventy-weeks prophecy. It affirms that Matthew 24, Mark 13, and 2 Thessalonians 2 will all be fulfilled in that coming brief period. It teaches that all the terrible events in the book of Revelation from chapters 6 to 18 will be fulfilled in that seven-year period.

The question that few people ask is, "Which tribulation?" Careful Bible study reveals that there is no such thing as one solitary Tribulation.

"Many Tribulations"

"Tribulation" is not a word that most of us use frequently, but neither is it a strange or technical term. It simply means great affliction, oppression, or suffering. "Tribulation" in the singular is found twenty-one times in the New Testament.[1] The plural is found seven additional times. These texts refer to great suffering in many different times and places.

Paul and Barnabas made it plain to the new Christians in what is now Turkey: "We must through many tribulations enter the kingdom of God" (Acts 14:22). "Must . . . many." In 2 Thess. 1:4 Paul speaks of "all your persecutions and tribulations that you endure." "All your . . . tribulations."

It is a mistake to think that tribulation cannot touch Christians. The gospel message is not one that promises a life of leisure. Tribulation is not one definite period in our future. Tribulation can come frequently to followers of Christ.

"Yes," futurism says, "but when we speak of the Tribulation we have in mind the Great Tribulation." Actually, "great tribulation" is a topic in and of itself deserving lengthy treatment. Chapter 8, "Three Great Tribulations," will show that the Bible uses the term "great tribulation" only three times. Furthermore, the Bible never uses this expression to refer to a seven-year period yet in our future.

Various Premillennial Views

Futuristic premillennialism is divided into three camps based on the timing of the Rapture in relation to the Tribulation: pre-tribulationism, mid-tribulationism, and post-tribulationism. Pre-tribulationism is by far the largest and most popular group. This view is *pre*-millennial because it holds that Jesus will come to earth *before* a literal Millennium. It is *pre*-tribulational because it affirms that the coming of Jesus in the Rapture will take place *before* the

Tribulation. Thus, the events are seen as taking place in this order: the Rapture, the Tribulation, the Second Coming, and finally the Millennium. Since this is the most popular view today, it is the view being discussed here.

Hal Lindsey explains the difficulty facing all three camps:

> As an example, Dr. Gundry [a post-tribulationist] repeatedly says that pre-Tribulationism is based largely on arguments from inference and silence. This is in some measure true. But here is the big point: *All* [italics by Lindsey] of the views have to be developed to some degree on arguments from inference and silence.
>
> The truth of the matter is that neither a post-, mid-, or pre-Tribulationist can point to any single verse that clearly says the Rapture will occur before, in the middle of, or after the Tribulation.[2]

It would be beneficial to examine these inferences to determine if they are indeed justified or if they are contrary to the Bible.

Are Christians Protected from Wrath?

One common inference mentioned by various teachers of futurism (pretribulational-premillennialism) goes something like this: The Tribulation is a time of wrath; God promised to deliver Christians from wrath; therefore, the Rapture will take Christians out of the world before the Tribulation. Two of the main texts used as proof are 1 Thess. 1:10 and 5:9:

> To wait for His Son from heaven, whom He raised from the dead, even Jesus who delivers us from the wrath to come . . .
> For God did not appoint us to wrath, but to obtain salvation through our Lord Jesus Christ.

The unproven assumption in this popular argument is that when these texts speak of wrath, they refer to a future seven-year Tribulation on earth. The argument assumes what needs to be proved. Wrath is mentioned in many different contexts from Genesis to Revelation. It is another general word like tribulation, which is in no way limited to an exclusive event or period. Wrath is simply great anger. In any given situation, one person's wrath may be the cause of another person's tribulation, but each individual situation must be examined to learn the time, the place, and the people involved in that particular tribulation or wrath.

The texts just quoted indicate that saints are protected from wrath. Yes, but we must ask from what wrath they are protected. Christians are certainly not protected from all wrath. Moses, a saint under the old covenant, experienced the wrath of Pharaoh (Heb. 11:27). Jesus experienced the wrath of the Nazarenes (Luke 4:28-29). Early Christians experienced the wrath of the Ephesian pagans (Acts 19:28). The book of Revelation speaks of true believers suffering the wrath of Satan (12:12; 14:8; and 18:3). Clearly, the followers of God are not protected from all wrath.

Aside from such examples of wrath, it is true that the majority of the forty-seven times that wrath is mentioned in the New Testament it refers to the wrath of God. The question remains: When Scripture speaks of Christians being protected from God's future wrath, what wrath is it talking about? Rather than being protected from a mere seven years of wrath, could it not be protection from God's eternal wrath? Several texts clearly point out God's eternal wrath upon the lost—in contrast to eternal life for the redeemed.

John 3:36 says: "He who believes in the Son has everlasting life; and he who does not believe the Son shall not see life, but the wrath of God abides on him." Thus, Jesus contrasts the wrath of God with eternal life. This clearly parallels such texts as Matt. 25:46: "And these will go away into everlasting punishment, but the righteous into eternal life."

Likewise, Rom. 2:7-9 contrasts those on the one hand who will receive "indignation and wrath, tribulation and anguish," with those on the other hand who will receive "eternal life." Two groups: one lost, one saved; one to perish, one to live; one to suffer the eternal wrath of God, and the other to enjoy eternal life from God.

After considering such verses, we can never assume that a verse about wrath is talking about a supposed seven-year period in the future. It is much more likely that such passages are talking about eternal wrath, also called "the second death," "the lake of fire," and "hell." This is the wrath from which Jesus saves us by His death on the cross.

Is the Church Missing
from Revelation 4 to 18?

There is another claimed inference by which futurism arrives at the conclusion that the Rapture will take place before the Tribulation. The futurist view teaches that Revelation chapters 6 through 18 is talking about a future seven-year Tribulation. It argues that the church is not present in all these chapters but rather was taken away in the Rapture at the beginning of chapter 4. John Walvoord, former president of Dallas Theological Seminary for thirty-four years, is a leading spokesman for this view. He writes:

> The word 'church,' prominent in chapters 2-3, does not reoccur until 22:16 though the bride mentioned in 19:7, no doubt, is a reference to the church. The total absence of any reference to the church or any synonym of the church in chapters 4-18 is highly significant.[3]

This statement needs careful scrutiny. Mr. Walvoord is correct in indicating that the word "church(es)" does not appear in chapters 4-18. He is also correct in accepting "bride" in 19:7 as a reference to the church. (Some versions, such as the NKJV, read "wife," instead of "bride.") However, his statement of "the total absence of any reference to the church *or any synonym of the church* in chapters 4-18" requires careful investigation (italics mine). Yes, the specific word "church" is absent. However, he himself says the bride is a reference to the church, and he acknowledges the validity of synonyms of the church. Therefore, based on his own arguments, the total absence of the precise word "church" is not at all equivalent to the total absence of any reference to the church in these chapters.

Mr. Walvoord correctly accepts "bride" ("wife") as a reference to the "church." This makes it clear that he does not consider the church to be a building as many people do. Rather, he correctly understands that Jesus' church is made up of people, in this case collectively called the bride or wife of the Lamb. What student of Scripture does not know that there are many terms in the New Testament that refer to the church—bride and wife are among the less common ones. There are such terms as Christians, body of Christ, disciples, family of God, and saints. These terms refer to the church both as a collective body and as individuals that make up that body.

In the New Testament, saints are not dead individuals to whom we pray for miracles. In all the New Testament excluding Revelation, the saints mentioned are nearly always Christians on earth, the church of Jesus Christ. The equivalency between church and saints, as well as the definition of saints, is seen in 1 Cor. 1:2: "To the *church* of God which is at Corinth, to those who are *sanctified* in Christ Jesus, called to be *saints*" (italics mine). Later in the same epistle, Paul makes mention of "all the churches of the saints" (14:33). In 15:9 he says, "I persecuted the church," while in Acts 26:10 he states, "many of the saints I shut up in prison." Shutting saints in prison was the same as persecuting the church. Futurism itself clearly understands that the church is made up of saints—one of its strong arguments for the Rapture is the contrast between Jesus coming "for the saints" and His coming "with the saints." Futurism teaches that Jesus will come for the saints at the time of the Rapture of the church. It teaches that Jesus will come with the saints when He returns to earth with the church. In both of these cases, futurism clearly equates the saints with the church. (For more on "for the saints" and "with the saints," see Chapter 15, "The Rapture.")

In Acts and the Epistles, the term "saints" is found in

forty-eight verses. Who would dispute that in nearly all those texts the saints mentioned are the members of the church of Jesus Christ? In all but one case, the term is plural referring to the collective body. Even the one time it is in the singular, it says "every saint" (Phil. 4:21). When Acts and the Epistles refer to saints, they are nearly always making "a reference to the church."

With this in mind, turn to the chapters in question— Revelation 4 to 18. Here we read of "the prayers of all the saints" (8:3-4), "the patience and the faith of the saints" (13:10), and the great harlot being "drunk with the blood of the saints" (17:6). Altogether, the term "saints" is found eleven times in these chapters. This is more times than "saints" is found in the book of Acts or any individual Epistle. Consequently, with these eleven direct references to saints, the assumption must be that the "church" *is* referred to in Revelation 4 to 18. Indeed, in Rev. 19:7-8 where the bride/wife is mentioned, we are told: "'The marriage of the Lamb has come, and His wife has made herself ready.' And to her it was granted to be arrayed in fine linen, clean and bright, for the fine linen is the righteous acts of the saints." Futurism accepts the wife as the church, and this text, immediately after the chapters in question, shows that the wife/church is made up of saints. There simply is no truth to futurism's claim that there is a "total absence" of "any synonym of the church" in Revelation 4-18.

Does Jesus Have Two Bodies?

Scripture proclaims, "There is one body" (Eph. 4:4). In contrast to this doctrine, the false assumption that Revelation 6 to 18 refers to a seven-year Tribulation without the church being present has led futurists to promote a false teaching involving two bodies. Rev. 7:9-14 indicates that multitudes will be saved during the great tribulation. Because the church is supposedly absent, futurism is forced to claim there are two bodies of saints. Futurism places "church saints" in one body of believers and "Tribulation saints" into another body of believers.

According to futurism:

1. "Church saints" are saved from wrath, which is the equivalent of a future seven years of Tribulation.

2. "Tribulation saints" can and will suffer wrath.

3. "Church saints" and "Tribulation saints" are two classes of saints, making up two bodies of saved souls.

It must be kept in mind that no interpretation of prophecy is acceptable if it contradicts the clear doctrine of the New Testament.

According to Scriptures already quoted and others to follow:

1. Church saints are saved from eternal wrath but *do* suffer tribulation in this world.

2. Tribulation saints do not suffer God's *eternal* wrath.

3. Church saints *are* tribulation saints. Jesus has only one body.

All Saints are Tribulation Saints

Futurism fails to distinguish between wrath and tribulation. As we have seen, the word "wrath" in the New Testament most often refers to the wrath of God upon those who disobey Him. In contrast, "tribulation" in the New Testament most often refers to what Christians suffer at the hands of the enemies of God. For example, in Matt. 24:9 Jesus told His disciples: "They will deliver you up to tribulation and kill you." He elsewhere referred to times "when tribulation or persecution arises for the word's sake" (Mark 4:17). Paul said of himself: "Chains and tribulations await me" (Acts 20:23). Heb. 10:33 speaks of Christians who "were made a spectacle both by reproaches and tribulations." In fact, twenty out of twenty-seven times in the New Testament, "tribulation" refers to persecution, afflictions, and suffering experienced by the faithful followers of Jesus Christ. It is a great mistake, therefore, to consider wrath as an equivalent of tribulation. The Scriptural teaching on Christians being protected from the "wrath to come" has nothing to do with Christians being protected from tribulation on earth. As with all other words, each text that mentions wrath or tribulation must be studied in its own context to learn exactly the topic of that text.

Paul writes in 2 Thess. 1:4: "So that we ourselves boast of you among the churches of God for your patience and faith in all your persecutions and tribulations that you endure." Rev. 2:9 tells of the tribulation of the church in Smyrna: "I know your works, tribulation, and poverty (but you are rich)."

Far from teaching that God will not allow Christians to experience tribulation, the Word teaches that tribulation can even be beneficial spiritually, regardless of its source: "And not only that, but we also glory in tribulations, knowing that tribulation produces perseverance; and perseverance, character; and character, hope" (Rom. 5:3-4). Tribulation develops Christian character if we are willing for it to produce that result. Rom. 12:12 commands us to be "patient in tribulation." If we allow it, tribulation can help us grow in Christ.

Jesus Promised It

Jesus not only walked in the path of suffering, He promised the same to us: "These things I have spoken to you, that in Me you may have peace. In the world you will have tribulation; but be of good cheer, I have overcome the world" (John 16:33). "In the world you will have tribulation." Jesus said it, and that settles it.

Jesus' parable of the sower can be considered a generalized prophecy of what will happen as the gospel is preached. Consider the seed sown in the stony ground: "Afterward, when tribulation or persecution arises for the word's sake, immediately they stumble" (Mark 4:17). Thus, Christians should not be surprised when fellow Christians fall away due to tribulation. At the same time, we ourselves are warned, so that we do not fall away in like manner. Superficial Christians look for a life where God solves all their problems. They expect the Christian life to be a continual emotional high. When hard times come because of serving God, they often quit.

Mature Christians, however, learn to handle tribulation with the help of the Savior, who led the way in all of His own sufferings. Mature Christians learn to move beyond murmuring and complaining. They learn to say with the apostle Paul:

> I know how to be abased, and I know how to abound. Everywhere and in all things I have learned both to be full and to be hungry, both to abound and to suffer need. I can do all things through Christ who strengthens me (Phil. 4:12-13).

The Scripture tells us to depend on our "God . . . who comforts us in all our tribulation, that we may be able to comfort those who are in any trouble" (2 Cor. 1:3-4).

The Apostle John was *in* the Tribulation

The apostle John wrote the book of Revelation some twenty-five years after the destruction of Jerusalem. At that time, he was in exile by order of Domitian, the Roman emperor. How did he view his situation?

> I, John, both your brother and *companion in the tribulation* and kingdom and patience of Jesus Christ, was on the island that is called Patmos for the word of God and for the testimony of Jesus Christ (1:9, italics mine).

John clearly said he was already in the tribulation and in the kingdom! As far as the apostle John was concerned, neither the tribulation nor the kingdom was two thousand years in the future. He was already in the kingdom. He was already in the tribulation. These introductory remarks of John certainly have a great bearing on the proper understanding of tribulation and kingdom in the entire book of Revelation.

Synonyms

There is not sufficient time to discuss all the texts of the New Testament that use the word "tribulation," much less to discuss all the texts that use synonyms of tribulation. One dictionary defines tribulation as "distress or suffering resulting from oppression or persecution."[4] To these four words (distress, suffering, oppression, and persecution) can be added four more: trial, affliction, trouble, and bearing the cross. These eight terms are all closely related to each other and to tribulation. All of them must be taken into account to adequately understand the Bible teaching on tribulation. For example, the apostle Paul grouped many kindred terms together with tribulation in 2 Cor. 6:4-5: "But in all things we commend ourselves as ministers of God: in much patience, in tribulations, in needs, in distresses, in stripes, in imprisonments, in tumults."

Paul in 2 Tim. 3:12 wrote: "Yes, and all who desire to live godly in Christ Jesus will suffer persecution." That tells us that if a person does not know through personal experience what it means to suffer persecution, then that person must not know what it means to "live godly in Christ Jesus." Strong words? Nevertheless, they are words of the Holy Spirit. The concept of escaping the Tribulation is contrary to both the letter and the spirit of Scripture.

Then there are the powerfully beautiful words in Romans 8:

> Who shall separate us from the love of Christ? Shall tribulation, or distress, or persecution, or famine, or nakedness, or peril, or sword? As it is written:
>
> 'For Your sake we are killed all day long;
> We are accounted as sheep for the slaughter.'
>
> Yet in all these things we are more than conquerors through Him who loved us (Rom. 8:35-37).

"More than conquerors" in tribulation. Today we, the

church, are the tribulation saints. We should not promise people that they can accept Jesus and be raptured out of the world before the Tribulation. Rather, we should encourage people that they can be more than conquerors in the very midst of tribulation.

Tribulation in Past Centuries

History demonstrates that in times of ease believers can easily be deceived by the idea that Christians will not suffer tribulation. However, such an attitude can be maintained only by ignoring the horrendous tribulations that Christians have endured in the past twenty centuries. Who does not have some knowledge of the persecutions and tribulations endured by the Christians in the first three centuries of the Christian era? It began with the persecutions conducted by unbelieving Jews as recorded in the book of Acts. It was continued by the hands of the Roman Empire from the time of Nero to that of Diocletian. Chapter 8, "Three Great Tribulations," discusses the second 'great' tribulation and quotes from Philip Schaff's classic *History of the Christian Church*. Schaff details some of the horrors suffered by Christians early in the fourth century when Diocletian attempted to blot Christianity off the face of the earth.

Later, when the Church of Rome held absolute power in Europe during the Dark Ages, the infamous Inquisition was instituted and continued for centuries. All "heretics" were at risk—a heretic was anyone who disagreed with Rome. The final two sections of Chapter 14, "666: the Mark of the Beast," document some of the details of this infamous period of church history when torture and death held sway over the enemies of Rome.

Twentieth-Century Tribulation

All such persecution is past history, right? Wrong. As recent as 1997, *The Reader's Digest* carried an article entitled "The Global War on Christians." The author begins with three specific examples: in China a woman murdered, in Pakistan a man shot, and in Bangladesh a man beaten until

Real Tribulation

Famous skyline view of the ruins of Rome's Colosseum for gladiators and Christian martyrs

Use Your Imagination

Visualize your father, daughter, wife, or husband waiting unarmed in one of the cells below. Visualize hungry lions pacing in another cell. Visualize their encounter in the arena. No, you cannot!

No! It is too much—too much tribulation; but that is the kind of tribulation the early church experienced!

Inside view of the Colosseum today with underground passageways exposed

his leg was broken. "Their crime? They are Christians. Never before have so many Christians been persecuted for their beliefs." Mention is made of "torture, enslavement, rape, imprisonment, forcible separation of children from parents."[5] The two main enemies of believers today are Muslim militants and communist oppressors. But communism collapsed when the Berlin Wall fell, right? Try posing that question to believers in China today.

Tribulation varies with time and place. Today there are believers in Christ who are suffering great tribulation, even unto death. Even in the "free" United States, incidents where individuals get into trouble with the authorities for speaking out in the name of Christ appear to be on the increase. Also, do not forget that Christian tribulation may be as simple as being laughed at or losing one's job for refusing to lie. Whatever form it takes, God has warned us that persecution and tribulation are part of the Christian walk.

According to the Word of God, tribulation cannot be limited to a seven-year period. According to the Word of God, the church cannot escape tribulation. Saints will not be free from trials, anguish, tribulation, and wrath until the end of the world and the arrival of eternity.

In the world you will have tribulation;
but be of good cheer, I have overcome the world.
— Jesus

Chapter 5

The Jews' Time Has Run Out

Then there will be great tribulation, such as has not been since the beginning of the world until this time, no, nor ever shall be. — Matt. 24:21

The imagination is stirred! Of what time is the Word of God speaking? Is it past, present, or future? The only way to find out is to study the context. The immediate context is Matthew 24. However, it is of utmost importance to notice that in this context, Jesus calls attention to a prophecy of Daniel. An in-depth study of Daniel 9 prepares the student for a better understanding of this "great tribulation."

The contexts of both Daniel 9 and Matthew 24 deal with the children of Israel, the Jews. Some people have special feelings in favor of these unique people, the Jews. Others have special feelings against them. Some believe the Jews are God's chosen people. Others would like to annihilate the Jews from the face of the earth.

Why are there Jews in the world anyway? Who are they? Where did they come from? Are the Jews God's special nation?

Nothing to Brag About

Without question, the Jewish nation is the dominant nation, not only of Daniel 9, but also of the entire Old Testament. They were the focus of God's dealings with man for two thousand years—from the time God promised Abraham that a special nation would rise up from his descendents until New Testament times. But why was so much attention given to the Jews? Was it because God simply wanted to especially bless only one nation out of all the nations of the earth? Or did God have another purpose in mind?

Upon careful examination, we can find nothing superior about the Jewish nation in and of itself. The only reason Israel stands out in the Bible and in history is because Almighty God's attention was focused upon them for two thousand years. As a matter of fact, the Jews would never have even existed without the special intervention of God. Consider the following facts:

Fact one: To get the children of Israel off to a start, God promised a son to a woman who was childless and past menopause. She laughed behind His back. In spite of her initial reaction, Sarah had sexual relations with Abraham and gave birth to a son. It was only by the power of God. Read about it in Genesis 18 and 21.

Fact two: The children of Israel came out of slavery in Egypt and developed into the leading nation of the Middle East. This only happened through innumerable interventions of God. From the ten plagues in Egypt to the fall of Jericho and beyond, God's power was the moving force all the way.

As the Jewish nation grew and prospered, it still was in no way superior, in and of itself. The Jews' greatness was a direct result of God's continual intervention. As for their level of morality and spirituality, time would fail to list all the sins of the Israelites from the day they came out of Egypt until God sent them into captivity. From the start, it is clear that God did not bless them because of their own goodness: "Therefore understand that the LORD your God is not giving you this good land to possess because of your righteousness, for you are a stiff-necked people" (Deut. 9:6). Centuries later in the opening chapters of the Epistle to the Romans, Paul discussed the spiritual condition of the whole world. After considerable discussion, he posed this question: "What then? Are we [Jews] better than they [Gentiles]? Not at all. For we have previously charged both Jews and Greeks that they are all under sin" (Rom. 3:9). Jews or Gentiles, we are all sinners; we are all in need of God's mercy and grace.

These truths are not to suggest that there have not been good people among the Jews. Consider such giants of faith as Daniel, Hezekiah, Esther, Nathan, Mary, Peter, and Paul. Nevertheless, the Jewish nation as a whole became and remained special solely because Almighty God made them special. One of the reasons Daniel 9 is so important is that it predicted both the ultimate purpose and the end of that special relationship.

Chosen with the World in View

The Jews were often quite near-sighted. Today, futurism also seems to be near-sighted on behalf of the Jews. It views God's blessing of the Jews as an end in itself. It makes a distinction between God's plans for the Jews and God's plans for the church and for the whole world. Is this what Scripture teaches? Or did God work with the Jews from beginning to end because He had a much bigger plan in mind?

The reality is that from the outset, Almighty God chose Israel with the whole world in view. When God first called Abraham, He promised him, "I will make you a great nation." Then He quickly added, "In you all the families of the earth shall be blessed" (Gen. 12:2-3). Later, at God's command, Abraham was willing to do the unbelievable by sacrificing his only son. Because of such faith, God intervened and confirmed His promise: "In your seed all the nations of the earth shall be blessed" (Gen. 22:18).

But how would all the nations of the earth be blessed through Abraham's seed? Would it be through the nation that would descend from Abraham, Isaac, and Jacob (Israel)? Or, would it be through the Messiah who would descend from them? Was it God's plan to focus on one nation solely for their own benefit? Or, did God decide to focus on one nation—for a time—with the purpose of using that nation to bring the Messiah into the world and thereby to bless all nations? Numerous Scriptures give us the answer to these vital questions. Not the least of those Scriptures is Daniel's seventy-weeks prophecy (Dan. 9:24-27).

God Sets a Time Limit

The seventy-weeks prophecy is a prediction of certain events that were to transpire in the nation of Israel. This extraordinary prophecy even dares to predict *when!* Verse 24 sets a time limit on God's working through the Jews and Jerusalem, while verse 25 sets the time for the arrival of the Messiah:

> Seventy weeks are determined
> For your people and for your holy city . . .
> Know therefore and understand,
> That from the going forth of the command
> To restore and build Jerusalem
> Until Messiah the Prince,
> There shall be seven weeks and sixty-two weeks.

Seven plus sixty-two makes sixty-nine weeks. That's about one year and four months. But sixty-nine weeks from when to when? According to the text, the sixty-nine weeks begin with a command to restore and build Jerusalem. They end with the arrival of the Messiah.

Daniel received this prophecy in the first year of Darius, 538 B.C. Two years later (536 B.C.), a Persian monarch gave the first command "to restore and build Jerusalem." As a result, the Jews began returning from captivity in Babylon to Jerusalem. The process of rebuilding the temple and the city of Jerusalem was very long, some one hundred years. Altogether there were four commands issued related to the reconstruction and restoration of Jerusalem and the temple. The final command of a Persian king to restore and build Jerusalem was issued in 444 B.C. The counting of the sixty-nine (and seventy) weeks has to begin sometime during this nearly one hundred year period.

There are those who would like us to believe that they interpret all prophecy literally. That simply is not so. Nobody does! Believers in Christ, whatever their prophetic viewpoint, agree on this point: the sixty-nine (and seventy) weeks cannot be interpreted literally. Why? Because the Messiah did not come sixty-nine literal weeks (sixteen months) after any of the four commands to restore Jerusalem. No one can find a fulfillment of the prophecy within that time frame—no Messiah, nothing. The truth is that God's Word, including prophecy, is similar to our everyday speech. It is filled with figurative language.

Whenever possible, we must allow Scripture itself to give us the keys to figurative interpretations. As for time prophecies, there is no better key than that which God gave Ezekiel: "I have laid on you a day for each year" (Ezek. 4:6). Sixty-nine weeks equals 483 days. Using the "day for each year" key, 483 days becomes 483 years. If you start from 536 B.C., when the first command was given, and count 483 years, you arrive at 53 B.C. On the other hand, if you start from 444 B.C., when the last command was given, and count 483 years, you arrive at A.D. 39. Thus, Daniel prophesied that the Messiah would come sometime between 53 B.C. and A.D. 39. The promised Messiah certainly did come during that time! Further calculations and dates related to this amazing prophecy will be examined in detail in Chapter 6, "Jesus Fulfilled God's Timetable."

The Jews a Blessing

A study of the precise years Daniel was predicting is both interesting and valuable. Nevertheless, of equal or more importance is the realization that no later than the first century A.D. God was going to work in a very special way with the Jews and their holy city, Jerusalem—all of which revolved around the arrival and work of the Messiah.

It is no secret that Jesus was a Jew: of the tribe of Judah, of the house of David, of the lineage of Abraham. It is no secret that the most important way the Jews have blessed all nations is by giving us Jesus in the flesh. Though the Jews often thought (and still think) that the Messianic hope was solely for them, it is no secret that the Messianic hope was and is the hope of the whole world. Jesus of Nazareth is the Jew who is the Messiah—the Prophet, Priest, and King—for all the nations of the earth!

In seventy weeks (490 years), the Jews would produce, humanly speaking, the Messiah just as Daniel prophesied. What would the Messiah accomplish? That is the subject of the opening verse of the prophecy (9:24). Gabriel announced to Daniel that God had reserved 490 years in which to accomplish His most important work for the human race.

Gabriel told Daniel that God had seventy weeks set aside "for your people and for your holy city" (9:24). That is, God had 490 years left in which to use the Jews. He prophesied that God, through the Jews and Jerusalem, would accomplish six vital goals within the first century of the Christian era. Almighty God, indeed, did fulfill this wonderful prophecy. He kept His word.

The Work of the Jewish Messiah

Six things were to be accomplished through the Jews and Jerusalem (Dan. 9:24). Indeed, they would be accomplished specifically through their Messiah the Prince (9:25). Then the Messiah would be "cut off" (9:26).

Seventy weeks are determined
For your people and for your holy city,
To finish the transgression,
To make an end of sins,
To make reconciliation for iniquity,

To bring in everlasting righteousness,
To seal up vision and prophecy,
And to anoint the Most Holy (Dan. 9:24).

In the first three items, Daniel foretells the solution to the problem of "transgression," "sins," and "iniquity." A century and a half earlier, Isaiah had prophesied the same thing:

But He was wounded for our transgressions . . .
And the LORD has laid on Him the iniquity of us all . . .
When You make His soul an offering for sin . . .
And He bore the sin of many,
And made intercession for the transgressors (Isa. 53:5-6, 10, 12).

With these words, Isaiah predicted the supreme sacrifice of Jesus on Calvary's cross. To accomplish this great cleansing of sins, the Messiah had to be "cut off" (Isa. 53:8; Dan. 9:26). These two great texts prophesy one great sacrificial death.

Notice that the six items to be accomplished are all spiritual in nature. The Jews had 490 more years. Within that time, they would be used by God to bring great spiritual blessings to the whole world. The first four of the items are such basic gospel doctrines that for the Christian little discussion is needed to verify their fulfillment.

Number One: "To finish the transgression."

For this reason He is the Mediator of the new covenant, by means of death, for the redemption of the transgressions under the first covenant, that those who are called may receive the promise of the eternal inheritance (Heb. 9:15).

Number Two: "To make an end of sins."

John saw Jesus coming toward him, and said, "Behold! The Lamb of God who takes away the sin of the world!" (John 1:29).

Predicted by Daniel

Fulfilled by Christ

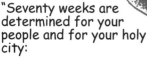

"Seventy weeks are determined for your people and for your holy city:

- To finish the transgression,
- To **make an end of sins,**
- To make reconciliation for iniquity,
- To **bring in everlasting righteousness** . . .
- Messiah shall be cut off, but not for Himself . . .
- But in the middle of the week He shall **bring an end to sacrifice and offering.**"

– Dan. 9:24-27

"Christ **died for our sins** according to the Scriptures."
– 1 Cor. 15:3

"Now the **righteousness** of God apart from the law is **revealed**, being witnessed by the Law and the Prophets."
– Rom. 3:21

"Now where there is remission of these [sins], there is **no longer an offering** for sin."
– Heb. 10:18
(God tore the temple veil in two.)

In the middle of the seventieth week, Jesus fulfilled it all on Calvary.

The earth trembled; the sun hid its face.
The plan of the ages was fulfilled.
Daniel 9 is glorious history!

Our old man was crucified with Him, that the body of sin might
be done away with, that we should no longer be slaves of sin.
For he who has died has been freed from sin (Rom. 6:6-7).

At the end of the ages, He [Jesus] has appeared to put away sin
by the sacrifice of Himself (Heb. 9:26).

Number Three: "To make reconciliation for iniquity."

We also rejoice in God through our Lord Jesus Christ, through
whom we have now received the reconciliation (Rom. 5:11).

Now all things are of God, who has reconciled us to Himself
through Jesus Christ, and has given us the ministry of reconciliation, that is, that God was in Christ reconciling the world to
Himself, not imputing their trespasses to them, and has committed to us the word of reconciliation (2 Cor. 5:18-19).

Number Four: "To bring in everlasting righteousness."

Now the righteousness of God apart from the law is revealed,
being witnessed by the Law and the Prophets [including Isaiah
53 and Daniel 9], even the righteousness of God, through faith
in Jesus Christ . . . whom God set forth as a propitiation by His
blood, through faith, to demonstrate His righteousness . . . so
that as sin reigned in death, even so grace might reign through
righteousness to eternal life through Jesus Christ our Lord
(Rom. 3:21-22, 25; 5:21).

These four items may be summed up in one verse: "Christ
died for our sins according to the Scriptures" (1 Cor. 15:3).
These "Scriptures" include Isaiah 53 and Daniel 9.

The Sealing of Vision and Prophecy

The final two items of the six are more difficult to understand. They are open to various interpretations; therefore,
they require deeper study.

Number Five: "To seal up vision and prophecy." The word "seal" may mean to affix a seal so as to authenticate or establish official approval. (Esther 8:8 is an example of this in ancient times.) Even today, certain documents require seals to make them legally binding. On the other hand, "seal" may mean to fasten up by sealing. Such sealing may be symbolic and authoritative in nature as when Christ's tomb was sealed, or it may be more physical in nature like using glue or tape to seal something shut. (Job 41:1, 15-17 describes how the scales of Leviathan were so tightly sealed.)

Which is the meaning in Daniel? Does it mean to give approval *or* to close up tight? Not an easy question. Perhaps both are correct. Remember that the prophecy has to do with Daniel's people, the Jews. God allotted them seventy weeks of years, which had to terminate no later than the first century A.D. By the first century, Jewish vision and prophecy had to be either authenticated or closed up—or both. The fulfillment clarifies that both took place.

In the first century, the Prophet of prophets came, and Almighty "God the Father has set His seal on Him" (John 6:27). This seal of approval was expressed by the Father from heaven when He proclaimed: "You are My beloved Son; in You I am well pleased" (Luke 3:22).

God also put His stamp of approval on all the Old Testament prophets by fulfilling their prophecies. As Jesus explained to His apostles:

> "O foolish ones, and slow of heart to believe in all that the prophets have spoken! Ought not the Christ to have suffered these things and to enter into His glory?" And beginning at Moses and all the Prophets, He expounded to them in all the Scriptures the things concerning Himself (Luke 24:25-27).

Thus, Old Testament vision and prophecy were sealed in the sense of receiving the best possible stamp of approval: fulfillment.

In addition, Jewish vision and prophecy were sealed up

by coming to an end: "All the prophets and the law prophesied until John" (Matt. 11:13). These words have a ring of finality to them. John the Baptizer was the last prophet of the Jewish nation. "God, who at various times and in various ways spoke in time past to the fathers by the prophets, has in these last days spoken to us by His Son" (Heb. 1:1-2). John made the final preparation for Jesus, the Messiah. Jesus was the great Prophet of "these last days," God's supreme and final Messenger for the final age, the church age.

For a limited time there were lesser prophets in the Lord's church. Nevertheless, these latter prophets were not prophets of physical Israel. They were prophets of the Lord's church, without regard to nationality. In the Lord's church, "there is neither Jew nor Greek" (Gal. 3:28). Physical Israel had ceased being God's message bearer to the world.

Jewish vision and prophecy were sealed in both senses: They were sealed with the divine stamp of approval via the fulfillment of so many prophecies. At the same time, they were sealed shut in the sense of coming to an end. This is not to say that all Old Testament prophecies were fulfilled by the time of Christ. Rather, no new prophecies were to be proclaimed by the Jewish nation after Christ ascended.

The Anointing of the Most Holy

Number Six: "To anoint the Most Holy." To anoint the *most holy* what or whom? Even the translators do not agree on how best to render the expression into English. Such translations may be found as, "the holy of holies," "a most holy place," "most holy One," and "the Most Holy."

Anointing was very common in Old Testament times in a wide variety of situations involving both sacred and common persons and things. The words "most holy," on the other hand, naturally had a quite restricted use. How many things or persons can be considered most holy? "Most holy" is the common translation of those cases where the Hebrew text doubles the word "holy." This occurs about forty-five times in the Old Testament, albeit with grammatical variations. A study of these forty-five times reveals that the expression is always used to describe the tabernacle (temple) or things directly connected to it. It is especially used of offerings and sacrifices, including the sin offering and the trespass offering. From time to time, the most holy things were anointed. All parts of the tabernacle were anointed as well as the priests who ministered there.

The seventy-weeks prophecy foretells the rebuilding of the temple, but it also foretells the utter destruction of that rebuilt temple sometime after the arrival of the Messiah. Some believe that "anoint the Most Holy" predicts the anointing of that rebuilt temple. They say it was anointed by Jesus' physical presence. However, this seems contrary to reality. Although Jesus did teach in the temple and did cleanse it twice, those were temporary situations. When Jesus gave up His life for us on Calvary, the veil of the temple was miraculously torn from top to bottom. Far from specially anointing that temple, far from considering that temple most holy, God Himself desecrated it by tearing the veil.

Other believers think that the anointing of the most holy refers to the Holy Spirit filling the New Testament temple, that is, the church. Although several arguments can be made in favor of this view, yet others consider these arguments to be deficient. They are much more in favor of a third view, namely, that the anointing of the Most Holy is a reference to Jesus.

In this case, the anointing of the Most Holy, similar to the first five items of Dan. 9:24, finds its fulfillment in the redemptive work of Christ. Among other things, Jesus replaced the most holy sin offerings of the temple with the sacrifice of Himself. The book of Hebrews is filled with such teaching:

> Every priest stands ministering daily and offering repeatedly the same sacrifices, which can never take away sins. But this

Man, after He had offered one sacrifice for sins forever, sat down at the right hand of God (Heb. 10:11-12).

Jesus is also the veil (10:20); Jesus is also the High Priest (9:11); Jesus is also the "propitiation" ("mercy seat") (compare Heb. 9:5 with Rom. 3:25 in the Greek). Jesus Himself, the Most Holy One, replaced these old most holy items and functions of the old covenant temple.

"Christ" means anointed one. The same word in Hebrew is "Messiah" (John 1:41). When we confess that Jesus is the Christ, we are confessing that Jesus is the Anointed One. The apostle Peter explained that "God anointed Jesus of Nazareth with the Holy Spirit" (Acts 10:38) following His baptism by John.

Daniel's prophecy uses the term "Messiah" ("Christ," "Anointed One") in both 9:25 and 26. No believer would question that Jesus is most holy. Joining both concepts, it seems natural to consider that "anoint the Most Holy" refers to the anointing of our Holy Jesus, who is also the One who brought fulfillment to the other five items predicted in Dan. 9:24.

The Jews' Time Has Run Out

In and of themselves, the Jews are not more nor less important than any other nation. God never choose them with the view that they would be the only people to receive special blessings. God brought them into existence to bless the whole world. That blessing could come only through the promised Messiah.

More than five centuries before the Messiah came, God's angel Gabriel revealed to Daniel that the Jews, Jerusalem, and the temple were to begin a countdown. There would be only 490 years left for God to complete His purposes through them.

Near the end of those 490 years, the Messiah, in fact, did come. Subsequently, He was cut off to take away the sin of the world. Once the Messiah's church was well established and the Jews had ample opportunity to repent and surrender to Him, God used the Roman armies to utterly destroy their temple and city in A.D. 70. The Jews who survived were scattered to the four winds. Their allotted time had come to an end.

Now that the Messiah has come for the salvation of the whole world, "there is neither Jew nor Greek." The Jews are now on the same footing as everyone else. As a special people, they have served their purpose. God chose the Jewish nation to bless you and me. He kept His promise. He did it on time.

Chapter 6

Jesus Fulfilled God's Timetable

Can you imagine predicting the arrival of a world leader several centuries before his actual arrival? Imagine predicting not only his arrival, but also the exact year of his arrival!

490 Years

Daniel's famous seventy-weeks prophecy (9:24-27) foretold the rebuilding of Jerusalem and the arrival of the Messiah, followed by a second destruction of Jerusalem. If this were the total prophecy, it would be sufficient to build one's faith. However, the prophecy is even more precise. When we consider the detailed chronological elements of this prophecy, our souls are overcome with wonder!

At the outset, it must be noted that the possibility of a literal seventy weeks (less than one and one-half years) must be discarded. If one insists on a literal interpretation, the prophecy simply fails. That is why all Bible believers accept some type of figurative interpretation.

To discover how to interpret time prophecies, serious Bible students will first search the Scriptures for clues. In this case, the clue comes from Ezekiel. God told Ezekiel to lie on his left side for 390 days and on his right side for 40 days. Why? "For I have laid on you the years of their iniquity, according to the number of the days . . . I have laid on you a day for each year" (Ezek. 4:5-6).

Therefore, "a day for each year" is a solid Bible precedent for the figurative interpretation of time prophecies. This does not mean that we should apply this key to every prophecy. Rather, it is a divinely given key that we should take into consideration every time the literal meaning of a prophecy does not make sense.

One week is 7 days; 7 days multiplied by 70 weeks equals 490 days. According to the key, one day equals one year. Therefore, 490 prophetic days become 490 calendar years. This interpretation offers real possibilities.

Notice what is said about the various periods in this prophecy. The six spiritual items listed in Dan. 9:24 had to occur within the 70 weeks (490 years). According to verse 25, the Messiah had to come in exactly "seven weeks and sixty-two weeks." Calculating according to Ezekiel's rule, 69 weeks becomes 483 years (7+62=69; 69x7=483). During the last week (7 years), a covenant would be confirmed. In the middle of that "week" the sacrifices would cease. All these things are prophesied to take place within 490 years.

The prophecy mentions two other items that might or might not occur during the 490 years. Verse 26 predicts both the death of the Messiah and the destruction of Jerusalem. The text introduces both events with these words: "And after the sixty-two weeks." It does not specify if "after" refers to the final week or some time later.

In short, the wording of the prophecy requires that many of the details be fulfilled within 490 years. However, the wording does not require that everything take place within that period.

The Start of the Timetable

In order to count a period of time, we must know when to start counting. Gabriel told Daniel in 9:25:

DANIEL'S SEVENTY-WEEKS PROPHECY

What God PROMISED to do in 490 years, He DID in 490 years.

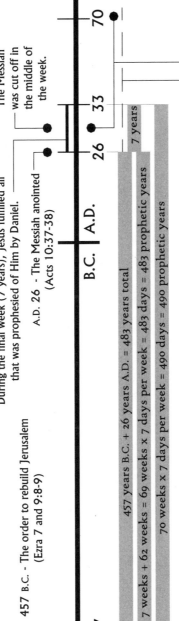

457 B.C. - The order to rebuild Jerusalem
(Ezra 7 and 9:8-9)

During the final week (7 years), Jesus fulfilled all
that was prophesied of Him by Daniel.

The Messiah
was cut off in
the middle of
the week.

A.D. 26 - The Messiah anointed
(Acts 10:37-38)

B.C. | A.D.

457

26   33

70

7 years

457 years B.C. + 26 years A.D. = 483 years total

7 weeks + 62 weeks = 69 weeks x 7 days per week = 483 days = 483 prophetic years

70 weeks x 7 days per week = 490 days = 490 prophetic years

An important profetic key:
A DAY = A YEAR
(see Ezekiel 4:6)
Daniel's 70 weeks = 490 years

The destruction of Jerusalem was predicted to take place
in an unspecified length of time after the 483 years.

Although Jerusalem was destroyed 43 years later, its doom
was sealed during the final week (Luke 19:41-44).

The fulfillment of the seventy-weeks prophecy is proof that Jesus is the Messiah.

-GOD DID NOT FAIL-   -JESUS DID NOT FAIL-   -SCRIPTURE DID NOT FAIL-

That from the going forth of the command
To restore and build Jerusalem
Until Messiah the Prince,
There shall be seven weeks and sixty-two weeks.

As already seen, 7 plus 62 equals 69 weeks which is 483 days. Using the day-for-a-year key, 483 days becomes 483 years. That is, 483 years "until" the Messiah. Starting when? Starting from the time there is a command "to restore and build Jerusalem."

When Gabriel was talking to Daniel, Jerusalem was in total ruins. It was time for the Jews to return to their Promised Land. A command would be given to "restore and build Jerusalem." Since the Bible records several such commands, we need to search for the specific one that is referred to in this prophecy.

First command, 536 B.C.:

Now in the first year of Cyrus king of Persia . . . Cyrus . . . made a proclamation throughout all his kingdom . . . saying,

> Thus says Cyrus king of Persia: All the kingdoms of the earth the LORD God of heaven has given me. And He has commanded me to build Him a house at Jerusalem which is in Judah . . . All His people . . . go up to Jerusalem which is in Judah, and build the house of the LORD God of Israel (Ezra 1:1-3).

This command had to do with the temple, which was the most important part of Jerusalem. Ezra proceeds to tell of this first return and of the building of the temple foundation. However, when local opposition developed, the next king of Persia issued a command to stop the building. The work ceased.

Second command, 520 B.C.:

Then King Darius issued a decree . . .

> Let the work of this house of God alone; let the governor of the Jews and the elders of the Jews build this house of God

on its site. Moreover . . . for the building of this house of
God: Let the cost be paid at the king's expense from taxes
. . . that they may offer sacrifices of sweet aroma to the
God of heaven (Ezra 6:1, 7-8, 10).

Similar to the first command, this second one also dealt
with the temple. Darius, another king of Persia, issued the
decree to stop the opposing forces. This time the work went
forward. Aided by the prophesying of Haggai and Zechariah,
the Jews completed and dedicated the temple in 516 B.C.

Third command, 457 B.C.:
This is a copy of the letter that King Artaxerxes gave Ezra the
priest . . .

> Artaxerxes, king of kings,
> To Ezra the priest . . .
> I issue a decree that all those of the people of Israel and
> the priests and Levites in my realm, who volunteer to go
> up to Jerusalem, may go with you . . . And you, Ezra, ac-
> cording to your God-given wisdom, set magistrates and
> judges who may judge all the people (Ezra 7:11-13, 25).

Ezra later reflects on Israel's blessings:

> Our God . . . extended mercy to us in the sight of the kings of
> Persia, to revive us, to repair the house of our God, to rebuild its
> ruins, and to give us a wall in Judah and Jerusalem (Ezra 9:9).

These two texts cover a full range of activities to "restore
and build" Jerusalem. They speak of establishing local law
and order, as well as rebuilding the ruins of the temple and
the wall.

Fourth command, 444 B.C.:
In the twentieth year of King Artaxerxes . . . I [Nehemiah] . . .
said to the king . . . "the city, the place of my fathers' tombs, lies
waste, and its gates are burned with fire . . . I ask that you send
me to Judah, to the city of my fathers' tombs, that I may rebuild
it" . . . So it pleased the king to send me (Neh. 2:1, 3, 5-6).

This final command of a Persian monarch dealt with the building of Jerusalem's walls. Nearly one hundred years had passed since the first command, and the walls were still in ruins. Now, finally, Nehemiah stirred up the people to rebuild the walls.

Which Command is the Starting Point?

Which of these four commands to "restore and build" Jerusalem is the one referred to in Daniel's prophecy? Not an easy question! There are those who favor one or another of these commands based on their concept of the nature of each command. However, it must be noted that the temple, the government, and the walls—all three are involved in the complete restoring and rebuilding of Jerusalem. Therefore, the words of the prophecy can be satisfied as long as any one of these commands becomes the starting point.

Daniel's seventy-weeks prophecy clearly foretells three important historical events:

1. The city and temple would be restored and rebuilt.
2. The Messiah would come.
3. The city and the temple would again be destroyed.

The prophecy further reveals that there would be 483 days/years from "the command . . . until Messiah."

Let us take each of the commands and count forward 483 years to see if there is any fulfillment. Keep in mind that counting years from B.C. to A.D. is much like counting temperature from below zero to above zero. If it was forty degrees below zero and warmed up twenty-five degrees, you actually subtract to arrive at the new temperature of fifteen degrees below zero. If it was ten degrees below zero and is now ten degrees above zero, you add the two figures. It warmed up twenty degrees.

1. Starting with 536 B.C. and counting forward 483 years, we arrive at 53 B.C. No Messiah there. He had not come yet.

2. Starting with 520 B.C. and counting forward 483 years, we arrive at 37 B.C. Still no Messiah.

3. Starting with 457 B.C. and counting forward 483 years,

we arrive at A.D. 26. Right on target for Jesus!

4. Starting with 444 B.C. and counting forward 483 years, we arrive at A.D. 39. No Messiah there either. He had come and gone by that date.

The first two are much too early, while the fourth is several years too late. No one suggests that the Messiah was on earth for any of these three dates. Therefore, of the four possible dates, only the third remains for examination.

"Until Messiah"

"Until Messiah." When Jesus was baptized, "The Holy Spirit descended in bodily form like a dove upon Him, and a voice came from heaven which said, 'You are My beloved Son; in You I am well pleased'" (Luke 3:22).

Several years later, Peter explained the same event this way: "That word . . . began from Galilee after the baptism which John preached: how God anointed Jesus of Nazareth with the Holy Spirit and with power, who went about doing good" (Acts 10:37-38). Peter mentioned these three events in the following order:

1. John's baptism.

2. Jesus being anointed with the Holy Spirit.

3. Jesus' ministry.

This leaves only one possible explanation for the anointing that Peter spoke of. After John baptized Him, Jesus was anointed with the Holy Spirit, who descended upon Him in the form of a dove.

Anointed! "Messiah" is the Hebrew word meaning anointed. "Christ" is the Greek word. The usual method of anointing was with oil; but Peter, by inspiration, says that Jesus was anointed with the Holy Spirit. This means that, in a real sense, Jesus became the Messiah/Christ at that moment.

Many scholars today would place Jesus' baptism in A.D. 26. Among various pieces of evidence is the reconstruction of Jerusalem's temple, which was still in progress during Jesus' ministry. Based on information from Josephus (Jewish historian of the first century), Herod the Great began the reconstruction in 21-20 B.C. According to John 2:13-20, the first Passover in Jesus' ministry was 46 years later, which would be in the spring of A.D. 27. This would place Jesus' baptism sometime in the latter part of A.D. 26 in order to allow time for the events to occur between His baptism and that first Passover.

The year A.D. 26 is precisely the date we arrived at when starting with the command of 457 B.C.! This is more than just an interesting coincidence. It is an amazing prediction and fulfillment! It leaves no room for doubt that Jesus of Nazareth is the promised Messiah of God. It leaves no room for doubt that the gospel of Jesus Christ is the only authentic religion in the entire world. It leaves no room for doubt that Jesus is the One who accomplished what Gabriel foretold would be accomplished within the 490 years; namely:

To finish the transgression,
To make an end of sins,
To make reconciliation for iniquity,
To bring in everlasting righteousness,
To seal up vision and prophecy,
And to anoint the Most Holy (Dan. 9:24).

The Final Week of Daniel

Daniel's final week (seven days/years) is singled out in the prophecy for special attention. The final week starts with the arrival of the Messiah. It is common knowledge that Jesus' earthly ministry lasted three and one-half years. That is half of the prophetic week. Daniel's prophecy does not specifically say when the Messiah would "be cut off." He just indicates "after" the seven plus sixty-two weeks. Now we can see that the cutting off took place exactly in the middle of the last week when He died on the cross.

With that in mind, notice what else Daniel says would take place "in the middle of the week": "He shall bring an end to sacrifice and offering" (9:27). The death of Jesus on the cross put an end to the sacrificial system of the law:

> Previously saying, "Sacrifice and offering, burnt offerings, and offerings for sin You did not desire, nor had pleasure in them" (which are offered according to the law) . . . He takes away the first that He may establish the second. By that will we have been sanctified through the offering of the body of Jesus Christ once for all . . . For by one offering He has perfected forever those who are being sanctified . . . for after He had said before, "This is the covenant that I will make with them after those days, says the LORD . . . then He adds, "Their sins and their lawless deeds I will remember no more." Now where there is remission of these, there is no longer an offering for sin (Heb. 10:8-10, 14-18).

As a matter of fact, those old offerings and sacrifices still physically existed when Hebrews was written; but, as far as God was concerned, they were meaningless in comparison with Jesus' sacrifice.

God not only said this through His inspired writer, He confirmed it with action: "And Jesus . . . yielded up His spirit. Then, behold, the veil of the temple was torn in two from top to bottom" (Matt. 27:50-51). The temple was no longer God's house. The sacrifices of the temple no longer had value. The cloth veil was torn in two because Jesus became the real veil—the Mediator between the true Holy Place and the true Holy of Holies: "Therefore, brethren, having boldness to enter the Holiest by the blood of Jesus, by a new and living way which He consecrated for us, through the veil, that is, His flesh" (Heb. 10:19-20). By His death, resurrection, and ascension, Jesus brought "an end to sacrifice and offering." It only remained for God to physically destroy the temple a few years later as His final proof that the old sacrificial system was no longer valid. It had been replaced by the sacrifice of His beloved Son.

The Covenant Confirmed

Before speaking of the middle of the week, Gabriel said that the Messiah "shall confirm a covenant with many for one week." This statement brings to mind Jeremiah's prediction of a new covenant (Jer. 31:31-34). There is no question that Jesus brought in a new covenant. At the Last Supper He declared: "For this is My blood of the new covenant, which is shed for many for the remission of sins" (Matt. 26:28).

It thus seems easy to think of Jesus confirming the covenant for the first half of the week, that is, during his three and one-half-year ministry. However, what about the second half—the three and one-half years following His ascension? There should be no difficulty in understanding that Jesus continued to confirm His new covenant through the work of His apostles after His ascension. However, why is the confirming predicted to last only three and one-half years following His ascension? What event could end the three and one-half years and thus close the seventy weeks?

That event cannot be the destruction of Jerusalem because that did not happen until A.D. 70. It is highly unlikely that the event is the conversion of the first Gentile, Cornelius, recorded in Acts 10. While we do not know the exact year of his conversion, the book of Acts places Cornelius' conversion after the conversion of Saul of Tarsus (Acts 9). Scholars place Saul's conversion about A.D. 35, five years after Jesus' death in A.D. 30. Since Cornelius' and Saul's conversions are too late to fit the prophecy, we must seek some significant event or condition prior to Acts 9.

Prophecy had predicted and Jesus had commanded that the gospel first be preached in Jerusalem (Joel 2:28-32; Luke 24:46-49). The church started with three thousand souls, and it quickly grew to five thousand men—all Jews—all in Jerusalem. Who knows how long the Christians would have remained in Jerusalem had it not been for the great persecution that followed the murder of Stephen. As a result of that persecution, the believers "were all scattered throughout the regions of Judea and Samaria" (Acts 8:1).

We do not know the exact date of Stephen's death and the resulting dispersion. Nevertheless, it must have been about

A.D. 33-34, to allow time for Saul's persecution of the church before his conversion about A.D. 35.

According to this data, this dispersion from Jerusalem appears to have taken place right at the end of the 70 weeks (490 years). Much of the seventy-weeks prophecy deals specifically with Jerusalem. It would appear that three and one-half years was precisely the length of time God set aside for the new covenant to be confirmed exclusively in Jerusalem and exclusively among Jews. This was Jerusalem's moment. Large numbers were converted before the Jews, led by Saul of Tarsus, tried to stamp out the new message.

Instead of stamping it out, they caused it to spread beyond Jerusalem. The first place mentioned which then received the Word was Samaria. The Jews hated the mixed-race Samaritans. The apostle John had wanted to call fire from heaven to consume a Samaritan village. Now, this same John laid hands on Samaritans so they could receive the Holy Spirit.

The day of preaching the gospel exclusively in Jerusalem and exclusively to pure Jews and proselytes was over. The seventy weeks had come to an end. World evangelism had begun. Jerusalem had had its golden opportunity. Many seized the opportunity; others only further sealed the doom of their city.

The Desolation of Jerusalem

Much of the seventy-weeks prophecy is about that doom. That doom would come "after" the sixty-nine (seven plus sixty-two) weeks. The language of the prophecy requires that the removal of sin take place within the seventy weeks. It requires that the Messiah come within the seventy weeks. It requires the confirmation of a covenant during the last week. However, it does not require that Jerusalem and the temple be destroyed within that time. The prophecy states, "After." In no way does it specify how long after.

Nevertheless, we cannot help noticing that the doom of Jerusalem was sealed during the seventy weeks. The tearing of the veil was proof that God was finished with the temple. In addition, the Jews proclaimed their own doom at the trial of Jesus: "And all the people answered and said, 'His blood be on us and on our children'" (Matt. 27:25).

During His last week, Jesus lamented:

> O Jerusalem, Jerusalem, the one who kills the prophets and stones those who are sent to her! How often I wanted to gather your children together, as a hen gathers her chicks under her wings, but you were not willing! See! Your house is left to you desolate (Matt. 23:37-38).

"Your house." No longer "My Father's house." "Your house . . . desolate" puts us right back in Daniel 9 with "abominations . . . makes desolate." The Jew's rejection of Jesus during the seventieth week ensured that the desolation would come; it could not be prevented.

When Jesus looked upon Jerusalem from the Mount of Olives,

> He . . . wept over it, saying . . . "days will come upon you when your enemies will build an embankment around you . . . and they will not leave in you one stone upon another, because you did not know the time of your visitation" (Luke 19:41-44).

"You did not know the time." They rejected God's timetable! They crucified their Messiah! The fate of Jerusalem was sealed during the seventieth week.

Why the Delay

When Jesus died, the temple sacrifices no longer had value as far as God was concerned. Nevertheless, God granted forty years of grace to the temple and Jerusalem. It was Jerusalem that crucified Jesus. It was right outside Jerusalem where Jesus arose from the dead, and it was in Jerusalem where the apostles were baptized with the Holy Spirit. The gospel had to begin in Jerusalem. The temple area was an important meeting place to preach the gospel.

Being thus empowered from on high, the apostles preached the Good News to Jews who had gathered for the annual feast of Pentecost. These Jews were present from all parts of the Roman Empire (Acts 2:8-11). "For out of Zion shall go forth the law," wrote Isaiah, "And the word of the LORD from Jerusalem" (Isa. 2:3). The Lord's church needed time to become established. The Jewish Christians needed time to understand the passing away of the law.

For the sake of the gospel, God was gracious to Jerusalem for forty years. For the sake of those Jews who would open their hearts to their Messiah, God was gracious to Jerusalem for forty years. During those forty years, God allowed the temple sacrifices to continue even though they no longer had any meaning for Him. However, the time was fast approaching when God would put a definitive end to those sacrifices. Not only would they be a thing of the past in God's mind, they would also become a thing of the past in historical reality. After forty years of grace, God sent the Romans to wipe the Mosaic system of sacrifice off the face of the earth. God sent the Romans to put a definitive end to Jerusalem as His dwelling place.

Jesus Fulfilled God's Timetable

The climax of Daniel's prophecy is the seventieth week. In the seventieth week the Messiah comes, He brings salvation, and He makes an everlasting covenant with His followers. It is the high point of human history. It is God reaching down to mankind in an unbelievable act of love. The seventy weeks end in triumph! The grand work of redemption is accomplished. In the city of Jerusalem thousands of believing Jews are born again, thus ushering in the eternal kingdom of God.

The Messiah came right on schedule. Jesus of Nazareth entered His Messianic ministry at the start of the seventieth week, precisely according to God's timetable. He was cut off in the middle of that week, ending the Mosaic system of sacrifices, precisely according to God's timetable. Jesus' death on the cross brought in reconciliation and righteousness, precisely according to God's timetable. The time for confirming the new covenant exclusively with Jews in Jerusalem was completed by the end of the seventieth week, precisely according to God's timetable. As Jewish Christians left Jerusalem to begin preaching all over the world, the seventy weeks for the Jews and Jerusalem came to an end. World evangelism had begun. Only God could make and predict such a timetable! Only through the Son of God could the predictions be fulfilled!

Chapter 7

"Not One Stone upon Another"

The Jews no longer offer animal sacrifices as they did centuries ago. Why? They can't. God commanded them to offer those sacrifices only in the temple in Jerusalem. The Jews have no temple. They have had no temple for more than nineteen centuries!

Jesus Prophesied It

The year A.D. 70 marked the end. The Roman armies under Titus leveled the magnificent temple as well as the entire city of Jerusalem. Forty years before it became history, Jesus had predicted this earth-shaking event:

Then Jesus went out and departed from the temple, and His disciples came up to show Him the buildings of the temple. And Jesus said to them, "Do you not see all these things? Assuredly, I say to you, not one stone shall be left here upon another, that shall not be thrown down" (Matt. 24:1-2).

These astounding words were only the introduction to Jesus' discourse on the future of Jerusalem and the temple. Among other things, He called attention to the fact that this destruction was already the subject of a former prophecy:

"Therefore when you see the 'abomination of desolation,' spoken of by Daniel the prophet, standing in the holy place" (whoever reads, let him understand), "then let those who are in
Judea flee to the mountains" (Matt. 24:15-16).

Jesus both confirmed and enlarged upon the prophecy
made by Daniel six centuries earlier. What was the importance of the temple in Jerusalem anyway?

The World's Most Holy City

Jerusalem is a unique city because thousands of years
ago the Creator of the universe chose it as His dwelling
place! God told the Jews through Moses:

You shall seek the place where the LORD your God chooses, out
of all your tribes, to put His name for His dwelling place; and
there you shall go. There you shall take your burnt offerings,
your sacrifices (Deut. 12:5-6).

Five hundred years later—one thousand years before
Christ— God revealed His choice to King David. A few years
later at the dedication of the temple in Jerusalem, King
Solomon quoted what God had said to his father, David: "I
have chosen Jerusalem, that My name may be there . . .
Your son [Solomon] who will come from your body, he shall
build the temple for My name" (2 Chron. 6:6, 9).

It was Jehovah God who chose Jerusalem and the temple. It was Jehovah God who chose when and how to bless
Jerusalem and the temple. It was the same Jehovah God
who would choose how and when to punish Jerusalem and
destroy the very temple that was His dwelling place.

The First Temple Destroyed

About two hundred and fifty years later, Hezekiah came
to power. He was one of the best kings Judah ever had.
However, Hezekiah's son Manasseh was one of the worst:

He [Manasseh] even set a carved image of Asherah that he had
made, in the house of which the LORD had said to David and to

Solomon his son, "In this house and in Jerusalem, which I have chosen out of all the tribes of Israel, I will put My name forever . . . *only if* they are careful to do according to all that I have commanded" . . . "Because Manasseh king of Judah has done these abominations . . . therefore thus says the LORD God of Israel: 'Behold, I am bringing such calamity upon Jerusalem and Judah, that whoever hears of it, both his ears will tingle'" (2 Kings 21:7-8, 11-12, italics mine).

Even though Manasseh's grandson, Josiah, was a very good king,

Nevertheless the LORD did not turn from the fierceness of His great wrath . . . And the LORD said, "I . . . will cast off this city Jerusalem which I have chosen, and the house of which I said, 'My name shall be there'" (2 Kings 23:26-27).

Disaster came by the hands of the famous Babylonian king, Nebuchadnezzar. You can read about it in 2 Kings 24 and 25 and 2 Chronicles 36. The forces of Nebuchadnezzar came up against Jerusalem four times. They carried away the best of the people of Judah to Babylon. They carried away countless treasures of gold, silver, and bronze, including all the articles of the temple. They slaughtered multitudes, burned the temple and palaces, and broke down the walls. Jerusalem was in total ruin.

Restoration Had Been Promised

Since the prophet Jeremiah was in Jerusalem, he was an eyewitness of this devastation. He had repeatedly told the people that such devastation was a certainty. In addition, he foretold that after seventy years God would punish the Babylonians and bring His people back from captivity. (See Jer. 25:1-12; 29:10-14.)

One of the good-looking youths who were carried captive to Babylon was Daniel. He was well aware of Jeremiah's prophecies, and he reached old age without forgetting them. In time, the Persians conquered Babylon. Daniel realized that this political change coincided with the completion of the seventy years that Jeremiah had foretold.

It was time for prayer with fasting, sackcloth, and ashes. Daniel's prayer (Dan. 9:2-19) has three leading themes. First, God is faithful, righteous, and forgiving. Second, Judah and Israel are wicked sinners deserving God's punishment. Third, Daniel pleads with God to now remember the desolation of Jerusalem. In the latter part of the prayer, Daniel speaks to God of "Your city," "Your holy mountain," "Your people," and "Your sanctuary." These are Jerusalem, Zion, Judah (Israel), and the temple. The seventy years were accomplished. Daniel longed for the restoration of Jerusalem and the people of God.

While Daniel was still praying, the angel Gabriel came and spoke to him. Gabriel's prophetic words are found in Dan. 9:24-27, the famous seventy-weeks prophecy. Do not forget the setting of this great prophecy—Jerusalem is in ruins, the temple is no more, and the people of Judah are in captivity.

Prophecy of the Second Temple

First, notice that this prophecy (Dan. 9:24-27) has to do with "your people" and "your holy city." The prophecy is inseparably connected to Daniel's prayer. Second, notice that "abominations" is mentioned once in the prophecy. "Desolate (or desolations)" is mentioned three times. These terms connect this prophecy to Jesus' prophecy in Matt. 24:15: "The 'abomination of desolation' spoken of by Daniel the prophet."

Gabriel explained (Dan. 9:25):

Know therefore and understand,
That from the going forth of the command
To restore and build Jerusalem . . .

There it is! This is the answer to Daniel's prayer. This is all he wanted. He wanted God to remember His promise to restore Jerusalem after seventy years. God did not directly answer Daniel with a "yes." Rather, God's reply *assumed* a "yes" answer. He used "yes" as simply *the starting point* to reveal greater events.

Daniel got more than he asked for. Yes, Jerusalem would be rebuilt. However, in addition, one day in the distant future someone would *again* "destroy the city and the sanctuary" (9:26). Was Daniel's desire therefore futile? Why rebuild Jerusalem and the temple of God only to have them destroyed again? Nevertheless, that is exactly what the prophecy said. It is to that part of the prophecy that Jesus referred in Matthew 24 when He declared: "Not one stone shall be left here upon another." Nebuchadnezzar had destroyed Solomon's temple. A second temple would be built to replace the destroyed one. However, it too would be destroyed. God said so!

The Arrival of the Promised Messiah

The seventy-weeks prophecy foretold that the Second Temple would end up like the First Temple. If that were the sum total of this prophecy, it would be a rather dismal picture. However, there is much more. Daniel asked about the temple, Mount Zion, Jerusalem, and Israel. In reality, none of these in themselves are important. The important thing is that they were the means by which God would bring the Messiah into the world.

Gabriel told Daniel *when* the promised Messiah would come. Aside from precise calculations of dates, the Messiah would come sometime between the building and destruction of the Second Temple! Gabriel said:

That from the going forth of the command
To restore and build Jerusalem
Until Messiah the Prince,
There shall be seven weeks and sixty-two weeks (9:25).

After that time, "Messiah shall be cut off" (9:26). The same verse adds that someone would come to "destroy the city and the sanctuary." The main historical outline of the prophecy is quite clear:

1. A command would be given to rebuild Jerusalem.
2. The Messiah would come and be cut off (killed).
3. The Second Temple and Jerusalem would be destroyed.

Gabriel revealed these things in 538 B.C., the first year of the Persian Empire. Jerusalem and the Second Temple were destroyed in A.D. 70 by the Romans. The Messiah had to come before A.D. 70.

And come He did! "When the fullness of the time had come, God sent forth His Son" (Gal. 4:4). As Jesus started His preaching campaign, he proclaimed: "The time is fulfilled, and the kingdom of God is at hand. Repent, and believe in the gospel" (Mark 1:15). Some believed. Many did not.

As His ministry drew to a close, Jesus approached Jerusalem in His "triumphal entry" surrounded by multitudes loudly praising God for their King. But when Jesus saw Jerusalem, He openly wept over it. The time for the Messiah had come, but because the Jews would crucify Him within the week, Jerusalem's doom was sealed:

> Now as He drew near, He saw the city and wept over it, saying, "If you had known, even you, especially in this your day, the things that make for your peace . . . For days will come upon you when your enemies will . . . level you . . . to the ground; and they will not leave in you one stone upon another, *because you did not know the time of your visitation*" (Luke 19:41-44, italics mine).

The fullness of time had come. The time for the Messiah had come. The time for the kingdom of God had come. However, the Jews did not recognize the time. Jesus gave them all kinds of proof that He was the Messiah. The crowning proof was His resurrection. Yet another great proof would come in A.D. 70, with the destruction of Jerusalem and the Second Temple. With this destruction, God closed the door on any future possibility of the Messiah coming. The Jews today who are still awaiting their Messiah might as well rip

Daniel 9 out of their Scriptures! Daniel 9 forever proves them wrong. The Messiah had to come before the Second Temple was destroyed.

The Siege of Jerusalem

Daniel and Jesus prophesied it. Secular history records it. Many times we must search records other than the Bible in order to appreciate the Bible fully. The Bible records in detail the fulfillment of the prophecy that Jerusalem would be rebuilt. (See the books of Ezra and Nehemiah.) The Bible records in detail the fulfillment of the prophecy that the Messiah would come and be cut off. (See the four Gospels.) However, what about the prophecy that the *Second* Temple and all Jerusalem would be leveled to the ground after the death of the Messiah? The Bible nowhere records the fulfillment of that prophecy. We must look elsewhere for this information.

We are especially indebted to Flavius Josephus at this point. Josephus, a Jew, was born seven years after Jesus' death. Some thirty years later when the fever of war greatly increased between the Jews and the Romans, Josephus led the Jewish forces in Galilee. When he was overtaken there, he surrendered to Vespasian, who thereafter became Emperor in Rome. Vespasian left his son Titus in command of the campaign in Palestine. Because Josephus accompanied Titus to Jerusalem, he was an eyewitness of the war.

Josephus dedicated his last thirty years to writing about the Jews. In his first work, the *History of the Jewish Wars,* he describes in great detail their war with Rome in A.D. 66-70.

Josephus tells of all the infighting among the Jews. He describes the siege of the city by the Romans and their conquest of the city wall by wall. He tells of famine, robbers, misery, and death. Many of the people wanted to surrender to the Romans, but others were determined to battle the Romans at all costs. These hard-liner Jews (Josephus calls them the "seditious") would not hear of surrender. Many

Jews tried to escape the city, but when the hard-liners even suspected that someone was about to attempt escape, they would slit his throat!

The Second Temple Destroyed

The Romans had respect for the holy sites of the nations they conquered. Titus did not want to destroy the temple in Jerusalem. As the Romans seized more and more of the city, the hard-liners retreated to the temple area itself as a last fortress from which to fight. Titus pled with them:

> If you will but change the place whereon you will fight, no Roman shall either come near your sanctuary, or offer any affront to it; nay, I will endeavour to preserve you your holy house, whether you will or not.[1]

The hard-liner Jews rejected Titus' offer. Thus, these hard-hearted and stubborn Jews, who fought to the death to save the temple, actually became the very cause of its destruction, thereby fulfilling the prophecies of Daniel and Jesus!

Court by court the Romans took the temple area until all that remained was the holy house itself with the surrounding cloisters. Some Roman soldiers set fire to these outer rooms. Titus attempted to intervene. However, his soldiers were so infuriated by the stubbornness of the Jews that no one could stop them. The temple could not be saved.

As the end neared, Titus took the opportunity to speak to the Jews who remained to see if they would surrender. As he opened his speech, he made a remarkable statement— remarkable because it reminds us of Daniel's prayer and Gabriel's prophecy. Titus exclaimed:

> I hope you, sirs, are now satiated with the miseries of your country, who have . . . like madmen, after a violent and inconsiderate manner, made such attempts, as to have brought *your people, your city, and your holy house to destruction* (italics mine).[2]

The Jews rejected the offer. The Almighty Creator God of the universe had decreed the destruction! Josephus opens book 7 with these words:

> Now, as soon as the army had no more people to slay or to plunder . . . Caesar gave orders that they should now demolish the entire city and temple, but should leave as many of the towers standing as were of the greatest eminence . . . and so much of the wall as enclosed the city on the west side. This wall was spared, in order to afford a camp for such as were to lie in garrison . . . but for all the rest of the wall, it was so thoroughly laid even with the ground by those that dug it up to the foundation, that there was left nothing to make those that came thither believe it had ever been inhabited.[3]

Titus returned to Rome. He and his father, Vespasian, and his brother Domitian were the center of a fabulous celebration. The seven-branched lampstand and the table of showbread that had been taken from the temple in Jerusalem were among many other things that were carried in the triumphal march. Later Domitian became emperor. In A.D. 81 he built the Arch of Titus in memory of Titus' capture of Jerusalem. If you visit Rome today, you can see a bas-relief on the inside of the arch depicting the Roman soldiers carrying the lampstand!

Why Did It Happen?

Parallel to Matthew 24 are Mark 13 and Luke 21. Our Savior said in Luke 21:20, 22: "But when you see Jerusalem surrounded by armies, then know that its desolation is near . . . For these are the days of vengeance, that *all things which are written may be fulfilled*" (italics mine). "Things which are written" especially include what Moses wrote in Deuteronomy 28 and what Daniel wrote in Daniel 9.

"The days of vengeance." The vengeance of the Almighty God of heaven. If you are not acquainted with the contents of Deuteronomy 28, you will want to read it. If a religious writer today were the first to write and publish the contents

ARCH OF TITUS IN ROME, ITALY

Arch of Titus with ruins of Colosseum in right background.

Sculpture on inside of arch depicting victory parade in Rome
when Titus returned from destroying Jerusalem in A.D. 70.
Soldiers can be seen carrying lampstand from temple.

of Deuteronomy 28, he would be strongly condemned for being anti-Semitic!

Josephus, a Jew who did not believe in Christ, over and again refers to the destruction of Jerusalem as being by the hand of God. For example, when Josephus himself was pleading with the Jews to surrender to the Romans, he said to them:

> . . . when the before-mentioned king of Babylon [Nebuchadnezzar] made war against us, and when he took the city and burnt the temple; while yet I believe the Jews of that age were not so impious as you are. Wherefore, I cannot but suppose that God is fled out of this sanctuary, and stands on the side of those against whom you fight.[4]

Much more to the point of the reason for God's vengeance are the remarks of an eighteenth century writer named Thomas Newton. In his *Dissertations on the Prophecies*, he says:

> The predictions [of Matthew 24] are the clearest, as the calamities were the greatest which the world ever saw: and what heinous sin was it, that could bring down such heavy judgments on the Jewish church and nation? Can any other with half so much probability be assigned, as what the Scripture assigns, their crucifying the Lord of glory? . . . and upon reflection, we shall find really some correspondence between their crime and their punishment. They put Jesus to death, when the nation was assembled to celebrate the passover; and when the nation was assembled too to celebrate the passover, Titus shut them up within the walls of Jerusalem. The rejection of the true Messiah was their crime; and the following of false Messiahs to their destruction was their punishment. They sold and bought Jesus as a slave; and they themselves were afterward sold and bought as slaves at the lowest prices. They preferred a robber and murderer to Jesus, whom they crucified between two thieves and they themselves were afterward infested with bands of thieves and robbers. They put Jesus to death, lest the Romans should come and take away their place and nation [see John 11:46-48]; and the

Romans did come and take away their place and nation. They crucified Jesus before the walls of Jerusalem; and before the walls of Jerusalem they themselves were crucified in such numbers that it is said room was wanting for the crosses, and crosses for the bodies. I should think it hardly possible for any man to lay these things together, and not conclude the Jews' own imprecation to be remarkably fulfilled upon them, (Matt. 27:25): "His blood be on us and on our children."[5]

Why was the temple in Jerusalem so totally destroyed that not one stone was left upon another? Because that is what God wanted! The Jewish nation rejected the Son of God. God rejected the Jewish nation. The sacrifices in the temple were no longer needed. The Son of God had made the perfect sacrifice.

Gabriel made it plain to Daniel. First, the temple and Jerusalem would be rebuilt. Then the Messiah would come and die. Finally, the temple and Jerusalem would again be destroyed. Only God could have that knowledge centuries ahead of time. Only God could bring it to pass. Jesus Christ is thus proven to be the Messiah long promised to Israel. The destruction of Jerusalem and the temple in A.D. 70 became the final and climactic proof that Jesus of Nazareth was and is, indeed, the Messiah, the Christ, the King and Lord of all. To serve Him is to invite salvation. To reject Him is to invite the wrath of God. Not one stone remained upon another!

Chapter 8

Three Great Tribulations

Not just one, not just two, but three "great" tribulations are found in the Bible. Examine them in Matthew 24, Revelation 2, and Revelation 7. These three texts predict three distinct times of suffering.

The New Testament teaches that from the first century to the end of time Christians can expect to suffer tribulation of many kinds (see Chapter 4, "Which Tribulation?"). Of all the tribulations mentioned in the N.T., three are termed "great." To understand these tribulations, we must study each prediction in its own context.

THE FIRST "GREAT" TRIBULATION

The best known of the three great tribulations is the one announced by Jesus in Matthew 24 shortly before His crucifixion. Futurism would push all of Matthew 24 into our future. Full preterism would push it all into our past. A third view says that neither extreme can satisfy the demands of the text, but rather that the chapter addresses two separate periods, one now past and one yet in our future. All views that interpret at least part of Matthew 24 as already fulfilled agree that the event predicted was the destruction of Jerusalem and its temple by the Romans in A.D. 70.

Once there is an awareness that Matthew 24, in whole or in part, was a prediction of A.D. 70, it is not too difficult to conclude that the "great tribulation" of this chapter (24:21) refers to the same period. The reality is that the context of Matthew 24 simply does not allow us to ignore the Roman destruction of Jerusalem in A.D. 70. Why? Notice the order of events:

1. The disciples showed Jesus the magnificent temple in Jerusalem.

2. Jesus shocked them by exclaiming: "Not one stone shall be left here upon another."

3. The disciples asked Jesus when "these things" would happen.

4. Jesus answered them.

5. Forty years later (A.D. 70), Jesus' prophecy about the stones was literally fulfilled.

Any acceptable interpretation of Matthew 24 must begin with these five facts. The first, second, and fifth are often ignored. However, it is impossible to understand the third and fourth points without taking into account the first two points. To express it another way, the disciples' questions and Jesus' replies must be seen in the context of the first two verses of the chapter:

> His disciples came up to show Him the buildings of the temple. And Jesus said to them, "Do you not see all these things? Assuredly, I say to you, not one stone shall be left here upon another, that shall not be thrown down" (24:1-2).

The whole context relates to the utter destruction of the temple then standing. Moreover, there is further likelihood of misunderstanding Matthew 24 if we ignore the parallel texts in Mark and Luke.

Often Gospel accounts have parallel passages. Mark 13 and Luke 21 are parallel passages to Matthew 24; each one offers further information. It is most helpful to examine what each Gospel records regarding the following:

1. Jesus' remark about the stones.
2. The disciples' questions about His remark.
3. Jesus' reply to their questions.

Jesus said, "Not one stone shall be left here upon another." The disciples then asked, "When will these things be?" According to Matthew 24:3 the disciples also asked, "And what will be the sign of Your coming, and of the end of the age?" However, there is no record of the disciples asking these latter two questions in either Mark or Luke. In Mark 13:4 they ask, "When will these things be? And what will be the sign when all these things will be fulfilled?" The account in Luke is almost identical to Mark. Matthew is the only Gospel that records the questions about Jesus' coming and the end of the age. Nobody really knows what the disciples' concepts were of Jesus' coming and the end of the age; it is of no benefit to speculate.

On the other hand, all three Gospels record the question, "When will these things be?" (of one stone not remaining upon another). Therefore, it must be concluded that the primary issue in the disciples' minds and in Jesus' response was the total destruction of the temple then standing. This is the simple and basic fact that is so often missed. In this context, "these things" can only refer to the complete destruction of the temple that was then standing in Jerusalem—"Not one stone shall be left here upon another."

Furthermore, in verses 15 and 16 of Matthew 24, Jesus specifically referred to "the holy place" and Judea. In verse 16, He told believers in Judea to "flee." In verse 20, He continued talking about "your flight." Verse 21 begins with the word "for," which introduces the reason for fleeing: "For then there will be great tribulation, such as has not been since the beginning of the world until this time, no, nor ever shall be."

Jesus was saying they should flee from the great tribulation in Judea when "the abomination of desolation" stood in "the holy place." Mark 13:14-19 reads almost identically to Matt. 24:15-21. However, the parallel verses in Luke 21:20-24

"O Jerusalem, Jerusalem...

Photograph © by Todd Bolen/BiblePlaces.com. Used by permission.

... How often I wanted to gather your children together, as a hen gathers her chicks under her wings, but you were not willing! See! Your house is left to you desolate" ... *and His disciples came up to show Him the buildings of the temple. And Jesus said to them, "Do you not see all these things? Assuredly, I say to you, not one stone shall be left here upon another, that shall not be thrown down."*

— Matthew 23:37–24:2

A.D. **30** – Jesus made the above lament and prophecy.

A.D. **70** – Romans destroyed the temple.

A.D. **691** – Muslims completed the Dome of the Rock.

Today – The Dome of the Rock still stands on the Temple Mount.

Today – The Wailing Wall is all that remains of the Temple Mount. It was not part of the temple itself but only part of a retaining wall to shore up the mount.

"See! Your house is left to you desolate."

contain several important variations. Instead of the words "great tribulation," we find "days of vengeance," "great distress in the land and wrath upon this people," and "Jerusalem will be trampled." Jesus spelled out the reason for the coming suffering: "Days of vengeance, that all things which are written may be fulfilled." It was a matter of God's vengeance upon Israel and Jerusalem for rejecting and crucifying the Messiah.

The "great tribulation (distress)" of Matthew 24, Mark 13, and Luke 21 was inseparably connected to Jesus' prediction of the utter destruction of the temple then standing in Jerusalem. The fulfillment of these shocking words took place in the year A.D. 70, at which time not one stone was left standing upon another—literally.

"Has Not Been . . . Nor Ever Shall Be"

What did Jesus mean when He said: "For then there will be great tribulation, such as has not been since the beginning of the world until this time, no, nor ever shall be"? Many believe these words could not refer to A.D. 70. However, it is essential for good Bible interpretation to keep these words in context. We have already seen that the context is the desolation of the temple that Jesus and the disciples had been looking at. These words, therefore, must somehow be connected to the destruction of that temple.

Some see the expression "never before and never again" as a Jewish proverbial expression. For example, two kings who faithfully followed God in Judah were Hezekiah and Josiah. Of Hezekiah it is said: "He trusted in the LORD God of Israel, so that after him was none like him among all the kings of Judah, nor who were before him" (2 Kings 18:5). Just five chapters later, the sacred writer speaks of Josiah:

> Now before him there was no king like him, who turned to the LORD with all his heart, with all his soul, and with all his might, according to all the Law of Moses; nor after him did any arise like him (2 Kings 23:25).

Nobody like him, before or after, is said of both kings! Thus, "never before . . . never after" in these cases must be the figure of speech called hyperbole (an exaggerated statement to emphasize a point). For a parallel example in modern English, how many times have you said, "I never saw anything like it"? On other occasions, Jesus unquestionably used hyperbole in such remarks as "a plank is in your own eye." Thus, hyperbole cannot be ruled out.

Others, however, prefer a different approach. They point out that whenever something is called "the greatest," we must ask, "greatest in what respect?" In magnitude? In duration? In nature? We may legitimately ask in what way the destruction of Jerusalem and the temple in A.D. 70 was the "greatest" of all tribulations. There are several possibilities.

First, keep in mind that this text is not discussing a world war. It is referring to one city. It is saying this would be the greatest tribulation ever for one city. Compare Hiroshima where about seventy-five thousand were killed by the atomic bomb in 1945. Horrible! However, in great contrast, over one million died in the siege of Jerusalem in A.D. 70!

Second, it was the greatest spiritual tribulation that Jerusalem and the entire Jewish nation ever suffered. The war of A.D. 70 once and for all destroyed what had been God's dwelling place on earth! It brought a complete end to the entire Mosaic system of animal sacrifices and temple rituals. The Jewish religion has never been the same since.

Third, throughout world history there have been tribulations caused by foreign invasions and tribulations caused by civil wars. The Jews suffered both at the same time. While the Romans besieged Jerusalem, the Jews suffered even worse fighting, destruction, and misery within the city at the hands of their very own countrymen, resulting in a time of very great tribulation if not the greatest ever. This will become clearer in the quotations that follow.

In various ways, there never has been anything like the

destruction of Jerusalem in A.D. 70. Whatever interpretation one may give to Jesus' prediction of "great tribulation, such as has not been . . . nor ever shall be," the context of Matthew 24 dictates that the interpretation must be related to the destruction of the very temple Jesus and the apostles were looking at.

Josephus Records It

John Chrysostom, famed fourth-century preacher in Antioch of Syria, certainly understood Matthew 24 better than today's futurism does. He saw that the chapter deals with both A.D. 70 and the second coming of Christ. He also recognized that studying the writings of Josephus was an important step toward full appreciation of Jesus' prophecies. Note what Chrysostom said of Josephus' testimony:

> And let not any man suppose this [Matt. 24:21] to have been spoken hyperbolically; but let him study the writings of Josephus, and learn the truth of the sayings. For neither can anyone say, that the man being a believer, in order to establish Christ's words, hath exaggerated the tragical history. For indeed he was both a Jew, and a determined Jew, and very zealous, and among them that lived after Christ's coming.
>
> What then saith this man? That those terrors surpassed all tragedy, and that no such had ever overtaken the nation.[1]

"Study the writings of Josephus"? Absolutely. We are indebted to Flavius Josephus for a detailed eyewitness account that dramatically documents the fulfillment of Jesus' and Daniel's prophecies. In Chapter 7, "Not One Stone upon Another," we examined some of Josephus' testimony. Chrysostom calls us to investigate further.

In his *History of the Jewish Wars,* Josephus wrote:

> O most wretched city, what misery so great as this didst thou suffer from the Romans, when they came to purify thee from thy intestine hatred! For thou couldst be no longer a place fit for God.[2]

Accordingly, it appears to me that the misfortunes of all men from the beginning of the world, if they be compared to these of the Jews, are not so considerable as they were.[3]

Josephus believed in God but not in Jesus. Therefore, his statement is all the more remarkable, inasmuch as it so nearly parallels what our Lord foretold.

Jew against Jew

Violence erupted between the Romans and the Jews in Palestine in A.D. 66. As things went from bad to worse, Nero sent Vespasian to conduct an all-out war against the Jewish nation. By the time Vespasian was proclaimed emperor in A.D. 69, he had subjugated all of Galilee and Judea except the capital. Returning to Rome, he left his son Titus to conquer Jerusalem. Before Titus and his armies arrived, multitudes of Jews entered Jerusalem to celebrate the Passover. Titus soon hemmed them in with a siege. On the inside of the walls there were three rival factions led by Eleazar, John, and Simon, who not only fought among themselves but also against any who opposed them. It was a dreadful situation. Josephus records that both John and Simon fought each other and

> set on fire those houses that were full of corn, and all other provisions . . . destroying what the city had laid up against the siege . . . almost all the corn was burnt, which would have been sufficient for a siege of many years (5.1.4).

> And now, as the city was engaged in a war on all sides, from these treacherous crowds of wicked men [the three factions], the people of the city, between them, were like a great body torn in pieces. The aged men and the women were in such distress by their internal calamities, that they wished for the Romans, and earnestly hoped for an external war, in order to their delivery from their domestic miseries (5.1.5).

> Now, while these factions fought one against another, the people were their prey on both sides . . . Simon held the upper city

. . . John held the temple . . . and fought it out, and did everything that the besiegers could desire them to do; for they never suffered any thing that was worse from the Romans than they made each other suffer . . . those that took it [Jerusalem] did it a greater kindness; for I venture to affirm, that the sedition destroyed the city, and the Romans destroyed the sedition (5.6.1).

But the famine was too hard for all other passions . . . insomuch that children pulled the very morsels that their fathers were eating out of their very mouths . . . the seditious . . . when they saw any house shut up, this was to them a signal that the people within had gotten some food; whereupon they broke open the doors, and ran in, and took pieces of what they were eating almost up out of their very throats, and this by force: the old men, who held their food fast, were beaten (5.10.3).

I shall, therefore, speak my mind here at once briefly:—That neither did any other city ever suffer such miseries, nor did any age ever breed a generation more fruitful in wickedness than this was, from the beginning of the world (5.10.5).

Jerusalem's End

The Roman soldiers captured escapees and crucified them—five hundred a day! The area outside the walls became filled with crosses. "Their multitude was so great that room was wanting for the crosses, and crosses wanting for the bodies" (5.11.1). Josephus continues:

The upper rooms were full of women and children that were dying by famine; and the lanes of the city were full of the dead bodies of the aged (5.12.3).

There was found among the Syrian deserters a certain person who was caught gathering pieces of gold out of the excrements of the Jews' bellies; for the deserters used to swallow such pieces of gold . . . So the multitude of the Arabians, with the Syrians, cut up those that came as supplicants, and searched their bellies (5.13.4).

No fewer than 600,000 were thrown out at the gates . . . when they were no longer able to carry out the dead bodies of the poor, they laid their corpses on heaps in very large houses, and shut them up therein . . . some persons were driven to that terrible distress as to search the common sewers and old dunghills of cattle, and to eat the dung which they got there (5.13.7).

I am going to relate a matter of fact, the like to which no history relates, either among the Greeks or Barbarians! It is horrible to speak of it, and incredible when heard . . .

There was a certain woman that dwelt beyond Jordan—her name was Mary; her father was Eleazar . . . and it was now become impossible for her any way to find any more food . . . she slew her son; and then roasted him, and ate the one half of him [see Deut. 28:52-57], and kept the other half by her concealed. Upon this the seditious came in presently, and smelling the horrid scent of this food, they threatened her that they would cut her throat immediately if she did not show them what food she had gotten ready. She replied that she had saved a very fine portion of it for them; and withal uncovered what was left of her son. Hereupon they were seized with a horror . . . and those already dead were esteemed happy, because they had not lived long enough either to hear or to see such miseries (6.3.3-4).

As for the rest of the multitude that were above seventeen years old, he put them into bonds, and sent them to the Egyptian mines [see Deut. 28:68; Luke 21:24]. Titus also sent a great number into the provinces, as a present to them, that they might be destroyed upon their theatres, by the sword and by the wild beasts; but those that were under seventeen years of age were sold for slaves . . .

Now the number of those that were carried captive during this whole war was collected to be 97,000; as was the number of those that perished during the whole siege 1,100,000, the greater part of whom were indeed of the same nation [with the citizens of Jerusalem], but not belonging to the city itself; for they were come up from all the country to the feast of unleavened bread, and were on a sudden shut up by an army . . .

. . . Accordingly, the multitude of those that therein perished exceed all the destructions that either men or God ever brought upon the world . . . And now the Romans set fire to the extreme parts of the city, and burnt them down, and entirely demolished its walls (6.9.2-4).

"Great tribulation." "Not one stone shall be left here upon another." History has spoken. Jesus' words are vindicated. The fulfillment of Daniel's and Jesus' prophecies offers a solid foundation for faith. The first "great tribulation" is an accomplished, horrible fact of history.

THE SECOND "GREAT" TRIBULATION

The second "great" tribulation was foretold in Rev. 7:14. It is impossible to combine the "great tribulation" of Matthew 24 with the "great tribulation" of Revelation 7. They include very different circumstances, and the accounts are contradictory rather than complimentary. Here are some highlights of Revelation 7:

> After these things I looked, and behold, a great multitude which no one could number, of all nations, tribes, peoples, and tongues, standing before the throne and before the Lamb, clothed with white robes . . . saying, "Salvation belongs to our God who sits on the throne, and to the Lamb!" . . . Then one of the elders answered, saying to me, "Who are these arrayed in white robes, and where did they come from?" And I said to him, "Sir, you know." So he said to me, "These are the ones who come out of the great tribulation, and washed their robes and made them white in the blood of the Lamb" (7:9-10, 13-14).

Consider the differences. In Matthew 24, Jews suffered the tribulation. In contrast, in Revelation 7, Gentiles (people "of all nations") suffered the tribulation. In Matthew 24, those who did not believe in Jesus and, therefore, did not heed His warning to flee from Jerusalem suffered the tribulation—they were unbelieving Jews. In contrast, in Revelation 7, people who fully believed in Jesus and had their sins cleansed in the blood of the Lamb suffered the tribulation— they were believing Gentiles. In the one case, unbelieving Jews suffered great tribulation as punishment from God; in the other case, believing Christians of all nations were eternally blessed by God for remaining faithful to Him in spite of great tribulation.

Revelation 7 speaks of those who have "come out of the great tribulation" (7:14). In context, what can that be? Starting with this verse, we must search backward until we find the answer. The first part of chapter 7 presents no tribulation of any kind. The sixth seal (6:12-17) is certainly a time of tribulation. It tells of the "wrath of the Lamb" (6:16) upon the kings and slaves alike. However, it offers no indication of faith or repentance for salvation.

Only when we back up to the fifth seal do we find satisfactory information. Here we read of "those who had been slain for the word of God" (6:9). Surely a time of tribulation. What did they wear in 6:11? "A white robe was given to each of them" just like it says in 7:13-14. In the context, what better reply can be found as to which great tribulation is being spoken of in Rev. 7:14? The tribulation of the saints of the fifth seal, who were killed "for the word of God and for the testimony which they held."

The historical interpretation of the book of Revelation sees the fulfillment of the fifth seal in the persecution of the early church by the Roman Empire. This persecution culminated in Emperor Diocletian's attempt to blot out Christianity, A.D. 303-311.

In his classic *History of the Christian Church,* Philip Schaff offers some details:

> All former persecutions of the faith were forgotten in the horror with which men looked back upon the last and greatest [of Diocletian] . . .
>
> . . . Christian churches were to be destroyed; all copies of the Bible were to be burned; all Christians were to be deprived of public office and civil rights; and at last all, without exception, were to sacrifice to the gods upon pain of death . . .
>
> . . . All the pains, which iron and steel, fire and sword, rack and cross, wild beasts and beastly men could inflict, were employed.[4]

Even if one rejects this as the specific fulfillment of the fifth seal, still the fifth seal is obviously a time of persecution of Christians to the death. The ones who received the white robes were the martyred Christians. After Rev. 6:11, those white robes are next mentioned in 7:14 as having been received by "the ones who come out of the great tribulation."

The great tribulation of Matthew 24 had to do with the Jews. It was God's punishment upon them for their unbelief and rejection of their Messiah. The great tribulation of Revelation 7 had to do with believers of all nations. It was the martyrdom of Christians perpetrated by unbelievers; but the martyrs are the real victors, given white robes, and dwelling in peace with God forever. Two different great tribulations totally unrelated to one another.

THE THIRD "GREAT" TRIBULATION

There is a third text that speaks of "great" tribulation. It is Rev. 2:20, 22 in the letter to the church of Thyatira:

> Nevertheless I have a few things against you, because you allow that woman Jezebel, who calls herself a prophetess, to teach and seduce My servants to commit sexual immorality . . . Indeed I will cast her into a sickbed, and those who commit adultery with her into great tribulation, unless they repent of their deeds.

This "great tribulation" was to punish a false prophetess in the Lord's church in Thyatira along with those who followed her. Christ warned that if she and her followers did not repent, He would cast them into "great tribulation." It would be the Lord's punishment on specific sinning Christians. There is no way to fit this situation into the context of either Matthew 24 or Revelation 7.

As far as I know, there is no record of the fulfillment of this great tribulation. In fact, it is not a direct prophecy but rather a warning of what would happen "unless." We do not know if there was repentance. We do not know if this tribulation became a reality. If it did, Jesus, the true author of

Revelation, said that it would be "great tribulation."

"YOU WILL HAVE TRIBULATION"

According to futurism, the Rapture is the Christian's hope because through the Rapture, the church will escape "the" Great Tribulation. However, not one—but three— "great" tribulations are mentioned in the N.T., and each one involves circumstances quite different from the others. Moreover, all three refer to times which are now history. The first tribulation involved unbelieving Jews of the first century. The second involved faithful Christians quite possibly of the first four centuries. The third, if it took place at all, involved wicked Christians late in the first century. As already seen in Chapter 4, "Which Tribulation?" tribulation to one degree or another is something to be expected in every Christian's life.

According to the Word of God, there is no way to limit tribulation to one future seven-year period. According to the Word of God, the church throughout all ages will suffer tribulation. In John 16:33, Jesus said to His disciples: "In the world you will have tribulation; but be of good cheer, I have overcome the world."

Chapter 9

Did God Stop the Prophetic Clock?

Daniel's seventy-weeks prophecy is one of the greatest proofs that Jesus of Nazareth is the Messiah! It is one of the clearest prophecies to detail the work of the Messiah. It is also an outstanding prediction of God's final judgment upon Jerusalem and the temple.

As seen in previous chapters, the final seventieth week of Daniel 9 is the heart of this prophetic message. Proof was given to show that this prophetic week was fulfilled from A.D. 26 to 33. Jesus' death for our sins occurred in the very middle of the prophetic week, in A.D. 30. Further proof was given that the balance of the prophecy was fulfilled by the year A.D. 70 when the Romans destroyed the temple and all Jerusalem. Daniel 9 has been totally and wonderfully fulfilled.

"Not so," says futurism. The futurist interpretation says that Daniel's final week is yet future!

"The Prophetic Clock Stopped"

According to the futurist view, "God's prophetic clock" ran

flawlessly for sixty-nine weeks (483 years). Then suddenly the clock stopped and has not ticked since.

Another metaphor frequently used by futurism is that our present church age is in a parenthesis or gap. Futurism claims God's major prophetic plan of all ages relates to physical Israel on the physical earth. It says that when the Jews rejected Jesus, God delayed these plans for Israel and instituted the church.

In his best-selling book *The Rapture*, Hal Lindsey writes:

> God obviously stopped "the prophetic stopwatch" after it had ticked off 483 years . . . Because Israel failed to accept her Messiah and instead "cut him off" by crucifying him, God stopped the countdown seven years short of completion. During the ensuing parenthesis in time, God turned His focus to the Gentiles and created the Church.[1]

Lindsey's statements raise serious concerns. He indicates that when the Jews crucified Jesus, God had to change plans! This means that Jesus' ministry was a failure, that Jesus did not accomplish what He came to do on earth. In other words, he says that God's millennial kingdom for the Jews had been on the launching pad for 483 years without a problem. The launch was just seven years away when suddenly God had to stop the countdown. God's plan for the Jews went on hold; it has been on hold for over nineteen hundred years! This concept is one of the foundation stones of the futurist (dispensational) system.

"At the Rapture, the Clock Will Start Again"

Futurism further says that God cannot continue His plans with Israel as long as Jesus' church remains in the world. Futurism says the Rapture must take place before God's prophetic plan can again move forward. Hal Lindsey explains it this way: "The Lord will Rapture the Church believers before the beginning of Daniel's Seventieth Week."[2]

With the church out of the way, futurism says, God can

resume His dealing with the Jews for seven more years thus completing the final week of Daniel. Futurism calls this seven-year period the Tribulation. Daniel 9 is the only text offered by futurism to uphold its idea that the Tribulation will be for seven years. Hal Lindsey writes of "this period, which will last seven years. Students of prophecy have commonly called this time 'the Tribulation' . . . The prophet Daniel gave the framework for the Tribulation era in Daniel 9:24-27."[3]

There exists a slight variation of the futurist interpretation which says the seven-year period does not begin exactly at the Rapture, but rather shortly after the Rapture when the Antichrist signs a pact with Israel. Speaking of this covenant between the Antichrist and Israel, Tim LaHaye says: "His signing will trigger the prophetic clock of God, and from that moment on only seven years will be left for the human race on earth."[4] Speaking of the same treaty in *Tribulation Force*, "Left Behind" #2, LaHaye and Jenkins put these words into the mouths of the Tribulation Force: "The seven-year treaty . . . actually signals the beginning of the seven-year period of tribulation . . . once it does, the clock starts ticking . . . toward Christ setting up his kingdom on earth."[5] Futurism is saying that until the Rapture and the signing of the treaty after the Rapture, God's prophetic clock is on hold.

To understand the importance of this issue in critiquing the "Left Behind" series, one must realize that the entire series is based upon it. The whole plot is built upon this futuristic assumption: God's clock stopped while Jesus was on earth the first time, and the clock will start again soon after the Rapture. If the stopping of God's clock is, in fact, an unproven theory, then there is no biblical foundation for the "Left Behind" series.

The futurist view says that none or only a portion of the six items mentioned in Dan. 9:24 were fulfilled in Jesus' first coming. It says Jesus must return to completely fulfill Dan. 9:24. Futurism teaches that the church is not the kingdom, that Israel is still God's chosen nation, and that the Millennial Age will see a future earthly Jewish kingdom that will begin after the Tribulation.

In short, the futurist view places the majority of Daniel's seventy-weeks prophecy in the same category that it places most of the book of Revelation and most of Bible prophecy—somewhere in our future. According to futurism, the Rapture must take place before the bulk of Bible prophecy can begin to be fulfilled. God's plans are presently on hold.

The Prophecy Does Not Say "350 Weeks"

Futuristic premillennial dispensationalism is the only method of prophetic interpretation that holds to the parenthesis (gap, stopped-clock) theory. It is also the method which so strongly asserts that the literal interpretation of the Bible is the bedrock principle of its system. Futurism says Old Testament prophecies about Israel must be interpreted literally.

How does this claim to literal interpretation hold up? Keep in mind that the seventy-weeks prophecy is one of the major prophetic texts dealing with Israel. How does futurism apply the literal principle to the seventy-weeks prophecy? First, futurism claims that days represent years; the historical view agrees. However, this is not a literal interpretation! Futurism teaches that once days are converted into years, 483 stands for 483 literal years from the order to rebuild Jerusalem to the arrival of the Messiah; the historical view agrees. Futurism claims the final seven years are seven literal years; the historical view agrees. However, agreement grinds to a halt at this point because futurism places a huge gap of time between the 483 years and the final 7 years. Is this gap in harmony with the literal method of interpretation? Consider the following:

The prophecy foretells seventy weeks. A week has seven days. Seventy times seven equals 490. Daniel 9 is a prophecy about 490 years. However, futurism stops the prophecy at 483 years and interjects more than 1,900 years claiming the last 7 years are yet in our future. Nearly 2,000 years are interjected! That is more than four times the total 490 years the prophecy is all about! To include the interjected years as literal numbers, Daniel should have said, "350 weeks are determined" (350 is the approximate number of "weeks" necessary to finalize the prophecy early in the twenty-first century). However, Daniel did not say "350 weeks." He said, "70 weeks are determined." Futurism simply is not as literal as it would have us believe. In effect, futurism affirms 70 = 350 even though it would never express it this way. The historical view affirms 70 = 70.

The concept of a prophetic clock is itself a figure, and indeed a figure nowhere found in Holy Scripture. What happened to this clock? Why did it stop? Was it defective or deceptive? Which? Asked another way, did God know the clock would stop, or did He not know? Neither choice is pleasant. According to futurism, for over nineteen hundred years God has not repaired His clock. What happened anyway? Which scenario would you be willing to defend?

First scenario: The clock was defective and failed; it did not work right. God did not know it was going to stop, and He was powerless to remedy the situation. The clock stopped; it was out of God's control.

Second scenario: The clock was built to deceive. God knew it was going to stop but did not want to change it. God allowed the clock to act for a while as a trustworthy time-piece knowing from the beginning that it was a deceptive product.

Which scenario could you live with? When you seriously consider the implications, it is preposterous to say that God's prophetic clock did not work right! Was it a surprise to God, or did He know all along that it would happen? Was God a helpless victim, or was it God's plan to deceive the Jews?

Does Seventy Equal Seventy?

Someone has explained the absurdity of the gap theory this way. You plan a trip from Los Angeles to Chicago. As

you leave Los Angeles, you see a sign that says: "Chicago—
70 miles." You travel 69 miles and see another sign pointing
back in the direction you came: "Los Angeles—69 miles."
Pointing forward, the sign says: "Chicago—1 mile." Below
that there is another line in small print that says: "(plus 2,000
miles)." Who would believe such a scenario?

Here is another way to look at it. Take a ruler and cut off
the last inch. Attach the inch to the rest of the ruler with a
piece of elastic. Now you have a new ruler. Just stretch the
elastic as little or as much as you like. This ruler is a very
literal ruler—it contains eleven literal inches plus one last
literal inch, a total of twelve inches. A literal ruler, right?
Oh, the elastic in between? No problem. It's still a good
ruler, isn't it, with all its twelve inches? Do you want to do
business with the owner of this ruler?

When I lived in Guatemala, I was teaching a young man
in his home. Since he was very knowledgeable in the Bible,
prophetic questions kept coming up, including Daniel 9.

One day I asked him: "Julio, what would you think if I
asked you to lend me one thousand quetzals [the national
currency]? I promise to pay you back in eight weeks. When
seven weeks pass, I come to you and say, 'Julio, there is a
little matter I didn't tell you. Between the seventh and
eighth weeks of our agreement, there is a space of ten years.'
What would you think of me?" Without hesitation Julio said,
"You would be a swindler."

With these examples in mind—the false mileage sign, the
fake ruler, and the swindler—it is easy to see that the futuristic method of dealing with the seventy weeks goes well
beyond the question of literal or figurative. There is no
symbolism that can convert 70 weeks into 350 weeks or
convert 490 years into 2,450 years. There is no figurative
interpretation that can accept a gap in a time prophecy. If it
is a prophecy about time, it is a prophecy about time. To
place a gap in that time period is to falsify the prophecy.
There is biblical warrant for a day symbolically representing
a year. There is no biblical warrant for converting 70 into

350. There *is* biblical warrant for gaps, jumping from one event to another, in some kinds of prophecies. There is *no* biblical warrant for a gap in a *time* prophecy. To place a gap in a time prophecy is to destroy the prophecy—the time predicted is invalidated.

Do you remember it was Jesus' apostles (not Jesus himself) who thought that everything came to a halt when their Master was crucified? Jesus then had to appear to them not only to prove His resurrection, but also to prove that nothing had stopped. Jesus told them that everything was on time exactly as God had prophesied:

> Thus it is written, and thus it was necessary for the Christ to suffer and to rise from the dead the third day, and that repentance and remission of sins should be preached in His name to all nations, beginning at Jerusalem (Luke 24:46-47).

No clock stopped. No plans changed. Nothing was thrown in parenthetically. Everything was exactly on schedule exactly as "it is written"—70 weeks is 70 weeks; 490 years is 490 years.

Inserting What is Not There

Futurism inserts various concepts into the seventy-weeks prophecy that simply are not there, such as the following:

1. The Antichrist will make a covenant with the Jews for seven years.

2. These seven years will be called the Tribulation.

3. Before or during the early part of the seven years, the Jews will rebuild the temple.

4. In the middle of the seven years, the Antichrist will break this covenant and stop the sacrifices.

5. Jerusalem and the third temple will be destroyed.

However, a careful reading of Dan. 9:26-27 reveals that none of these concepts are mentioned. There is no Tribulation, no second rebuilding of the temple, no second restoration of sacrifices, no Antichrist making a covenant with the Jews, no later breaking of such a covenant, and no Jerusalem being destroyed twice. None of these things are predicted. Rather, they are ideas that futurism has inserted into the text. They are ideas that are assumed to be true. The text is then read with these assumptions in mind. Reading the text without these assumptions results in a very different understanding of what Daniel was prophesying.

Furthermore, futurism attempts to impose an order of events in the text that is not warranted. Futurism says that things must take place in the order they are mentioned. That would often be true, but it is not necessarily so. In the seventy-weeks prophecy, futurism notices that four items are mentioned in the following order:

1. the sixty-nine weeks,
2. the death of the Messiah,
3. the destruction of Jerusalem, and
4. the seventieth week.

Based on this list, the claim is made that these four items must take place in the order in which they are listed. Therefore, since events #2 and #3 are mentioned between the sixty-ninth and seventieth weeks, futurism claims this proves there is a gap between the last two weeks of the prophecy. If that is so, there is a gap of at least forty years from A.D. 30, when the Messiah died, to A.D. 70, when Jerusalem was destroyed. Once futurism "discovered" a forty-year gap, it saw no problem in stretching the gap from forty years to two thousand years.

However, such an argument based on the order in which things are written simply is not a sound rule of interpretation for the Bible or any other literature. History and prophecy (the foretelling of history) frequently discuss events out of chronological order. For one biblical example, read the great Messianic prophecy of Isaiah 53 from beginning to end. Anyone can easily see that numerous statements are out of chronological order. When any text clearly indicates that one event follows another, then that order must be accepted. However, in the absence of such clear indications, we may or may not be able to discover the chronological order of events.

Indeed, it is not necessary to look beyond Daniel 9 to show that such an "order" argument cannot prove anything by itself. Notice the order of the items in verse 25:

1. seven weeks,
2. sixty-two weeks, and
3. building the street and wall.

Neither futurism nor any other view claims this word order proves the events were to take place in that order. All knowledgeable believers (including futurists) agree the building of the street and wall took place *during* the first seven weeks (which was centuries before Christ). It did not take place *after* the sixty-two weeks (which would put it in the time of Christ). We all need to take great care to not read ideas into a text that simply are not there.

Six Items in Seventy Weeks

The futurist view further says that not all six items listed in Dan. 9:24 were fulfilled during Jesus' first coming; therefore, the fulfillment must take place sometime in our future. For that reason, futurism says, a parenthesis is required between the sixty-ninth and seventieth weeks. The argument goes like this (taking the second item of Dan. 9:24 as an example): the prophecy says "to make an end of sins"; since there is still sin in Israel, the prophecy was not fulfilled; it will not be fulfilled until the Millennium.

In reply to this example of futurist teaching, consider a parallel text. John the Baptist said, "Behold! The Lamb of God who takes away the sin of the world!" If we force John's beautiful words as futurism forces Dan. 9:24, then we have to say that John's words were not fulfilled at Calvary. Why? Because there is still sin in the world. Who would dare teach such a thing? The major portion of Chapter 5, "The Jews' Time Has Run Out," demonstrates how all six items of Dan. 9:24 were fulfilled during Jesus' first coming on earth. Numerous New Testament texts are quoted to prove their fulfillment.

Verse 24 clearly says the six items are to be fulfilled during seventy weeks:

> Seventy weeks are determined
> For your people and for your holy city,
> To finish the transgression,
> To make an end of sins,
> To make reconciliation for iniquity,
> To bring in everlasting righteousness,
> To seal up vision and prophecy,
> And to anoint the Most Holy.

According to this prophecy, six important items must be accomplished within the seventy weeks (490 years). However, futurism places the fulfillment of some or all of the six items outside of the seventy weeks. The idea is that a gap is necessary between the sixty-ninth and seventieth weeks, so that whatever was not fulfilled during the sixty-nine weeks can be fulfilled in a future seventieth week. However, a careful look at futurism's own teaching shows that several of the six items are not fulfilled in any of the seventy weeks.

There are various interpretations within futurism on exactly how or when the six items of Dan. 9:24 are fulfilled. One view is that at least the basis for the fulfillment of the first three items was accomplished by Jesus on the cross. However, the usual futurist teaching is that the sixty-ninth week ended at the triumphal entry five days before Jesus' death. Therefore, according to the gap theory, Jesus died in the gap between the sixty-ninth and seventieth weeks. Think of it: futurism actually teaches that five days *after* God's prophetic clock stopped, His Son died on Calvary! That puts Jesus' death outside of God's prophetic plan. Futurism not only puts the church in the parenthesis, it places the death, burial, and resurrection of the Messiah in the parenthesis! This directly contradicts the fact that God planned the death of Jesus before the foundation of the world. Peter referred to "the precious blood of Christ, as of a lamb without blemish and without spot. He indeed was foreordained before the foundation of the world" (1 Pet. 1:19-20). Even more directly, Rev. 13:8 speaks of "the Lamb slain from the foundation of the world."

Futurism teaches that the seventieth week is a future Tribulation that will be followed by the Millennium. Although futurists do not agree on all aspects of the six items of Dan. 9:24, they seem to be unanimous in saying that at least some of the six will not be fully realized until the Millennium. This presents a real problem: According to futurism's own timetable, the Millennium comes *after* the seventieth week. Thus, if anything in Dan. 9:24 is to be fulfilled during the Millennium, it would again be outside of the seventy weeks demanded by the prophecy.

Dan. 9:24 indicates that all six items must be fulfilled *within* the seventy weeks. Though futurist teachers handle the six items in Dan. 9:24 in various ways, it seems they all place most of the fulfillment either in the gap itself or after the final week, rather than during the seventy weeks. This simply does not satisfy the requirements of the prophecy. Rather than accept such a theory, it is much easier to believe that God knew what He prophesied. It is much easier to believe that Dan. 9:24 was fulfilled by Jesus right on schedule—at His *first* coming.

The New Covenant Temple

The futurist viewpoint admits that nowhere does the Bible prophesy the rebuilding of the temple after A.D. 70. What, then, is the basis for the assumption there will be a third temple, not to mention a fourth temple in the Millennium? It is said that Daniel 9, Matthew 24, 2 Thessalonians 2, and Revelation 11 cannot be fulfilled without a rebuilt temple.

The first two texts, Daniel 9 and Matthew 24, are excellent examples of the need to examine prophecy in context. Even though futurism gives Dan. 9:26 scant attention, it agrees that Dan. 9:26 refers to the destruction of the second temple in A.D. 70. On the other hand, the futurist view says that the next verse, 9:27, refers to the destruction of a third temple in our future.

Any casual reading of Dan. 9:24-27 will highlight three great historical events. Remember that when Gabriel spoke this message to Daniel, Jerusalem and the temple were in ruins. In that setting, Gabriel predicted the following:

1. Jerusalem and the temple will be rebuilt.
2. The Messiah (Christ) will arrive and die.
3. The city and temple will be destroyed again.

That is it. Did you notice that between verses 26 and 27 the temple was rebuilt *again*? No, you did not, because it is not there. Even the futurist view recognizes that Daniel 9 speaks of only one reconstruction of Jerusalem—the one whose fulfillment is recorded in Ezra and Nehemiah. Since no second rebuilding is announced, verse 27 is necessarily offering more details of the destruction predicted in verse 26.

There is no place in the Old or New Testaments where any rebuilding of Jerusalem's temple is prophesied to take place after the destruction that was scheduled for A.D. 70. Daniel 9 prophesies one rebuilding, not two. Without a second rebuilding, there cannot be a second destruction. Until someone finds a Scripture that clearly predicts a second reconstruction, we will have to understand that Dan. 9:26-27 refers to A.D. 70.

As for Matthew 24, any statements that Jesus makes about Jerusalem and the temple must be understood in light of the context. While Jesus and His disciples were observing the second temple, Jesus said: "Not one stone shall be left here upon another" (24:2). He was obviously speaking of the temple then standing. He talked only about the destruction of that temple. He gave not the slightest hint of any later reconstruction. Until someone finds a Scripture that predicts a reconstruction after A.D. 70, anything Jesus said about the destruction of Jerusalem and the temple must refer to the temple He and the apostles were looking at when He made His declaration.

There are those today who are highly interested in seeing the temple in Jerusalem rebuilt. Even if it were rebuilt, it would not be in fulfillment of any prophecy of Scripture; none exists. Nor would it meet with any approval from God. On the contrary, it would be in direct defiance of the very God who used the Romans to destroy the temple in A.D. 70. If the Jews were to offer bulls and goats again, it would be an absolute insult to the Messiah Jesus, who two thousand years ago offered the perfect sacrifice for Jew and Gentile alike:

> We have been sanctified through the offering of the body of Jesus Christ once for all. And every priest stands ministering daily and offering repeatedly the same sacrifices, which can never take away sins. But this Man, after He had offered one sacrifice for sins forever, sat down at the right hand of God (Heb. 10:10-12).

The latter two texts which futurism uses to assume a future rebuilt temple, 2 Thessalonians 2 and Revelation 11, are excellent examples of the need to understand sound Scriptural doctrine before attempting to interpret prophecy. Both texts speak of "the temple of God." Both texts are part of the New Testament. The stone temple in Jerusalem ceased being the temple of God when God himself tore the inner veil in two at Jesus' death. As both Daniel and Jesus prophesied, that temple was doomed to destruction. No Scripture prophesies a rebuilding after that.

In the new covenant there is a new temple. Paul asked the church in Corinth: "Do you not know that you are the temple of God and that the Spirit of God dwells in you?" (1 Cor. 3:16). He told the Ephesian church:

> Now, therefore, you are . . . built on the foundation of the apostles and prophets, Jesus Christ Himself being the chief cornerstone, in whom the whole building, being joined together, grows into a holy temple in the Lord (Eph. 2:19-21).

With sound apostolic doctrine, there is no warrant nor necessity for inventing another rebuilding of the Jewish stone temple. Both 2 Thessalonians 2 and Revelation 11 contain prophecies of the Lord's church. That church is where God now dwells. That church is God's temple.

Jesus Did What He Came to Do

What opposition He faced! What obstacles He had to overcome! Yet, He did it. Jesus did what He came to do. The Jews could not stop Him. Satan and all his demons could not foil Him. Hades itself could not retain Him. Jesus did what He came to do.

The night He was betrayed, Jesus told the Father, "I have finished the work which You have given Me to do" (John 17:4). He had finished all—up to that moment, and He was ready to finish what lay just ahead. He previously had told His apostles:

> Behold, we are going up to Jerusalem, and all things that are written by the prophets concerning the Son of Man will be accomplished. For He will be delivered to the Gentiles and will be mocked . . . They will scourge Him and kill Him. And the third day He will rise again (Luke 18:31-33).

The prophets foretold it. Jesus foretold it. And He did it. The apostles preached that Jesus did what He came to do:

> For those who dwell in Jerusalem . . . have fulfilled them [the prophets] in condemning Him. And . . . they asked Pilate that He should be put to death. Now when they had fulfilled all that was written concerning Him, they took Him down from the tree and laid Him in a tomb . . . And we declare to you glad tidings— that promise which was made to the fathers. God has fulfilled this for us their children, in that He has raised up Jesus (Acts 13:27-29, 32-33).

Everything in Jesus' ministry went according to plan. The rejection by the Jews had been prophesied; it was part

Stop the "prophetic clock"?
God did not.
Man cannot.

Drawing © by CrossDaily.com (Ron Wheeler). Used by permission.

Jesus came <u>on time</u>.

Jesus died and rose <u>on time</u>.

Jesus started the kingdom <u>on time</u>.

Jesus said to the Father:
"I have finished the work
which You have given Me to do."
– John 17:4

of the plan. His death had been prophesied; it was necessary to redeem us from sin. The Jews could not stop God from fulfilling His promises, nor could Satan or Hades. We believe in and follow Jesus precisely because He was willing and able to do what He came to do.

Could Not Tell Time

Jesus cried. Not for himself but for Jerusalem. In His mind's eye, He skipped over His fast-approaching crucifixion and focused on the holy city's utter destruction scheduled for A.D. 70. In less than a week, the city would nail Jesus to a cross. However, Jesus was not crying because He was a failure. He was crying because the Jews failed to recognize their Messiah who loved them.

Futurism claims that because the Jews rejected Jesus, God made a drastic change of plans. It claims the kingdom Daniel predicted had to be postponed for thousands of years. Jesus, the real prophecy teacher, held a very different view. He never said the Jew's rejection would cause the kingdom to be postponed. Never! Rather, He said the Jew's rejection would cause the total destruction of Jerusalem. Listen to His words:

> He saw the city and wept over it, saying . . . "days will come upon you when your enemies will . . . level you . . . and they will not leave in you one stone upon another, because you did not know the time of your visitation" (Luke 19:41-44).

The Jews did not know the time. It was time for the Messiah to arrive. It was time for the kingdom to arrive. It was time to fulfill many great prophecies. God was visiting His people, but Jesus accused the Jews of not understanding God's timing.

If your little daughter cannot tell time, do you stop the clock until she can? Absurd. Neither did God stop His so-called prophetic clock when the Jews could not tell time. Rather, he destroyed their city! Daniel had already prophesied this. God knew centuries earlier what the reaction of the Jews would be. With God everything was right on schedule, but the Jews could not tell time. Can we tell time today?

The Real Parenthesis

The parenthesis or gap theory is upside down and backwards. Why? Because futurism has placed God's eternal plan in parentheses and has made God's parenthetical plan His major plan. According to futurism, God's plan with the Jews is the major theme of Bible prophecy. According to this view, the gospel age in which we live is just a parenthesis between God's former and future dealings with Israel.

However, the Scripture clearly sustains an opposite view. The main theme of the Bible is God's eternal plan for the church age. It is the old covenant of the Jews that was in parenthesis. The book of Galatians was written because some early Christians did not understand the proper place of the Mosaic Law. They did not understand the true biblical gap doctrine. They did not grasp what the promises to Abraham were all about. Paul explained to them:

> And the Scripture, foreseeing that God would justify the Gentiles by faith, preached the gospel to Abraham beforehand, saying, "In you all the nations shall be blessed" (Gal. 3:8).

Scripture foresaw the salvation of the Gentiles. All nations are blessed in Abraham. How? Through the preaching of the gospel. The Jews were a vessel used by God to bring us the Savior. Paul further explained:

> Now to Abraham and his Seed were the promises made. He does not say, "And to seeds," as of many, but as of one, "And to your Seed," who is Christ (Gal. 3:16).

The promise was made to Abraham. The fulfillment came through Christ. The real parenthesis in the Bible is the space of time between Abraham and Christ. Listen to the next verse:

> The law, which was four hundred and thirty years later, cannot annul the covenant that was confirmed before by God in Christ, that it should make the promise of no effect (Gal. 3:17).

Here is the order of events:
1. The covenant and promise are given to Abraham.
2. The Jewish nation receives the law.
3. Christ fulfills the promise to Abraham.

The law, item #2, filled in the gap. So the question arises:

> What purpose then does the law serve? It was added because of transgressions, till the Seed should come to whom the promise was made (Gal. 3:19).

There you have the gap (parenthesis) that the Bible teaches. The Law of Moses is the parenthesis between the promise to Abraham and the fulfillment of that promise through Christ. God's real parenthesis did not involve any clock stopping. There was no change of plans. Everything happened according to schedule:

> When the fullness of the time had come, God sent forth His Son, born of a woman, born under the law, to redeem those who were under the law, that we might receive the adoption as sons (Gal. 4:4-5).

God's Clock is Trustworthy

Jesus' death was not the start of a parenthesis. It was the end of the Divine Parenthesis that God placed between Abraham and Jesus. When Jesus died, God's prophetic clock did not stop. The Mosaic Law stopped! It was nailed to the cross. Acceptable temple sacrifices stopped! The veil of the temple was torn in two. It all happened according to God's timetable.

God gave the Jews seventy weeks (490 years). No trick clock can extend that time. Jesus told the Jews: "For days will come upon you when your enemies . . . will not leave in you one stone upon another, because you did not know the time of your visitation" (Luke 19:43-44). Before the 490 years ended, their doom was sealed. There was no problem with God's clock. The problem was with the Jews. They could not tell time!

God knew ahead of time that men would reject His Son. He predicted it in Psalm 2:

> Why do the nations rage,
> And the people plot a vain thing?
> The kings of the earth set themselves,
> And the rulers take counsel together,
> Against the LORD and against His Anointed [Messiah, Christ]
> . . .
> He who sits in the heavens shall laugh (2:1-2, 4).

This striking prophecy was fulfilled when Jesus came to earth the first time. In Acts 4:25-28, we can read where the apostles quote and explain a portion of these very verses:

> Who by the mouth of Your servant David have said:
> "Why did the nations rage,
> And the people plot vain things?
> The kings of the earth took their stand,
> And the rulers were gathered together
> Against the LORD and against His Christ."
> For truly against Your holy Servant Jesus, whom You anointed, both Herod and Pontius Pilate, with the Gentiles and the people of Israel, were gathered together to do whatever Your hand and Your purpose determined before to be done.

Did God stop His clock? Did God change His plans? Not at all! Rather, God did exactly what He had "determined before to be done" and laughed at those opposed to His Anointed One.

But wait! This is not the whole story. Throughout the Bible God has always worked with a remnant. Some of the Jews *did* figure out what time it was. They took advantage of the day of salvation that had been prophesied for so long. It was in Jewish Jerusalem that the church began. The twelve apostles were all Jews. The first three thousand converted were all Jews. Soon after, the number converted grew to five thousand men, all Jews. Most of the New Testament was written by Jews. It is just as Paul asked and replied: "Has God cast away His people? Certainly not! For I also am an Israelite, of the seed of Abraham, of the tribe of Benjamin" (Rom. 11:1).

The gospel and the church are not a parenthetically inserted program. They are God's real eternal program, open to Jew and Gentile alike. They are what the promise to Abraham was all about. They are the reason Jesus came to earth. Daniel's seventy-weeks prophecy has been gloriously fulfilled. Praise God!

Section Three

The Roman Connection

Chapter 10

Why Rome?

Most studies of Revelation mention Rome sooner or later. It may be Rome in the past, present, or future. It may be Rome as a political power or Rome as a religious power. It may be Rome as a major player or Rome as a minor player in the events predicted. One way or another, Rome is usually brought into the picture. Why Rome?

Nebuchadnezzar's Awesome Image

It all started twenty-six hundred years ago when the Creator of the universe used a Middle-Eastern tyrant to make an amazing revelation. Nebuchadnezzar, dictator of the ancient Babylonian Empire, was a special vessel utilized by God to punish Israel. He was also specially chosen by God to receive one of the best-known dreams of all times—not that he understood a word of it. In fact, he could not even remember it.

Like some modern politicians, Nebuchadnezzar called in his astrologers for consultation. He asked them to tell him what he had dreamed. The astrologers, of course, asked the king to tell them the dream so that they could give the interpretation. However, Nebuchadnezzar had much more common sense than do many gullible church members to-day. He was not going to believe just anything he was told even by respected spiritual authorities. He wanted evidence that the astrologers really did have power to interpret dreams. For this reason, he demanded of them: "Tell me the dream, and I shall know that you can give me its interpretation" (Dan. 2:9).

The "wise men" of Babylonia were understandably upset with the king's demand. "There is not a man on earth who can tell the king's matter," they said. "There is no other who can tell it to the king except the gods, whose dwelling is not with flesh" (Dan. 2:10-11). Later Daniel entered and agreed that the astrologers were incapable of making the dream known. However, Daniel demonstrated that they were wrong on the last point. The God of heaven, indeed, did dwell with men—specifically with the prophets of Israel. Thus, Daniel, inspired by God, was able to explain the dream.

Five Kingdoms

An awesome image . . . head of gold . . . chest of silver . . . belly of bronze . . . legs of iron. In addition, there was an extraordinary stone. After crushing the awesome image, this stone became such a great mountain that it filled the entire earth.

Daniel made it plain to Nebuchadnezzar: "You are this head of gold" (Dan. 2:38). Daniel continued: "After you shall arise another kingdom . . . then another, a third kingdom . . . And the fourth kingdom . . . [and last of all] the God of heaven will set up a kingdom" (2:39-40, 44)—five kingdoms in all. By saying a third and fourth *kingdom*, it is clear that the golden head was more than King Nebuchadnezzar alone. The head included the entire kingdom of Babylon. Five kingdoms in all are portrayed: the image represented four kingdoms of this world, and the stone represented the kingdom of God.

The identity of the first four kingdoms is the simplest

part of the prophecy. Virtually all Bible believers, from ancient to modern times, agree that these kingdoms are Babylon, Medo-Persia, Greece, and Rome. Are these believers right?

Years after Nebuchadnezzar's death, Belshazzar, king of Babylon, was having a royal party. Who has not heard the picturesque expression: "He saw the handwriting on the wall"? For Belshazzar it was far from picturesque. He was so terrified at the sight that his knees were knocking together. Included in Daniel's explanation of the writing were these words: "Your kingdom has been divided, and given to the Medes and Persians" (Dan. 5:28). Thus, the second kingdom is that of the Medes and Persians, a fact also confirmed in secular historical records.

Secular history confirms the third kingdom to be Greece; the book of Daniel agrees. Chapter 8 contains the vision of a goat totally overpowering and trampling a ram. Verses 20 and 21 point out: "The ram . . . the kings of Media and Persia. And the male goat is the kingdom of Greece." Positive identification. The great horn of the goat was, of course, Alexander the Great. Alexander died prematurely: "The large horn was broken, and in place of it four notable ones came up toward the four winds of heaven" (8:8). This is an obvious reference to the four-fold breakup of Alexander's empire among four of his generals.

The book of Daniel does not identify the fourth kingdom, but any student of history knows that the Roman Empire was the next one on the scene. Rome was the world power when Jesus of Nazareth walked this earth. Luke makes this clear when he records that Jesus was born in the days of Caesar Augustus (Luke 2:1). It is also seen in Luke's account of the beginning of Jesus' ministry: "Now in the fifteenth year of the reign of Tiberius Caesar, Pontius Pilate being governor of Judea" (Luke 3:1). Tiberius is well known as the second emperor of the Roman Empire. In the life of the apostle Paul, there are frequent references to the rule of Rome. Indeed, Paul used his Roman citizenship to seek a fair trial under Caesar in Rome (see Acts 25:10-12). Though not named in Scripture, the Caesar at that time was the infamous Nero.

Was Rome the Fourth Kingdom?

Since the Roman Empire was the next one on the world scene after the Grecian, it is only natural that believers consider Rome to be the fourth kingdom prophesied. However, not everyone believes that the fourth kingdom, represented by the legs of iron, was Rome. A few people today believe the legs of iron are yet in our future. Is that possible? They agree that the first three kingdoms were Babylon, Medo-Persia, and Greece. However, they place a gap of more than two thousand years between the image's belly of bronze and its legs of iron. Is that a feasible interpretation? Let us examine specific reasons why believers past and present are nearly unanimous in believing that the image's legs of iron were surely prophetic of the Roman Empire.

Nebuchadnezzar saw just one image in Daniel 2. It had the form of one man, complete with one head, one torso, two arms, and two legs. All believers agree the first three kingdoms (empires) immediately followed one another, thus fitting into the symbolism of one body. However, if the fourth empire does not immediately follow the third, then the fourth kingdom should have been a separate image. If there are two thousand years of world history between the third and fourth kingdoms, the dream should have portrayed two separate images. However, the dream was not like that. Nebuchadnezzar saw just one image, one complete man with all of his body parts normally connected to each other. God has not entrusted any of us with a hacksaw, setting us free to amputate the image's legs and to set them off by themselves.

The simple fact of numbering the kingdoms is a confirmation of their connectedness. After discussing the head of gold, Dan. 2:39-40 says, "after you shall arise another kingdom . . . then another, a third kingdom . . . And the fourth

Daniel 2	Fulfillment	Daniel 7	Revelation 13
	Babylon 606–538 B.C.	Lion	mouth like a **Lion**
	Medo-Persia 538–331 B.C.	Bear	feet like a **Bear**
	Greece 331–31 B.C.	Leopard	like a **Leopard**
	Rome 31 B.C.–A.D. 476	Beast	**BEAST**
	Rome after A.D. 476	with ten horns	with ten horns and seven heads

Drawing © by Holly Deyo, http://www.millennium-ark.net/News_Files/Trib_Time/Beasts.html. Used with permission.

kingdom." Both "third" and "fourth" are specified. The text does not say "eighth" or "twelfth," nor does it simply say "another" and "another." It says "third" and "fourth."

The close relationship between the four kingdoms is further expressed in the following words to Nebuchadnezzar: "head of gold . . . another kingdom . . . a third kingdom . . . the fourth kingdom . . . will break in pieces and crush all the others" (Dan. 2:38-40). In this context, "all the others" can only refer to the former three kingdoms. There is no way in this dream that "the others" can refer to some unnamed kingdoms two thousand years in the future. By saying that the fourth kingdom would break and crush the other three kingdoms, a historical connection to the first three kingdoms is required.

As will be discussed later, some argue that Rome was not a universal empire; therefore, they look for a future empire or kingdom to fulfill this part of the prophecy. However, Daniel 2 does not say, "the fourth universal kingdom." It simply says: "The fourth kingdom" (2:40). Whether we agree that Rome was universal or not, Daniel says, "the fourth kingdom." Whether we agree that Rome was as strong as iron or not, Daniel says, "the fourth kingdom." Regardless of our preconceived ideas of what that kingdom should be like, Daniel says that it would be the *fourth* kingdom. Historically speaking, there is no question that Rome was the fourth kingdom.

Daniel 7—The Five Kingdoms Revisited

Nebuchadnezzar's dream in Daniel 2 does not stand alone. In chapter 7, Daniel records related visions of his own. God told Daniel that four beasts represent four kings (7:17) or kingdoms (7:23). This sounds just like Daniel 2. The difference is that in one case there is an image and in the other case, four animals. However, there is a problem in chapter 7. None of the kingdoms is openly identified; so, where does the prophecy begin? Daniel 2 becomes the all-important key to unlock Daniel 7.

Both chapters predict four earthly kingdoms. Both prophecies were made during the Babylonian Empire. Both chapters place far more emphasis on the fourth kingdom than on the preceding three. Both chapters use iron as a symbol of the fourth kingdom—in one, the legs are of iron; in the other, the fourth beast has iron teeth. Both prophecies emphasize the strength and destruction caused by the fourth kingdom:

> The fourth kingdom shall be as strong as iron . . . will break in pieces and crush all the others (2:40).

> The fourth beast shall be
> A fourth kingdom . . .
> And shall devour the whole earth,
> Trample it and break it in pieces (7:23).

In addition, the kingdom of God is the next and only other kingdom portrayed in both chapters.

Combining all the evidence, the only meaningful way to interpret chapter 7 is to do it the way nearly everyone has always interpreted it. There is every reason to believe that the four kingdoms in the two prophecies are the same four kingdoms. Indeed, there is no reason to believe otherwise. Since Daniel 2 positively identifies the first kingdom as the Babylonian power, this becomes the only meaningful place to begin in chapter 7. Thus, the lion is Babylon, the bear is Persia, the leopard is Greece, and the terrible beast is Rome.

Testimony of Early Christians

Although the early Christians differed on many points regarding prophecy, there was wide agreement among them that they were living during the time of the iron legs of the image—the time of the fourth beast. They recognized Rome as a fulfillment of both Daniel 2 and Daniel 7. Hippolytus, who lived from A.D. 170 to 236, offers an example of this viewpoint. While discussing Daniel 2 and 7, he writes:

The golden head of the image and the lioness denoted the Babylonians; the shoulders and arms of silver, and the bear, represented the Persians and Medes; the belly and thighs of brass, and the leopard, meant the Greeks, who held the sovereignty from Alexander's time; the legs of iron, and the beast dreadful and terrible, expressed the Romans, who hold the sovereignty at present; the toes of the feet which were part clay and part iron, and the ten horns, were emblems of the kingdoms that are yet to rise.[1]

Several other direct quotes from early Christian writers are given in Chapter 12, "Man of Sin–the History." Thomas Newton wrote in the eighteenth century: "All ancient writers, both Jewish and Christian, agree with Jerome in explaining the fourth kingdom to be the Roman."[2]

In the third century A.D., the heathen Porphyry took an opposing view claiming the third kingdom was solely that of Alexander the Great, while the fourth kingdom consisted of Alexander's successors. Modern-day liberal "theologians" have followed that heathen example. Like Porphyry, they desperately attempt to rid Daniel of prophecy. Their method is to claim that the book of Daniel is a forgery written by an unknown Jew in the second century before Christ. They assert that Daniel's prophecies were already history by the time the book was written. At the opposite extreme are a few writers early in the nineteenth century who took the view that Rome was the third kingdom and the fourth is yet future. All the views that deny Rome as the fourth kingdom are views of a minority who are mostly unbelievers.

Almost all Bible believers throughout history have considered the fourth kingdom to be Rome. They have held this view for many excellent reasons that are being discussed in this chapter. However, once Rome is agreed upon, there is wide divergence as to the significance of that fact. Some believers place the entire fulfillment either in the first century or in the first four centuries. Other believers place the fulfillment throughout history from the first century until the present. Still others place most of the fulfillment yet in our future. So there is wide divergence. The point here is simply to substantiate the fact that Daniel did prophesy about Rome. This is the first vital step toward understanding many prophecies of both Daniel and Revelation.

"All the World"

In different ways, Daniel 2 and 7 indicate that the fourth kingdom would have power over the whole earth (2:40; 7:23). Some make the argument that this was not true of the Roman Empire; therefore, these prophecies cannot refer to Rome. However, there are similar statements of universality regarding both the first and third kingdoms (2:37-39). In addition, consider common every-day expressions such as "everybody was there," "the entire town turned out," and "he traveled all over the world." We all understand that such expressions are not one hundred percent absolutes. They are generalizations—exaggerations for emphasis. The technical term is "hyperbole." A good Bible example is Matt. 3:5: "Then Jerusalem, all Judea, and all the region around the Jordan went out to him."

In regard to the Roman Empire, notice what Luke states when he introduces Jesus' birth: "It came to pass in those days that a decree went out from Caesar Augustus that all the world should be registered . . . So all went to be registered, everyone to his own city" (Luke 2:1, 3). Whatever interpretation a person gives to the expressions in Daniel 2 and 7 regarding all the earth, the identical interpretation must be given to Luke 2. Whatever Daniel meant regarding the extent of the first, third, and fourth kingdoms, Luke 2 says the same thing concerning the kingdom then in power, the Roman Empire. In the days of Augustus, the first emperor of Rome, the Roman Empire was as universal as Daniel prophesied the fourth empire would be. The Bible tells us so.

Time for the Fifth Kingdom

During the early days of the Roman Empire, Jesus proclaimed that it was time for God's kingdom to be established:

"The time is fulfilled, and the kingdom of God is at hand" (Mark 1:15). To word it another way: "The time has come for the arrival of God's kingdom." Time has come? Time fulfilled? Kingdom of God? Without a doubt, Jesus was referring to the predictions of Israel's inspired prophets, many of whom spoke of that coming kingdom. Among these, there is no prophecy that highlights and pinpoints the time for the arrival of the kingdom as does Daniel.

After describing in considerable detail the legs, feet, and toes of the fourth kingdom, Daniel told Nebuchadnezzar: "In the days of these kings the God of heaven will set up a kingdom which shall never be destroyed" (2:44). God promised to set up His kingdom in the days of the fourth earthly kingdom. When Jesus said that the time had arrived for God's kingdom to be set up, He was claiming indirectly that He was living in the days of the kings of the fourth kingdom. The fourth kingdom had already arrived! If the fourth kingdom had not yet arrived, it would not be time for God's kingdom to arrive. No one disputes that Rome was the empire in power when Jesus spoke; therefore, the Roman Empire is the fourth kingdom of Daniel 2 and Daniel 7.

Jesus was not the only one who announced the nearness of the kingdom. John the Baptist, the apostles, and "the seventy" all went out preaching, "the kingdom of heaven is at hand," "the kingdom of God has come near" (Matt. 3:2; 4:17; 10:7; Luke 10:9). Furthermore, Jesus also predicted: "There are some standing here who will not taste death till they see the kingdom of God present with power" (Mark 9:1). In other words, the kingdom of God, prophesied in Daniel 2 and elsewhere, would arrive in the lifetime of those present. Since their lifetime was during the Roman Empire, the Roman Empire must be "these kings," the legs of iron.

One of several outstanding verses that confirm the arrival of Jesus' kingdom in the first century is the one Paul wrote to the brethren in Colosse while Nero was emperor: "He has delivered us from the power of darkness and conveyed us into the kingdom of the Son of His love" (Col. 1:13).

"Has delivered us . . . and conveyed us"—past tense, accomplished fact. "Into the kingdom." God's predicted kingdom was a present reality as Paul wrote. Consequently, Nero was one of "these kings" predicted in Daniel 2.

Extended Information in Chapter 7

As we dig deeper into these prophecies, we must keep in mind that Daniel 7 offers information regarding the fourth beast extending well beyond the information provided in chapter 2 regarding the legs and feet of the image. In chapter 7 we not only have a beast, but the beast has ten horns:

> The ten horns are ten kings
> Who shall arise from this kingdom.
> And another [little horn] shall rise after them;
> He shall be different from the first ones,
> And shall subdue three kings (7:24).

These ten horns provide us with information not included in the image of chapter 2.

Chapter 2, indeed, speaks of a "divided" kingdom. A careful Bible student, however, will notice that the text says nothing about ten toes representing ten divisions. The image's ten toes have no more prophetic meaning than do its ten fingers or its two ears. Chapter 2 clearly identifies the division: "Whereas you saw the feet and toes, partly of potter's clay and partly of iron, the kingdom shall be divided . . . the kingdom shall be partly strong and partly fragile" (Dan. 2:41-42). The division is not the ten toes, but the iron and the clay. The kingdom will at first be as strong as iron (the legs). However, in its later stages (the feet and toes), it will weaken as represented by a mixture of clay with iron. Nothing in chapter 2 deals with events in Rome after the fall of the Roman Empire. All that is represented in the image is the Roman Empire itself and its fall when broken in pieces by the stone. Indeed, chapter 2 does not even say the image had ten toes; we just assume it. "Ten" is a non-issue in chapter 2.

In contrast, the ten horns of the dreadful beast in chapter 7 are definitely an issue. As already seen, this chapter specifically says the ten horns are "ten kings." But, what is meant by "kings"? Since a king is the head and chief representative of a kingdom, "king" can sometimes actually mean "kingdom." Dan. 7:17 says that the four beasts are four kings. Yet 7:23 says the fourth beast is a "fourth kingdom." The fourth beast is a fourth king who stands for a fourth kingdom. Therefore, the ten horns are not necessarily ten individual kings, but rather may well be a prediction of ten kingdoms that would arise out of the Roman Empire. Many students of the Word understand that these ten horns and the little horn (7:8) take us prophetically into historical times following the fall of the Roman Empire, describing its division into many parts. That is to say, the power of Rome continued but in a different form. Many of us see clearly that this little horn represents the organized religious power that arose in Rome from the ashes of the Roman Empire.

The Beasts of Revelation 13

Most people are far more interested in the book of Revelation than in the book of Daniel. However, much of Revelation would be even more difficult to interpret than it is were it not for the foundation laid in Daniel. This is particularly true regarding the beasts of Revelation 13 and 17.

Daniel offers the biblical key for interpreting symbolical beasts. Accounts of beasts in prophecy cannot be treated like parables as some believers teach. Parables teach general spiritual truths applicable to many times and places. Bible prophecy, on the other hand, predicts specific events at specific times and places. Daniel's use of beasts offers clear proof of this truth. In Daniel 7 and 8, God tells us these prophetic beasts refer to specific political powers at specific times in history (7:17, 23; 8:20-21). In other words, these visions depicting beasts are not simply a generalized essay on the battle between good and evil—they are prophecy! They foretell specific political powers at specific times in history: Babylon, Medo-Persia, Greece, and Rome. Besides being prophecies in their own right, Daniel 7 and 8 are the biblical key for unlocking our understanding of the beasts in Revelation 13 and 17. With Daniel as the authority, the beasts in Revelation must be interpreted as specific world powers at specific times in history.

If this key to interpreting prophetic beasts were the only help Daniel offered us for the interpretation of Revelation, that would be substantial. However, Daniel 7 offers far more aid than that. In Revelation 13, the first beast is described as "having seven heads and ten horns . . . like a leopard . . . a bear, and . . . a lion" (13:1-2). Remarkable! The four beasts named in Revelation 13 are exactly the same four beasts of Daniel 7. Moreover, they are listed precisely in order, albeit reverse order. Surely, Revelation is pointing us to Daniel 7 for the key to interpretation. The beast of Revelation 13 has certain characteristics of all four beasts of Daniel 7. The only kingdom that would have characteristics of all four kingdoms would be the last one. Since the last one mentioned in Daniel 7 is the Roman Empire, obviously the first beast of Revelation 13 is none other than that same power.

Rome in Later Developments

Rome was the world power at the time John wrote the book of Revelation, near the end of the first century. In chapter 17, we again find a beast "having seven heads and ten horns" (17:3). Though this beast is scarlet, surely there is a connection with the seven-headed and ten-horned beast of chapter 13. The information about the ten horns in chapter 17 is most instructive: "The ten horns which you saw are ten kings who have received no kingdom as yet" (17:12). We have learned that the beast is Rome, which was then in power. However, here the text says the ten horns of the beast (also mentioned in Daniel 7 and Revelation 13) were yet in John's future. They were a development that was to take place in the second century or later. The beast already existed, but the ten-horn phase had not yet begun.

Irenaeus, writing in the second century, continued to see the ten horns as a later development of the Roman Empire. He tells of John in Revelation writing "concerning the ten kings who shall then arise, among whom the empire which now rules [the earth] shall be partitioned."[3] In other words, the ten horns have to do with the breakup of the Roman Empire. Early in the third century, Hippolytus saw himself as living under the fourth kingdom but with the ten horns as something yet in his future: "The ten horns, were emblems of the kingdoms that are yet to rise."[4]

By the fifth century A.D., the declining Roman Empire disintegrated into ten barbaric parts ushering in the Middle Ages. It was a time of upheaval; powers and borders were in flux. For this reason, not all scholars will list all the same names, nor exactly ten. Nonetheless, the following typical list of the peoples involved can generally be confirmed by any history book covering the fall of the Roman Empire: Burgundians, Franks, Heruli, Huns, Lombards, Ostrogoths, Saxons, Suevi, Vandals, and Visigoths. The Western Roman Empire had disintegrated; the predicted ten horns had become a historical reality.

In the image of Daniel 2, there was nothing to take us beyond the Roman Empire per se, which fell in A.D. 476 when the last emperor of Rome was overthrown. However, Daniel 7 and Revelation clearly take us well beyond that point in history. The Imperial Roman Empire is only the starting place for interpreting the beasts of Daniel 7 and those of Revelation 13 and 17.

A Revived Roman Empire

Regarding the first beast, Rev. 13:3 says: "And I saw one of his heads as if it had been mortally wounded, and his deadly wound was healed." Then in verses 11 and 12 another beast is presented: "Then I saw another beast . . . like a lamb . . . And he exercises all the authority of the first beast in his presence . . . the first beast, whose deadly wound was healed." The first beast, Imperial Rome, is to be "mortally wounded." *Mortal* means fatal, causing death. Yet, the wound was healed.

Revelation thus prophesied that Imperial Rome would practically die; yet, Roman power would live on. This takes us past A.D. 476. After that time, a lamb-like beast was to arise that would have all the authority of Imperial Rome and would exercise that power in the presence of a revived Rome. All one has to do is read history to see clearly what happened in Rome after the fall of the Western Roman Empire. Although detailing that history is beyond the scope of *Nobody Left Behind,* some highlights will be given in the next four chapters.

The developments prophesied in Revelation 13 and 17 are the same as those already referred to in Daniel 7. In Daniel 7, there is a powerful little horn that supplants three of the ten horns and acts brutally and blasphemously. A careful study and comparison of the texts leads to the conclusion that this little horn of Daniel 7 is prophetic of the same power as the lamb-like beast of Revelation 13. The little horn is a development related to Rome that takes place sometime following the breakup of the Roman Empire into ten parts.

Among other deficiencies, the futurist theory of a modern-day "revived Roman Empire" totally ignores the facts of ancient and medieval history. A revived Roman Empire is not something to look for in modern times; it is already history. Imperial Rome fell. However, unlike ancient Nineveh and Babylon, the *city* of Rome did not sink into ruins. On the contrary, Rome revived after A.D. 476 and continued to exercise great power over Europe and far beyond. The mortal wound was healed, and the beast lived on after it should have been dead.

These truths in Daniel 7 and Revelation 13 are expressed in yet another way in Rev. 17:8: "The beast that was, and is not, and yet is." Notice the three stages:

1. "The beast that was": the Roman Empire.
2. "And is not": Rome fell.

3. "And yet is": the emperor of Rome was replaced by the bishop of Rome, who was later called the Pope.

Rome lived on, and during the Middle Ages (the Dark Ages), Rome ruled the possessions and souls of men. Although Rome's power is now much diminished, to this day there are loyal subjects in most nations of the world who give their allegiance to the man who sits in the Vatican Palace in Rome.

Great City of Seven Hills

Rev. 17:9 interprets: "The seven heads are seven mountains on which the woman sits." Later, verse 18 says: "And the woman whom you saw is that great city which reigns over the kings of the earth." The woman sits on seven mountains, and the woman is a great city. Since ancient times, Rome has been known as the city of seven hills: the Palatine, the Aventine, the Caelian, the Esquiline, the Viminal, the Quirinal, and the Capitoline Hills. Although these names mean nothing to most of us, the fact that Rome is a seven-hilled city is widely known. Can there be any doubt that the harlot and scarlet beast are related to Rome?

Further identification of Rome is found in the "666" and the "man of sin" prophecies. The following three chapters offer an in-depth study of the "man of sin" prophecy. Chapter 14 explores the intriguing "666" prophecy.

Chapter 11

Man of Sin–the Prophecy

We are all sinners. Yet, one man in all history is singled out as "the man of sin . . . the son of perdition . . . the lawless one." Not a pleasant description. Why talk about him? Because the Word of God talks about him.

Most students of Scripture, past and present, see a connection between the "man of sin" of 2 Thessalonians 2 and the "little" "horn" of Daniel 7. They also see a connection with one or more of the beasts in Revelation 13 and with "the great harlot" and "Babylon" in Revelation 17 and 18. From ancient times, these outstanding prophecies have been lumped together under the common title Antichrist.

In spite of such agreement, views regarding the fulfillment vary widely. Is this enemy of God someone in the past, present, or future? The most popular view today, futurism, says that he is yet in the future. At the opposite extreme is a view gaining in popularity, preterism, which believes that he is a relic of ancient history. Howbeit, for hundreds of years, the vast majority of Bible believers unswervingly have proclaimed that the man of sin is a present reality.

Since there are so many conflicting views, many believers do not bother to try to figure out who the man of sin is in

2 Thessalonians 2. If we carefully read the text, however, we find that this is not just an idle study to be done out of curiosity. Eternal issues are at stake here.

What Difference Does it Make?

Number One: "Christ" *versus* **"the man of sin"** (verses 2-3). It is our Lord Jesus Christ on the one side and the man of sin on the other. Paul assures his readers that not only is Christ coming, but that the man of sin is also coming. The best and the worst. The Son of God versus a son of Satan (verse 9). Nothing less is involved than the eternal battle between the forces of good and evil. The eternal battle between God and Satan.

Number Two: "Not to be soon shaken" *versus* **"falling away"** (verses 2-3). Some people think the study of prophecy has little to do with "practical" Christianity. How much more practical can we get than standing firm or falling away? The problem is that many believers think that falling away relates only to drunkenness, adultery, forsaking the assembly, and the like. However, Paul speaks of being shaken by not knowing if the day of Christ is past or future. Paul speaks of the falling away that involves worship in the temple of God. We need to investigate what this is all about.

Number Three: "The love of the truth" *versus* **"not receive the love of the truth"** (verse 10). Love God. Love Jesus. Love your brother. Love your spouse. Love your neighbor. Love your enemy. Also—love the truth. To some people, love means sex. To others, love means unconditional acceptance of whatever a person believes or does. "Love of the truth" is not at all popular in our relativistic-materialistic age. It is not at all popular with the do-it-if-it-makes-you-feel-good club. If you love the truth, you will search for it as diligently as for a hidden treasure (Prov. 2:1-4).

Number Four: "Truth" *versus* **"deception," "delusion," and a "lie"** (verses 10-11). Living the Christian life is more than morality. It has to do with what we believe. It has to do with truth versus error. In the Garden of Eden, it was God's truth versus Satan's lie. It still is. Eve let her desires cloud the truth. Paul tells both Timothy and the Corinthians that Eve was deceived (1 Tim. 2:13-14; 2 Cor. 11:3). In like manner, millions today are deceived by the man of sin. We are not dealing here with idle prophetic curiosity. We are dealing with the issue of truth versus lies. Jesus is truth. Satan is the father of lies. That is what this prophecy is all about.

Number Five: "Saved" *versus* "condemned" (verses 10, 12). Eternity is involved in the man-of-sin prophecy. Saved or lost; blessed or condemned. Many Christians sidestep various questions, including the interpretation of prophecy, by retorting, "Well, it isn't a matter of salvation." However, the concerns in this particular prophecy are very much a matter of salvation. This prophecy has very much to do with understanding the characteristics of those who are saved and those who are condemned. It is an issue with eternal consequences.

Number Six: Righteousness *versus* "unrighteousness" (verse 12). Yes, morality does count. You cannot believe right and live wrong. At issue here are those who have "pleasure in unrighteousness." This reminds us of "lovers of pleasure" in 2 Tim. 3:4. Sin is fun—fun now; pay later. If it were not fun now, why would people bother with it? Moses chose to suffer with the people of God rather than "enjoy the passing pleasures of sin" (Heb. 11:25). The man of sin has to do with fun religion. It is fun because you can have one foot in a church and another foot in the world. They worship yet have "pleasure in unrighteousness."

These are six solid reasons why the man-of-sin prophecy merits serious study on the part of every person who cares about his relationship with the God of the universe and His precious Son.

Clarifying Important Issues

Before attempting to find the fulfillment of the man-of-sin prophecy, we must give careful attention to exactly what is predicted. All the elements of the prophecy must be taken into consideration, not just a selected few. Words and expressions must be defined properly. An English dictionary can be helpful; but also, terms must be properly interpreted in the light of what the rest of the Bible teaches. The interpretation of prophecy must always agree with sound Scriptural doctrine. In addition, prophecies elsewhere in the Bible may offer important keys to the correct interpretation of prophetic symbolisms. With these considerations in mind, let us examine a number of important issues in the man-of-sin prophecy, paying careful attention to the text itself as well as the rest of Scripture.

Which "Temple of God"?

One of the most important questions in this prophecy is the meaning of "the temple of God," since that is where the man of sin would sit. A millennium before Christ, Solomon built a great temple for God in Jerusalem. Four centuries later, God sent Nebuchadnezzar, king of Babylonia, to devastate that temple and all Jerusalem due to the sins of Judah. Three great prophets of God, Isaiah, Jeremiah, and Daniel, foretold the rebuilding of Jerusalem and the temple following that devastation. Ezra and Nehemiah record the historical facts of the rebuilding, which was completed more than four centuries before Christ.

Even though the temple was rebuilt, both Daniel and Jesus prophesied the destruction of that second temple, just like the destruction of the first one. These predictions were powerfully fulfilled in A.D. 70 when the Romans crushed the Jewish rebellion. Actually it was God who brought judgment upon Jerusalem and the temple because of the Jewish nation's rejection of Christ (Luke 19:41-44).

Those who claim that a third temple is going to be built in the future base their views solely upon inference. Their arguments run like this: since the man of sin will sit in the temple of God, the temple in Jerusalem has to be rebuilt in order to fulfill the prophecy. However, one may well ask: What is the proof that "the temple of God" in 2 Thessalonians 2 is to be a physical temple in physical Jerusalem?

Indeed, there are at least three reasons for rejecting such an interpretation.

First of all, it is a plain fact that no Scripture makes such a prediction. There is not a single Bible prophecy foretelling a rebuilding of Jerusalem's temple after its destruction in A.D. 70.

Secondly, one must consider the nature of the Jerusalem temple in the New Testament. Everyone understands that the temple in Jerusalem was the temple of God when Jesus arrived on the scene. Jesus himself said of the temple, "Do not make My Father's house a house of merchandise!" (John 2:16). It was in the temple that animals were sacrificed and their blood shed for the remission of the people's sins. However, Jesus came into the world to offer His own body and blood as the perfect sacrifice for sins. Thus, at the moment of Jesus' death, God acted in an unprecedented manner: "Then, behold, the veil of the temple was torn in two from top to bottom; and the earth quaked" (Matt. 27:51). In this graphic fashion God declared that He was finished with the physical temple when Jesus died.

After the tearing of the veil, the term "house of God" never again refers to the temple in Jerusalem. A physical temple has not existed for over nineteen hundred years. Any physical temple built today to restore the Old Testament worship would be a slap in the face to Jesus, who shed His blood to do away with the temple's animal sacrifices. The second temple, which existed in Jesus' day, ceased being the temple of God the moment Jesus died. Forty years later God sent the Romans to totally destroy that temple. If a third temple were built, it would not be a temple of God for even one minute.

Thirdly, 1 Tim. 3:15 clearly states: "That you may know how you ought to conduct yourself in *the house of God, which is the church* of the living God, the pillar and ground of the truth" (italics mine). Scripture could not say more clearly what the house of God is today—God's church.

The same is true of the expression "temple of God."

"The Temple of God"

The Old Way (a building)

"The descendants of the captivity were building the temple of the LORD God" (Ezra 4:1).

"Jesus went into the temple of God and drove out all those who bought and sold in the temple" (Matt. 21:12).

The Cross Made the Difference

- God tore the old temple veil in two when Jesus died.
- God replaced the old temple sacrifices with Jesus' blood.
- God used the Romans to destroy the old temple in A.D. 70.
- God now dwells in His people. The church is His temple now.

The New Way (people)

"You are the temple of God" (1 Cor. 3:16).

"A holy temple in the Lord, in whom you also are being built together for a dwelling place of God" (Eph. 2:21-22).

Persons depicted are models; photograph used for illustrative purposes only.

"House of God, which is the church of the living God" (1 Tim. 3:15).

Therefore: After the cross, any prophecy about the temple of God cannot refer to the temple destroyed in A.D. 70, but rather to the church of the living God.

Examination shows that after Jesus' death, "temple of God" never again refers to the physical temple in physical Jerusalem. Rather, it refers to the church of God. It seems that our brethren in Corinth were not quite clear on this point. So Paul asked them, "Do you not know that you are the temple of God and that the Spirit of God dwells in you?" (1 Cor. 3:16). Today we would ask people similar questions: When you study prophecy about the temple of God, do you not know that since Jesus' death the people of God are the temple of God? Do you not know that the house of God is the church of God?

This is sound doctrine. By using sound doctrine as the basis for the study of prophecy, the careful student of the New Testament will realize that when 2 Thessalonians 2 speaks prophetically of the temple of God, it must be a prophecy about the church. Something very evil was going to happen in Jesus' church.

What is Apostasy?

Another important concern is the meaning of the expression "the apostasy" (2 Thess. 2:3). Actually, several versions, including the NKJV, make it clear when they translate it as "the falling away." That is exactly what apostasy means.

A man cannot fall from a cliff he has never been on. A child cannot fall from a train she never boarded. Since this prophecy has something to do with the temple of God, the church, it is therefore predicting a falling away from the true church. It is a prophecy about apostasy, a prophecy about a departure from the faith "once for all delivered" (Jude 3). The prophecy cannot be talking about Judaism, because it preceded the church of Christ. It cannot be talking about Islam, because it is a wholly distinct religion unrelated to the gospel of Christ. We have to study church history to search for the falling away.

Neither is the prophecy about just any falling away. It prophesies "the" falling away, "the" apostasy. That would seem to tell us that to find fulfillment we must look for the most outstanding false church in all history.

Connected with the idea of falling away is "the lawless one" (2 Thess. 2:8-9). That is to say, he would turn his back on the law of Christ and establish his own laws. A person is a lawbreaker for breaking just one law. However, "lawless one" conveys the idea of someone who persistently opposes the commandments of the New Testament. This prophecy, then, is not dealing with just any slight deviation from the true gospel. It foretells a departure of major proportions.

Paul wrote to the Thessalonians more than nineteen hundred years ago. Before thinking that the man of sin might be future, a believer must search nineteen hundred years of church history to see if the prophecy has already been fulfilled. When people ignore nineteen centuries of Christianity, they are much more easily deceived by the idea that fulfillment is yet in the future.

One Man or a Group of Men?

How many people are involved in the expression "the man of sin"? That may sound like a strange question inasmuch as the text plainly says "the man" of sin (2 Thess. 2:3). However, in Bible prophecy, one person often represents an entire group of people. For example, most students agree that the four beasts in Daniel 7 represent Babylonia, Persia, Greece, and Rome. Each beast represents an entire empire. Daniel 7:23 says that the fourth beast would be "a fourth kingdom on earth." Yet verse 17 says, "Those great beasts, which are four, are four kings." Thus, a beast represents a man, and both represent a kingdom. This Bible symbolism is not nearly as strange as some seem to think it is. Ever hear of Uncle Sam? What about the elephant and donkey representing the Republicans and Democrats?

This same type of symbolism is found in Revelation 17. Who would assert that "the great harlot" is a prophecy of a red-light-district prostitute? Indeed, the prophecy itself clears up any doubt because verse 18 says, "And the woman whom you saw is that great city which reigns over the kings of the earth." One woman represents an entire city. She represents especially the power of the leaders of that city to exercise control over many nations.

Both Daniel and Revelation make clear that a prophetic individual may well represent an entire city or an entire empire, especially the governmental powers.

A Matter of Religion

It must not be overlooked that worship is involved in this prophecy (2 Thess. 2:4). Whatever political power he may have, the man of sin is a religious figure. He presents himself as God to be "worshiped." Moreover, he does this in the temple of God, which is the church.

God does not want just any religion. The very first murder in the human race was for religious motives: "The LORD respected Abel and his offering, but He did not respect Cain and his offering. And Cain was very angry" (Gen. 4:4-5). The first sin of Cain was not murder, not even hate for his brother. Cain's first recorded sin was false worship.

The Bible is filled with accounts of religious conflict. Jesus, for example, told the Samaritan woman, "You worship what you do not know" (John 4:22). Jesus told the religious leaders of his day that they worshiped God in vain because they were "teaching as doctrines the commandments of men" (Matt. 15:9). The man of sin is all about false worship.

Miracles by Satan

The predicted apostate church would be "the working of Satan, with all power, signs, and lying wonders" (2 Thess. 2:9). This eliminates many apostate people and organizations as candidates for the man of sin. The man of sin works miracles. Satan working miracles is nothing new to the Bible. As early as the time of the Exodus, Pharaoh's magicians were capable of duplicating Moses' signs of turning rods into snakes, of turning water into blood, and of producing a plague of frogs (Exod. 7:8 to 8:19). It is true that Moses by the hand of the Almighty outdid them. However, make no mistake about it: those pagan magicians worked real miracles.

There are numerous ways God's people can distinguish between the miracles of God and the miracles of Satan. One way is that recorded in Exod. 8:18: "Now the magicians so worked with their enchantments to bring forth lice, but they could not." They had worked many miracles, but they came to the point where they tried again and failed. Anyone who tries to work a miracle but fails is not of God. His failure shows that the miracles he succeeded in working were of Satanic origin.

Strong Delusion

We must not overlook the fact that "strong delusion" (2 Thess. 2:11) is a part of the picture. Do not expect the people of the world to be easily convinced that some false church is the man of sin. Do not expect the ecumenical movement to believe it. Do not expect those who put unity above purity of doctrine to believe it. The man of sin is very religious, he works miracles, and many consider him to be in the true church of our Lord. Multitudes will be deceived and strongly deluded.

Started in Paul's Day

Paul made it clear that in his day "the mystery of lawlessness is already at work" (2 Thess. 2:7). Therefore, in searching for the fulfillment of this prophecy, we must look for some spirit or some activity that was already at work in the first century. It makes no sense to start our search with the year 2000 and work backward. It makes even less sense to theorize about some future possibility. How can we believe that something which was already at work in Paul's day has not been able to break out into the open for over nineteen hundred years?

Rather, the sensible thing is to start our search in the first century and move forward in time. We must examine the development of church history from its origin. We must search for something already working in Paul's day that in time became the full-blown apostate church. When we find that, if it fulfills all the details of the prophecy, then we have found the man of sin.

Comes Before Jesus Comes

Who will come first, Jesus or the man of sin? The Scripture plainly tells us: "The lawless one will be revealed, whom the Lord will . . . destroy with the brightness of His coming" (2 Thess. 2:8). Inasmuch as Jesus will destroy the lawless one when He comes again, the lawless one has to be here first.

Futurism claims the "coming" in verse 1 of 2 Thessalonians 2 is the Rapture, and the "coming" in verse 8 is "the Second Coming" seven years later. However, the Greek word for "coming" in verse 1 is the same as in verse 8. The text gives no hint of two different comings of Jesus, a second coming followed by a third coming. In verse 1, Paul introduces the topic: "Now, brethren, concerning the coming of our Lord Jesus Christ . . ." In verses 1 and 2, Paul simply says they should not think that Jesus' coming had already happened. In verse 3 he gives one reason why they should not think Jesus had already come: Jesus will not return until after the man of sin comes. In verses 4-7, Paul gives many details concerning this man of sin. In verse 8 Paul declares, "then the lawless one will be revealed, whom the Lord will . . . destroy with the brightness of His coming." In short, Paul teaches that the Lord is not coming until the man of sin comes, and when the Lord does come he will destroy the man of sin, the lawless one. The man of sin comes first, Jesus comes later.

What to Search For

A careful study of the man-of-sin prophecy in its Biblical context results in a number of important conclusions:

• After the death of Christ, the expression "temple of God" in Scripture always refers to Jesus' church.

• The word "apostasy" means a falling away. The prophecy is about a fallen or apostate church.

• "Worship" is involved, but it would be a false worship of someone presenting himself as God.

• The one leading this apostate church is called the man of sin or lawless one. A comparison with other prophetic Scripture shows that a "man," singular, can represent a group of men.

• This apostate church and its leadership would have the power to work miracles.

• The trends leading in this direction were already at work in Paul's day and would fully develop before Jesus returns.

The search for the fulfillment of the man-of-sin prophecy must take into consideration all these Bible-based conclusions. The man-of-sin prophecy is a prediction of a fully developed apostate church and leadership which would take place before Jesus returns for His church. There was already movement towards that apostasy before Paul wrote. The search for fulfillment must begin in Paul's day and continue forward in church history until a great miracle-working apostate church is found that has a leadership claiming to have the characteristics of God.

Chapter 12

Man of Sin–the History

Paul warned: "The mystery of lawlessness is already at work" (2 Thess. 2:7). Thus, the fulfillment of this prophecy had begun in the first century. Something was already working in Paul's day that in time would produce "the man of sin . . . the son of perdition . . . the lawless one" (2:3, 8).

"All Roads Lead to Rome"

From the second to the twenty-first century, most students of prophecy have understood that the little horn of Daniel 7 and the beasts of Revelation 13 and 17 are related to Rome. Today there are three major views regarding the time in history when Rome fulfills these prophecies. Preterism places the fulfillment in our past, futurism places it in our future, and historicism places it in our past, present, and future.

Most agree that 2 Thessalonians 2 is part of this same prophetic picture. This means that the man of sin will be found in Rome. The evidence already presented in Chapter 11 points to the conclusion that "the man of sin . . . the son of perdition" refers to the most outstanding apostate church in history. Add Rome to the equation, and the fulfillment of the prophecy becomes obvious.

"I Told You . . . You Know"

The Bible was not sealed in a vacuum as soon as it was written, unread and unstudied until it reached each of us in the twenty-first century. To ignore the intervening centuries is shortsighted and egotistical. If we do not learn from others, why should we expect others to learn from us?

"I told you . . . you know," said Paul, "what is restraining" (2 Thess. 2:5-6). This is amazing. The saints in Thessalonica knew. Paul had taught them in person, but the Holy Spirit prevented Paul from writing it down. Is there any other place in Scripture like this? The writer says his readers know what he is talking about, but he shrinks from writing it down. It becomes irresistible to scan early Christian writings to learn what they can tell us. Can you conceive that the first-century Christians would not pass on the information?

Before examining these early Christian writers, we need to be aware of three things:

1. They were not inspired. Therefore, they express many contradictory views on prophecy as well as on other matters.

2. Before a particular prophecy is fulfilled, we cannot expect Christians to understand it completely. For example, the apostles did not have the correct views of many messianic prophecies even though Jesus was in their midst.

3. After a prophecy is fulfilled, there will always be those who will deny its fulfillment. For example, to this very day the Jews deny that Jesus of Nazareth is the promised Messiah.

With these precautions in mind, it is still very enlightening to discover what Christians through the ages have believed regarding various prophecies. This is especially true here where Paul said, "You know . . ."

Not Fulfilled in the First Century

The preterist view teaches that the man of sin appeared

in the first century. It applies all the details of 2 Thessalonians 2 to events surrounding the destruction of Jerusalem in A.D. 70. It quotes authorities with identical views, but never any authority earlier than the seventeenth century. Why not earlier? The reason is simple. There are no earlier authorities that hold such a view.

Not one writer before A.D. 1600 mentions anyone who believed the man-of-sin prophecy had been fulfilled in the first century. Notice:

1. The Thessalonians knew who was restraining the lawless one from being revealed.

2. Many Christian writers in the second to fifth centuries wrote in detail about this prophecy.

3. Not one early writer thought the man-of-sin prophecy was fulfilled in the first century.

4. The early writers often discuss views contrary to their own. None of them mention anyone who applied this prophecy to the first century.

In the eighteenth century, Thomas Newton discussed 2 Thessalonians 2 at length in his famous *Dissertations on the Prophecies*. He mentions five writers of the seventeenth and eighteenth centuries who claimed that the man-of-sin prophecy was fulfilled in the first century. He points out that they not only disagree with the majority of interpreters, but also disagree with each other as well as with all who were before them. Then he remarks:

> If this prophecy [2 Thessalonians 2] was fulfilled, as these critics conceive, before the destruction of Jerusalem, it is surprising that none of the fathers [early Christian writers] should agree with any of them in the same application, and that the discovery should first be made sixteen or seventeen hundred years after the completion. The fathers might differ and be mistaken in the circumstances of a prophecy which was yet to be fulfilled; but that a prophecy should be remarkably accomplished before their time, and they be totally ignorant of it, and speak of the accomplishment as still future, is not very credible.[1]

The Early Christians Speak

A search into early Christian writings reveals that many believers had a definite view as to what was restraining or withholding the appearance of the man of sin. No, there is no writer who claims to quote the apostle Paul or one who heard the apostle Paul say what was restraining. Nevertheless, these early Christians lived infinitely closer to the source than we do. Therefore, they were in a far better position than we are today of being in touch with the information Paul imparted to the saints in Thessalonica. Surely, we should investigate what early Christian writers thought Paul was talking about before we consider novel interpretations of the twenty-first century.

In light of the many divergent views on prophecy that we find among the early Christian writers, it is impressive that there is so much agreement on the question of what was restraining-withholding-hindering. In the end, of course, their views have to be tested by both Scripture and history. With that in mind, as we follow their views and look at the development of history, we cannot help but be impressed with the fact that the early Christians were on the right track regarding much of this prophecy—well before it was fulfilled.

Irenaeus, A.D. 130 to 202

Irenaeus was born about 30 years after the apostle John died. He heard the teaching of Polycarp, who had heard the teaching of the apostle John. Irenaeus devoted several chapters to Daniel 7, Revelation 13, and 2 Thessalonians 2 in his extensive work, *Against Heresies*. Typical of believers in all ages, he understood that the three prophecies are related. Irenaeus wrote:

> Daniel too, looking forward to the end of the last kingdom, i.e., the ten last kings, amongst whom the kingdom of those men shall be partitioned, and upon whom *the son of perdition shall come,* declares that ten horns shall spring from the beast, and that another little horn shall arise in the midst of them (italics mine).[2]

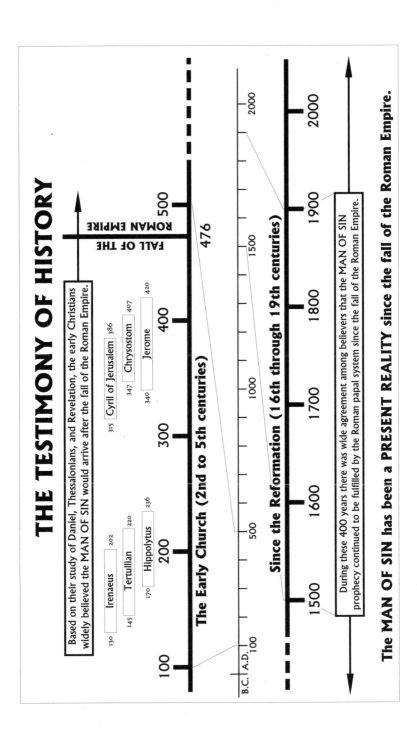

THE TESTIMONY OF HISTORY

Based on their study of Daniel, Thessalonians, and Revelation, the early Christians widely believed the MAN OF SIN would arrive after the fall of the Roman Empire.

FALL OF THE ROMAN EMPIRE

476

The Early Church (2nd to 5th centuries)

Irenaeus 130–202
Tertullian 145–220
Hippolytus 170–236
Cyril of Jerusalem 315–386
Chrysostom 347–407
Jerome 340–420

Since the Reformation (16th through 19th centuries)

During these 400 years there was wide agreement among believers that the MAN OF SIN prophecy continued to be fulfilled by the Roman papal system since the fall of the Roman Empire.

The MAN OF SIN has been a PRESENT REALITY since the fall of the Roman Empire.

In a still clearer light has John, in the Apocalypse, indicated to the Lord's disciples what shall happen in the last times, and concerning the ten kings who shall then arise, among whom *the empire which now rules [the earth] shall be partitioned* (italics mine).[3]

Based on Daniel, Thessalonians, and Revelation, Irenaeus believed that the Roman Empire of his day would one day be divided ten ways, and that out of this division would arise the son of perdition, the man of sin.

Tertullian, A.D. 145 to 220

Not many years later, Tertullian quoted and commented on 2 Thessalonians 2. He blended the man-of-sin prophecy with the prophecies of the ten-horned beast.

Again, in the second epistle he [Paul] addresses them with even greater earnestness . . . "For that day shall not come, unless indeed there first come a falling away," he means indeed of this present empire, "and that man of sin be revealed," that is to say, Antichrist, "the son of perdition, who opposeth and exalteth himself above all that is called God . . . And now ye know what detaineth, that he might be revealed in his time. For the mystery of iniquity doth already work; only he who now hinders must hinder, until he be taken out of the way." *What obstacle is there but the Roman state, the falling away of which, by being scattered into ten kingdoms, shall introduce Antichrist* upon (its own ruins)? (italics mine).[4]

Hippolytus, A.D. 170 to 236

A few years later, Hippolytus wrote a *Treatise on Christ and Antichrist*. While discussing Daniel 2 and 7, he wrote:

The golden head of the image and the lioness denoted the Babylonians; the shoulders and arms of silver, and the bear, represented the Persians and Medes; the belly and thighs of brass, and the leopard, meant the Greeks, who held the sovereignty from Alexander's time; the legs of iron, and the beast dreadful and terrible, expressed the *Romans, who hold the sovereignty at present;* the toes of the feet which were part clay and part iron, and the ten horns, were emblems of the kingdoms that are *yet to rise; the other little horn that grows up among them meant the Antichrist* in their midst (italics mine).[5]

Cyril of Jerusalem, A.D. 315 to 386

Moving to the fourth century, Cyril, after quoting 2 Thessalonians 2, said the following:

Thus wrote Paul, and now is the 'falling away' . . . now the Church is filled with heretics in disguise. For men have fallen away from the truth, and 'have itching ears' . . . This therefore is 'the falling away,' and the enemy is soon to be looked for.[6]

But this aforesaid *Antichrist is to come when the times of the Roman empire shall have been fulfilled,* and the end of the world is now drawing near. There shall rise up together ten kings of the Romans, reigning in different parts perhaps, but all about the same time; and after these an eleventh, the Antichrist, who by his magical craft *shall seize upon the Roman power* (italics mine).[7]

"So that he seateth himself in the temple of God." What temple then? He means, the Temple of the Jews which has been destroyed. For God forbid that it should be the one in which we are![8]

Cyril, living before the fulfillment, preferred to think that "the temple of God" meant a rebuilt temple of the Jews. That is where he envisioned the man of sin sitting. Why? Because he recoiled from the idea of the man of sin sitting in the church. Nevertheless, the manner in which he expresses himself shows that he did understand that the term "the temple of God" could apply to the church. Many today completely overlook this important point by assuming, without proof, that "the temple of God" must apply to a rebuilt Jewish temple in Jerusalem.

Chrysostom, A.D. 347 to 407

Later in the fourth century, Chrysostom wrote multitudes of homilies based on Scripture texts. In his Homily on 2 Thess. 2:6-9, he says:

> What then is it that withholdeth, that is, hindereth him from being revealed? Some indeed say, the grace of the Spirit, but others the Roman empire, to whom I most of all accede. Wherefore? Because if he meant to say the Spirit, he would not have spoken obscurely, but plainly . . . But because he said this of the Roman empire, he naturally glanced at it, and speaks covertly and darkly. For he did not wish to bring upon himself superfluous enmities, and useless dangers.[9]

> "Only there is one that restraineth now, until he be taken out of the way," that is, *when the Roman empire is taken out of the way, then he shall come.* And naturally. For as long as the fear of this empire lasts, no one will willingly exit himself, but when that is dissolved, he will attack the anarchy, and endeavor to *seize upon the government both of man and of God* (italics mine).[10]

Jerome, A.D. 340 to 420

Jerome wrote the first letter quoted here in A.D. 396 and the second in A.D. 409. Already the Roman Empire was in deep trouble from the barbarians.

> I shudder when I think of the catastrophes of our time . . . *The Roman world is falling:* yet we hold up our heads instead of bowing them . . . Rome's army, once victor and Lord of the world, now trembles with terror at the sight of the foe (italics mine).[11]

> But what am I doing? Whilst I talk about the cargo, the vessel itself founders. *He that letteth [restrains] is taken out of the way, and yet we do not realize that Antichrist is near.* Yes, Antichrist is near whom the Lord Jesus Christ "shall consume with the spirit of his mouth" . . . For thirty years the barbarians burst the barrier of the Danube and fought in the heart of the Roman Empire . . . Rome has to fight within her own borders not for glory but for bare life (italics mine).[12]

Augustine, A.D. 354 to 430

In his famous *City of God,* Augustine wrote:

> I can on no account omit what the Apostle Paul says, in writing to the Thessalonians, "We beseech you, brethren, by the coming of our Lord Jesus Christ," etc.
>
> No one can doubt that he wrote this of Antichrist and of the day of judgment, which he here calls the day of the Lord, nor that he declared that this day should not come unless he first came who is called the apostate . . . Then as for the words, "And now ye know what withholdeth," i.e., ye know what hindrance or cause of delay there is, "that he might be revealed in his own time;" they show that he was unwilling to make an explicit statement, because he said that they knew . . . I frankly confess I do not know what he means. I will nevertheless mention such conjectures as I have heard or read.
>
> Some think that the Apostle Paul referred to the Roman empire, and that he was unwilling to use language more explicit, lest he should incur the calumnious charge of wishing ill to the empire which it was hoped would be eternal . . . But others think that the words, "Ye know what withholdeth," and "The mystery of iniquity worketh," refer only to the wicked and the hypocrites who are in the Church, until they reach a number so great as to furnish Antichrist with a great people, and that this is the mystery of iniquity.[13]

Christian writers of the second, third, and fourth centuries have spoken. From these brief excerpts, we can make the following general observations of what was widely believed during those centuries:

1. It was widely believed that Daniel 7, 2 Thessalonians 2, and Revelation 13 and 17 are interrelated, all prophesying about Rome.

2. It was widely believed that the little horn of Daniel 7 and the man of sin of 2 Thessalonians 2 referred to the Antichrist in their future.

3. It was widely believed that the Antichrist would appear when Rome fell, and that the Roman Empire under

which they lived was that which was restraining the rise of the man of sin.

A Word Regarding the Middle Ages

Before the prophecies were actually fulfilled in history, it was impossible for the early Christians to understand exactly what was going to transpire. Nevertheless, what is very impressive is that there was general agreement among students of the Word throughout the ages that the man of sin would appear when Rome fell.

Rome did fall in A.D. 476. The bishop of Rome stepped into the power vacuum taking the place of the Emperor. As the years went by, the popes, as the Roman bishops were then called, gained incredible powers over the bodies and souls of men. Such power lasted for centuries. The history of this period, often called the Dark Ages, is covered in detail in innumerable, easily available history books. Not surprisingly, it is difficult to find writings during the Dark Ages identifying the Roman Church as the Antichrist. Obviously Rome would not identify itself as the Antichrist, and those who would identify it as such were successfully suppressed.

The Reformers Knew the Truth about Rome

As early as the thirteenth century, one voice after another began to cry: the Pope of Rome is the Antichrist, the Pope is the man of sin. The voices grew louder and louder until the full-blown Reformation Movement took shape. From that day until recent times, Protestants were united in calling the Roman Pontiff the man of sin.

Rather than prove this with endless quotations from Protestants over the centuries, let us rather take notice that both preterism and futurism admits this historical fact.

Gary DeMar, a modern preterist, totally rejects the idea that the Pope is the man of sin. He thinks 2 Thessalonians 2 and related prophecies were fulfilled in the first century by Nero and the Jews, among others. Nevertheless, he admits this historical fact:

For centuries the papacy was the unanimous candidate for the Antichrist. The papal system was identified as "both the 'man of sin' and the Babylonian whore of which Scripture forewarns (2 Thessalonians 2; Revelation 19). In the conviction of the sixteenth-century Protestants, Rome was the great Anti-Christ, and so firmly did this belief become established that it was not until the nineteenth century that it was seriously questioned by evangelicals."[14]

The Reformers, almost without exception, believed the "man of lawlessness" to be the Roman Pontiff. In their dedication to the King James Version of the Bible (1611) the translators identified the Pope as the "man of sin" of 2 Thessalonians 2: "The zeal of your majesty [King James] toward the house of God doth not slack or go backward but is more and more kindled, manifesting itself abroad in the farthest parts of Christendom by writing a defence of the truth which hath given *such a blow to that man of sin* as will not be healed" (italics his).[15]

These words addressed to King James can be found in the "Dedicatory" in the front of some King James Bibles. Later in the same "Dedicatory," the translators speak of "Popish Persons" on the one hand and "Brethren" on the other hand.

On the other end of the prophetic spectrum is Dave Hunt, a well-known futurist. Using the terminology of the old King James Version, he believes the Roman Catholic Church is the "whore" called Babylon in Revelation 17. However, being a futurist, he believes the beasts of Revelation 13 and 17 are in the future, as are the little horns of Daniel 7 and 8 and the man of sin of 2 Thessalonians 2. Hunt believes the Antichrist is probably alive now, but that he will not be revealed until during the Tribulation after the Rapture. In spite of all these beliefs, he yet admits:

Early Protestant creeds unanimously called the Pope Antichrist.[16]

It was only after the Russian Revolution that Christians began to view Communism as the Antichrist system. Yet for 400 years before 1917, Catholicism was so identified by Protestants.[17]

Turning Their Backs on History

History records that the early Christians believed the Antichrist would arise when Rome fell. History demonstrates they were right. History shows that when the Reformation came, preachers, politicians, and the populace were convinced the Pope of Rome was the man of sin, the Antichrist. History tells us that the vast majority of Bible believers continued in that conviction until recent times. History proves that futurism preaches a novel doctrine when it refuses to believe that the Pope of Rome is the man of sin.

To deny that the Pope of Rome is the son of perdition is to turn one's back on the thousands of martyrs whose bodies were twisted and wrenched by the "Holy" Inquisition. To deny that the Roman Church is the falling away (the apostasy) is to gloss over the gross perversion of sound doctrine that still emanates from the Vatican. To deny that each Pope of Rome is the man of sin is to ignore the blasphemy involved in calling a human being "Head of the Church," "Supreme Pontiff," "Vicar of Christ," and "Holy Father."

Tim LaHaye, in his commentary on Revelation 17, takes about half a chapter to discuss the false doctrines and practices of the Roman Church including its persecution of those who opposed Rome. In the midst of the discussion he says: "In some respects the religion of Rome is more dangerous than no religion."[18] In *Tribulation Force*, #2 of the "Left Behind" series, the authors invent the "Enigma Babylon One World Faith" which is "headed by the new Pope" during the Tribulation.[19] These views demonstrate some knowledge of the true nature of the Roman Church and the Roman Pope.

In spite of such views, LaHaye and Jenkins travel far in the opposite direction in the same novel. They paint the Pope at the time of the Rapture as actually being among those who disappeared in the Rapture: "A lot of Catholics were confused, because while many remained, some had disappeared—including the new pope, who had been installed just a few months before the vanishings."[20]

The "Left Behind" novels are admittedly that: novels. The subtitle of Number One is *A Novel of the Earth's Last Days*. Instead of producing prophecy novels, it would be a far more beneficial use of time, money, and energy to produce historical documentaries on the church of the Middle Ages. Truth is stranger and more startling than fiction. Those who think that a mere seven years of Tribulation in our future could possibly be worse than the realities of the Middle Ages need to brush the dust off their history books. Instead of devouring prophecy fiction, it would be a far more beneficial use of time, money, and energy for believers to realistically compare the teachings in their Bibles with the teachings of Rome. To begin such a study, turn now to Chapter 13, "Man of Sin–the Reality."

Witness of the Eighteenth Century

"No commentator ever conceived the whore of Babylon to be meant of a single woman: and why then should the man of sin be taken for a single man? . . . under the gospel dispensation the temple of God is the church of Christ: and the man of sin's sitting implies his ruling and presiding there, and sitting there as God implies his claiming divine authority in things spiritual as well as temporal, and showing himself that he is God implies his doing it with great pride and pomp, with great parade and ostentation."

— Thomas Newton, 1704-1782
Dissertations on the Prophecies, 390-91

Chapter 13

Man of Sin–the Reality

Throughout history, many believers have viewed the man of sin as somehow related to Rome. The early Christians believed the fall of Rome would precipitate the arrival of the man of sin. Centuries later the Protestants of the Reformation believed this is exactly what happened, and they identified the Pope of Rome as the man of sin. Were the Reformers correct in their view that the doctrines of the Roman Church and the office of the Roman Pope fulfill the details of the man-of-sin prophecy?

To begin to answer this question, Chapter 11 was dedicated to a careful study of exactly what 2 Thessalonians 2 predicted. Then Chapter 12 presented interpretations that Bible believers across the centuries have given to the prophecy. The probe gave evidence that from the Reformation until rather recent times, the prevailing view among non-catholic believers was that the man-of-sin prophecy was fulfilled in the popes of Rome.

Now the task in this chapter is to examine the beliefs and practices of the Roman church and papacy. Are those students of prophecy correct who say the beliefs and practices of Rome fulfill the details of the falling away and man-of-sin prophecy, or should we look for a future fulfillment? To find the answer, it is not necessary to resort to private information, secret accords, and hidden agendas of Rome. Rather, it is sufficient to examine the open, public, admitted claims of Rome that anyone can read in many available official Catholic sources.

"He Sits as God"

Central to the whole teaching on the man of sin is the fact that "he sits as God." The Holy Spirit said: "Who opposes and exalts himself above all that is called God or that is worshiped, so that he sits as God in the temple of God, showing himself that he is God" (2 Thess. 2:4). To claim the attributes of God is blasphemy (see Mark 2:5-7). Revelation says the beast is "full of names of blasphemy" (17:3). Are the Roman popes full of names of blasphemy? Is it true that each one "sits as God . . . showing himself that he is God"? Obviously, Rome denies that. However, consider the implications involved in the following terms and facts:

1. "Pope" means father: Jesus plainly said: "Do not call anyone on earth your father; for One is your Father, He who is in heaven" (Matt. 23:9). Catholic teaching counters this text with 1 Cor. 4:15: "For though you might have ten thousand instructors in Christ, yet you do not have many fathers; for in Christ Jesus I have begotten you through the gospel." In this and other texts, Paul expresses a father-son relationship between himself and his converts and very close co-workers such as Timothy. However, far from upholding the use of "father" as a title for a church office, this text denies it. Paul is saying that he is their father because they were converted through his teaching. He says they have many instructors but *not* many fathers. Nor do such special relationships in any way uphold the use of "father" as an official title. In Matthew 23, Jesus taught that in the church we should not call men by their titles, even when the title is a correct one, such as teacher (Matt. 23:10; Eph. 4:11). Even when churches have pastors, for example, the members should not address them by that title.

Contrary to this teaching, the popes of Rome freely accept the title "Holy Father" not only from multitudes of Catholics they have no personal knowledge of but even from non-Catholics who do not accept papal authority. Added to that is the fact that the very term "pope" means father. The Modern English word "pope" comes from the Old English *papa,* which in turn comes from the Late Latin. Of course, "papa" is still used by children in English as a familiar term for their father. In Spanish, the familiar word for father and the word for pope are identical except for an accent mark: *papá* and *papa.* In Greek, the word for father is *pappas.* This also explains the origin of the words "papacy" and "papal." In short, the most widely used term for the bishop of Rome is "Pope," which means father. This term is used as an honorary title expressing a man's fatherhood over the universal church.

Moreover, the local parish priests are openly called "Father" by both Catholics and non-Catholics. The term is not used to express a personal relationship with converts or co-workers. Rather, it is used as a title, giving glory to a particular class of men and placing them on a level that belongs only to the God of the universe. The Catholic Church is filled with fathers worldwide, while their father in Rome is the most important, universal, and "Holy Father." He is the father of their fathers. However, our father should not be in the local parish nor in Rome. Our Father should be the One in heaven. There is "one God and Father of all" (Eph. 4:6). "For us there is one God, the Father, of whom are all things" (1 Cor. 8:6). "One is your Father, He who is in heaven" (Matt. 23:9). Almighty God is the only one who is Father to us all. For a man to claim to be the father of the universal church is blasphemy. He is "showing himself that he is God."

2. The head of the church: The Roman Pope claims to be the head of the church. It is often said that he is the *visible* head of the church, with the obvious understanding that Christ is the invisible Head. What does that do to the frequent figure in Scripture of the church being the body of Christ? Can a body have two heads?

Scripture says of God's work through Christ: "He put all things under His feet, and gave Him to be head over all things to the church, which is His body" (Eph. 1:22-23). There are not two heads. Jesus is "head over *all* things to the church" (italics mine). To claim to be the visible head of the church is to make one's self equal to Christ, the Son of God.

3. Pontiff: The term "pontiff" comes from the ancient pagan Roman religion. The pontiffs were their chief priests. Since individual local clergy in the Roman churches all over the world are called priests, the one in Rome is considered the Supreme Pontiff. This is just another way of saying "high priest," and that presents a real problem. According to Scripture: "We have a great High Priest who has passed through the heavens, Jesus the Son of God . . . without sin" (Heb. 4:14-15). "For the law appoints as high priests men who have weakness, but the word of the oath, which came after the law, appoints the Son who has been perfected forever" (Heb. 7:28). Jesus is our one and only High Priest. To claim to be the chief priest is to claim a position that belongs only to Jesus Christ, the anointed Prophet, Priest, and King. Inasmuch as Jesus is our High Priest and is God, any human claim of being high priest (Supreme Pontiff) is a claim of being God. When the Pope of Rome sits as the Supreme Pontiff in the church, he is sitting "as God in the temple of God."

4. Vicar of Christ: A common term for the popes is "vicar of Christ." "Vicar" comes from the Latin meaning substitute. Rome claims that the Roman Pontiff is acting for and in the place of Christ. He is a substitute for Christ. Inasmuch as the popes claim to function in the place of Christ, they are showing themselves to be Christ on earth. The concept of "Vicar of Christ" is akin to that of the "visible head of the church." Their idea is that Christ is not here physically with us, but the Pope of Rome is here physically taking His place. Can anyone take the place of Christ?

5. The popes claim primacy: Rome talks much about the primacy of Peter, which it claims has been passed on to all the bishops of Rome. The words "primacy" and "primary" are not found in Scripture whether referring to Peter or anyone else. Yes, Peter was outstanding among the apostles, but he had no authority over the rest of them. Scripture says that "God has appointed these in the church: first apostles" (1 Cor. 12:28). It does not say, "first Peter." It says, "first apostles." It uses the plural form; Peter is only part of this group.

Though the word "primacy" is not in the Bible, the kindred word "preeminence" is recorded twice; however, neither time does it refer to Peter. Paul declares of Christ: "He is the head of the body, the church ... that *in all things* He may have the preeminence" (Col. 1:18, italics mine). In 3 John 9-10 we learn of "Diotrephes, who loves to have the preeminence among them ... I will call to mind his deeds which he does, prating against us with malicious words." These two texts make it clear that primacy belongs to Christ in all things, whereas it is evil when men in the church seek primacy.

Paul declared: "The mystery of lawlessness is already at work" (2 Thess. 2:7). Among other things, that mystery was the struggle of men to have first place, preeminence, and primacy in the Lord's church. In Jesus' lifetime the apostles themselves had this problem: "There was also a dispute among them, as to which of them should be considered the greatest" (Luke 22:24). As for Diotrephes, he only sought first place in one local church. Students of church history know that the struggle for primacy continued unabated, but not just in individual local churches. Men sought more and more power over more and more churches until someone claimed to have first place over all the churches of the world. That someone was the bishop of Rome. He claimed and continues to claim primacy. Such a claim to primacy is a challenge to the primacy of Christ and fulfills the prophecy in Thessalonians. Jesus has preeminence and primacy in the church "in all things" whether in heaven or on earth. No man can have primacy in the Lord's church.

6. The Pope of Rome is a king: The Roman Pontiff uses all the trappings of royalty. He lives in a palace. In fact, the Vatican Palace is the largest palace in the world. He has an ornate crown called the tiara. For solemn functions, he sits on a throne. His period of power is called a reign. The cardinals are considered princes of the church who are subject only to the Pope of Rome. Though most Catholics may not usually use the term "king" for the Pope of Rome, some do. They also use many other expressions that confirm this concept. However, our King is Jesus. One kingdom cannot have two kings.

7. This king has three crowns: The tiara can be traced back to A.D. 1100. By A.D. 1300 it contained not one but three jewel-bedecked crowns, one above another on a rounded cone headpiece. Each crown represents a realm over which the popes rule. Authorities do not fully agree on the explanation of what the three realms are, but it is obvious that the popes claim all kinds of kingship, both spiritual and temporal. Though John Paul II does not physically wear the tiara, he has in no way renounced the tiara and what it represents. Quite the contrary, the tiara appears on his papal seal and the Vatican flag. In this way, the Roman Pope still presents himself as a thrice-crowned monarch. Jesus on earth had only one crown. Remember what it was made of ?

8. Above the law: The Roman Pontiff makes himself so much like God that he places himself higher than the Son of God. When Jesus was upon earth, He voluntarily submitted to taxation (Matt. 17:24-27) as well as to the Jewish council, the Roman Governor Pontius Pilate, and the Roman soldiers. He had the power to resist but He did not.

The popes of Rome, however, submit to no man! The Pope is head of Vatican City, which is located totally within the borders of Rome, Italy. Vatican City is the smallest independent nation in the world, covering only 108.7 acres, about one sixth of a square mile. The Vatican receives ambassadors from about 170 nations. It is true that Vatican

City is tiny compared to the land holdings of the popes of the Middle Ages. Nonetheless, it is big enough to furnish the popes with absolute independence from all human authority. The reason openly stated for the existence of Vatican City is that the popes cannot rightly be made subject to any temporal power on earth. Did any man ever "sit as God in the temple of God" more than this?

The apostle Paul wrote to the same church we are examining, the church in Rome, during the reign of the infamous emperor Nero. In that setting, Paul commanded the brethren in Rome: "Let every soul be subject to the governing authorities" (Rom. 13:1). The popes of Rome refuse to obey this command of God. They set themselves outside of and above all earthly authority. In so doing, they set themselves above the Son of God Himself who did submit.

"The Falling Away"

The man of sin is only one person (at a time). Keep in mind, however, that 2 Thessalonians 2 predicts an entire system over which the man of sin rules. It predicts "lawlessness," "falling away (apostasy)," "unrighteousness," "deception," "strong delusion," and "the lie." Since this is a "falling away (apostasy)," it has to be a departure or falling away from the true gospel—keeping parts, omitting parts, and changing parts—an unholy mixture of truth and error. It cannot be fulfilled by unrelated religions such as Buddhism or Islam.

High on the list of these unrighteous deceptions are the numerous mediators that Rome places between man and God. Uncontested at the top of this list of mediators is "the Virgin."

Does God have a Mother?

The Mary of Rome is not the Mary of the Bible. While it is true that some teachings and practices of the Roman Church edged closer to Bible truth during the twentieth century, its doctrine of Mary was not one of them. John Paul II, indeed, has dedicated his pontificate to "the Virgin." He has everywhere tried to increase devotion to her by visiting most of the Marian shrines in the world. His motto is *"Totus tuus sum Maria:* Mary, I am all yours"!

Rome makes a goddess out of their Mary. The teaching goes this way:

1. Mary is the mother of Jesus;
2. Jesus is God; therefore,
3. Mary is the mother of God.

The problem with this supposedly logical argument is the second point. Yes, Jesus is God, but Jesus was also man. As Rom. 1:3 states: "Jesus Christ our Lord, who was born of the seed of David *according to the flesh"* (italics mine). With this in mind, it is also correct to say that Jesus was the son of Mary *according to the flesh.*

This reminds me of the question little children (and materialistic philosophers) ask: "Who made God?" Of course, if someone made God, the one who was made would not be God; his maker would be God. This brings us to mother and son. A mother is always before a son. If Mary is the mother of God, then she existed before God and she is God. This is blasphemy. John clarified: "In the beginning was the Word . . . And the Word became flesh" (John 1:1, 14). Yes, Mary was before Jesus *in the flesh,* but Jesus was before Mary *in the spirit.* Mary is not the mother of God; she was the mother of Jesus in the flesh. The reality is that the Lord Jesus Christ is Mary's Maker and Master!

This is just one of many falsehoods involved in Rome's teachings regarding Mary. They note that Gabriel told Mary, "Blessed are you among women!" Yes, and when a woman cried out to Jesus, "Blessed is the womb that bore You," Jesus replied, "More than that, blessed are those who hear the word of God and keep it!" (Luke 11:27-28). Rome says Mary was a perpetual virgin even though married. They say she was sinless like Jesus. They call her "queen of heaven" (see Jeremiah 44). Since God is King of heaven, that makes Rome's Mary a goddess. They call her the Mediatrix. Since Jesus is the Mediator, that makes her equal to Jesus.

In fact, the rosary contains ten "Hail Mary's" for every "Our Father." Ten to one. The teaching of Rome is "to Jesus through Mary." The teaching of the apostles is "to the Father through the Son" (John 14:6; 1 Tim. 2:5). Two different teachings. Two different gods.

Other examples of lawlessness

The Holy Spirit says: "A bishop then must be blameless, the husband of one wife" (1 Tim. 3:2). Rome says that a bishop must *not* be the husband of one wife. God requires bishops to be family men. Rome requires bishops to be bachelors.

Paul wrote to all the Christians in Corinth: "As often as you eat this bread and drink this cup" (1 Cor. 11:26). Rome says the common members may *not* drink the cup. Rome dares to withhold from its members one half of the Lord's Supper.

The Word says, "as often as you eat this bread." Rome says that their parishioners do not eat bread; they eat the actual body of Christ. When Jesus changed water into wine, it no longer looked like water; it no longer tasted like water. The feast master said, "You have kept the good wine until now!" (John 2:10). A miracle of changing one thing into another does just that—it changes one thing into another. Rome claims that the host (bread) is transformed into the actual body of Christ even though it still looks, smells, and tastes like bread. That is not a miracle. That is a fabrication, an untruth, a lie. Since so many millions worldwide believe such an obvious falsehood, this alone is sufficient to fulfill the prophecy regarding "strong" delusion. However, it is far from being the only one.

Time fails to even name all the falsehoods of Rome. These are not just minor errors of a few points of doctrine. This is "the" falling away, "the" apostasy. Among other things, Rome teaches that parishioners must confess their sins to a mortal priest whom they did not sin against. Rome teaches that every mass is a sacrifice in which Christ, without blood, offers himself to God via the officiating priest. Rome teaches the baptism of ignorant, sinless infants. It practices sprinkling rather than immersion. Rome fosters the "veneration of images" (their term for idol worship), including kneeling and praying before them, burning candles before them, and carrying them in street processions. Rome condones church-sponsored gambling, dancing, and drinking on the one hand and the charismatic speaking in tongues on the other.

Antichrist?

Is it proper to call the papacy the Antichrist? The term "antichrist" appears only in the epistles of John, who says that many antichrists were already existent in his day. The texts in question are 1 John 2:18-19, 22; 4:3; 2 John 7:

> As you have heard that the Antichrist is coming, even now many antichrists have come . . . They went out from us . . . Who is a liar but he who denies that Jesus is the Christ? He is antichrist who denies the Father and the Son . . . and every spirit that does not confess that Jesus Christ has come in the flesh is not of God. And this is the spirit of the Antichrist, which you have heard was coming, and is now already in the world . . . For many deceivers have gone out into the world who do not confess Jesus Christ as coming in the flesh. This is a deceiver and an antichrist.

Item 1. John states they had "heard that the Antichrist is coming." John does *not* deny that "the" Antichrist is coming. Rather, he clarifies that there are other antichrists in addition to "the" Antichrist that was coming.

Item 2. "They went out from us." This agrees perfectly with the man-of-sin prophecy, which predicted a falling away. Both texts speak of a development originating within the true body of Christ.

Item 3. "This is the *spirit* of the Antichrist, which you have heard was coming, and is now already in the world" (italics in NKJV, which indicates the translators have added a word that is not in the original Greek). With good reason the translators have added "spirit" in 1 John 4:3. The Greek text literally says: "This is the of the Antichrist." Of course that sounds strange, and we cannot help but ask, the what? Only the context can tell us. Starting with 4:1, the word "spirit(s)" appears five times before John writes verse 3. Read for yourself and you will see that when you come to "the of the Antichrist," "spirit" is the only sensible word to supply.

Therefore, John is saying "the spirit" of the Antichrist is already in the world. That is just another way of saying "the mystery of lawlessness is already at work" (2 Thess. 2:7)—*before* "the" man of sin or "the" Antichrist actually appears.

Item 4. "Many deceivers have gone out into the world who do not confess Jesus Christ as coming in the flesh. This is a deceiver and an antichrist." Is Rome one of the "many deceivers"?

Rome teaches that Jesus was not capable of sin—not just that he did not sin, but that he *could not sin.* As a consequence, Rome denies Jesus' full humanity. However, what does God say of His Son?

> Inasmuch then as the children have *partaken of flesh* and blood, He Himself likewise shared in *the same . . . in all things He had to be made like His brethren,* that He might be a merciful and faithful High Priest . . . For in that He Himself has *suffered, being tempted,* He is able to aid those who are tempted" (Heb. 2:14, 17-18; italics mine).

To become our High Priest, Jesus had to be made flesh "in all things" like us. One way His flesh was like ours was in suffering temptation. "God cannot be tempted by evil" (James 1:13), but human flesh can be. For that reason, when "the Word became flesh" (John 1:14), He "was in all points tempted as we are" (Heb. 4:15). Jesus became flesh like us, capable of being tempted, and therefore capable of sinning. Praise God He did not! Rome, however, teaches that Jesus *could not sin,* thus denying that Jesus came in flesh like our flesh.

Item 5. "Who is a liar but he who denies that Jesus is the

Christ?" "Christ" means the anointed Prophet, Priest, and King. The popes do not directly deny Jesus is the Christ. However, by claiming the same attributes for themselves, they in effect do deny it. The popes claim to be the infallible chief teachers (prophets) and rulers (kings) of the entire church as well as supreme pontiffs (high priests). As vicars of Christ, they take the place of Christ on earth. In this way they deny that Jesus *alone* is the Christ.

Item 6. "He is antichrist who denies the Father and the Son." Does this describe the popes of Rome? There are many ways to "deny" God. Paul wrote, "They profess to know God, but in works they deny Him" (Titus 1:16). By receiving the title "Holy Father," the popes deny that we have only one Holy Father. Since Rome attributes so many titles and characteristics of the Father and the Son to the popes and their Virgin, they fulfill this Scripture in that "they profess to know God, but in works they deny Him." Since Rome teaches and practices so many falsehoods, Scripture is fulfilled by them in that "they profess to know God, but in works they deny Him."

"Power, Signs, and Lying Wonders"

"The coming of the lawless one is according to the working of Satan, with all power, signs, and lying wonders" (2 Thess. 2:9). Any religious or political system that does not work miracles cannot possibly fulfill the man-of-sin prophecy. On the other hand, among those groups who do have superhuman manifestations, no church has claims of miracles like Rome.

In the mid-nineteenth century, their Virgin appeared to Bernadette in Lourdes, France. A whole century later, the shrine built there attracted 200,000 pilgrims a year. Many are the claims of miraculous cures. Other well-known locations of supposed supernatural appearances of their Virgin are Fatima in Portugal, Knock in Ireland, and Guadalupe in Mexico. All such places became shrines and centers for pilgrimages. The claims of miracles are numerous. The average Catholic believes in far more miracles than the hierarchy is willing to authenticate; however, it does authenticate many of them.

To discuss all the miracles claimed by the Roman Church would require another book. I think there is no evangelical church that can begin to compete with the Roman Church when it comes to claims of miracles. Rome has made such claims for centuries. Surely the Roman religion fulfills this part of the prophecy as well as all the other parts.

The Value of this Prophecy

The man-of-sin prophecy is valuable to us today in at least three ways.

This prophecy is a warning. We are all in danger. Satan can deceive us. Just as he did with Eve, Satan continues to mix truth with error. His arguments seem plausible. He offers benefits. He offers "the passing pleasures of sin" (Heb. 11:25). This prophecy is a warning of a false religion and an apostate church. It is a warning that Satan has power to work signs and wonders. It is a warning that there would be lies and strong delusions in the name of Christ.

Many Bible believers today do not heed this warning. For example, many charismatics today, disregarding all other doctrines, bind themselves together with one common denominator—the claim that "speaking in tongues" is evidence of baptism in the Holy Spirit. "Spirit-filled" evangelical charismatics have great fellowship with their "Spirit-filled" Catholic brethren—ignoring the fact that the latter still attend the sacrifice of the Mass, still pray to their Virgin, and still give allegiance to the Pontiff of Rome.

This prophecy is an explanation. How often do people ask, "Why are there so many religions?" How often do Catholics ask people of other churches, "Can you trace your church back to Peter in the first century like we can?" This prophecy offers some answers to such questions. It shows that Jesus did not have any illusions about what was going to happen to His glorious church. This prophecy shows that

God knew from the beginning that awful things would happen in His Son's church, that there would be a great departure from the true gospel.

Tracing a sequence of leaders from the apostles to the present offers no guarantee of uncorrupted doctrine. On the contrary, the prophecy foretells "the falling away." It is not a question of who comes after whom from generation to generation; rather it is a question of who retains or returns to the truth. This prophecy says the Lord's church would become corrupted. Tragic as that is, the fulfillment cannot be disregarded. The prophecy makes it clear that there would be an apostate, false church, no matter how unpopular and unpleasant that reality might be. When coupled with Daniel and Revelation, the Thessalonian prophecy makes it clear that the principal apostate church would be headquartered in Rome.

This prophecy is a promise. After saying, "The lawless one will be revealed," the prophecy continues, "whom the Lord will consume with the breath of His mouth and destroy with the brightness of His coming" (2 Thess. 2:8). There is victory in Jesus. The man of sin will not triumph in the end. Christ will. Jesus will return. He will destroy His enemy. He will reign victoriously. If we reject the man of sin and cling to Jesus, we will share in the victory.

Chapter 14

666: the Mark of the Beast

What number is more intriguing than 666? For those of us who like mental puzzles, this is among the best. Yet, this is not a game. Neither is it a vain pursuit. The book of Revelation instructs us: "Let him who has understanding calculate the number of the beast" (13:18).

Sadly, when it comes to wild ideas, it may be difficult to surpass the absurdities foisted on the public as solutions to the enigma of 666. Popular ultra-modern views include concepts of a cashless society, the universal use of bar codes, and the implantation of computer chips and biochips in each individual for identification and control. It is claimed that the Antichrist will control all commerce by such technology.

At the other extreme, many commentaries on Revelation assert that it is useless, foolish, or even dangerous to attempt to discover a specific name with a historical fulfillment of 666. They treat 666 and most items in Revelation as if they were parables devoid of specific predictions with historical significance.

It was no one less than Jesus Christ, the real author of Revelation, who directed John to write: "Here is wisdom. Let him who has understanding calculate the number of the beast, for it is the number of a man: His number is 666" (Rev. 13:18). We are commanded to "calculate" or "count," as other versions translate it. We are dealing here with a mathematical computation. The Greek word means "count," as illustrated in the only other text where it appears in the New Testament: "For which of you, intending to build a tower, does not sit down first and count the cost, whether he has enough to finish it"(Luke 14:28). This parable has a spiritual application, of course; but it is talking about a man counting his money.

Seldom does Revelation directly tell us to apply understanding to grasp the meaning of a particular symbol. It does not tell us to try to figure out who the lamb-like beast is. It does not tell us that if we have wisdom we can figure out the meaning of the third trumpet. However, when it mentions 666, it specifically tells us to calculate or count.

A Number is a Number

From ancient to modern times, numbers have fascinated both believers and unbelievers. Many people attribute mystical meanings or even mystical powers to numbers. Have you ever known people afraid of the number 13? Many people approach 666 with the same attitude—as if it were an unlucky, dangerous number. In contrast, the text of the Bible never gives mystical meanings to numbers; much less does it say they possess either evil or beneficial powers.

One of the earliest biblical prophetic interpretations was given by Joseph when he explained Pharaoh's dreams. The number seven appears in this prophecy. What does it mean? Joseph told Pharaoh, "The seven empty heads blighted by the east wind are seven years of famine" (Gen. 41:27). Each empty head of grain represented a year of famine. What did seven represent? Seven! Throughout the explanation of these dreams, seven is seven.

Daniel wrote: "Those great beasts, which are four, are four kings" (7:17). Beasts represent kings, but four is four. In the same chapter: "The ten horns are ten kings"(7:24). Horns, also, are kings but ten is ten.

Everyday English sometimes uses certain numbers in an indefinite way. Take, for example, "I told you a dozen times." What does that mean? Exactly twelve? Not at all. An English dictionary gives the second meaning of "dozen" as "an indefinite number; a great many."[1] In such cases, the number is not precise; nevertheless, it is still a question of quantity, of an unknown great number. Sometimes there is a round number. "I lived there ten years," when really I only lived there a little over nine years. The round number is not precise; nevertheless, it is a number. It is a question of quantity, nothing more.

The same is true in the Bible, which often uses seven in the same way we frequently use dozen. Prov. 26:16 says a lazy man thinks he knows more than "seven men who can answer sensibly." Who would argue that the lazy man thinks he is better than seven men, but not better than eight? No one. It is just a graphic way of saying "a lot." It still stands for quantity, even if the quantity is indefinite.

Ezekiel received an important key to the interpretation of many prophecies involving time. God told the prophet: "Lie also on your left side, and lay the iniquity of the house of Israel upon it . . . then you shall bear the iniquity of the house of Judah forty days. I have laid on you a day for each year" (4:4, 6). Very interesting and important. Each prophetic day Ezekiel lay on his side represented a year in historical reality. "A day for each year." However, the number in and of itself had no symbolism: forty was forty.

There simply is no hidden spiritual meaning in biblical numbers either inside or outside of prophetic texts. Contrary to what is often taught and accepted without examination, numbers are numbers in the Bible. There is absolutely no biblical basis for seeking some mystical meaning to 666, any more than for any other number. The Holy Spirit specifically commands us to calculate the number of the beast's name. This is not a mystical enigma; it is a mathematical puzzle.

The Number of Man?

There is a view that Rev. 13:18 should not be translated "the number of a man," but rather "the number of man" (without *a*). The reason given is that the indefinite article *a* is missing in the original. Of course, it is missing; Greek has no indefinite article. For this reason, we must examine the context to determine if the translation into English should include the indefinite article or not.

By translating the phrase "the number of man" (without *a*), the text is made to say that 666 is the number of the human race in general. If that is what the text is saying, there is nothing to calculate. If the text is simply using 666 as a mystical representation of the human race, the command to count is meaningless.

Besides saying "the number of a man" in verse 18, John spoke of "the number of his name" in verse 17. The beast's name has a number. In addition, the beast in chapter 13 cannot be all mankind because he fights against much of mankind. For all these reasons, the number cannot have reference to humanity in general. Rather, we are commanded to calculate the number of the name of this specific enemy of mankind.

The common belief is that seven is the number of completeness, perfection, and God. It is believed that since six is less than seven, it is less than perfect, less than divine: it is the number of imperfect man. It is said that since six is repeated three times in the number 666, it refers to man at his worst in opposition to God.

Is six the number of humanity in contrast to the holy, perfect God, whose number is seven? Take, for example, the creation of the world; God completed it in six days. "God saw everything that He had made, and indeed it was very good. So the evening and the morning were the sixth day" (Gen. 1:31). Nothing incomplete here. God made it in six days and only rested on the seventh (Exod. 20:11; 31:17). Some say that six is the number of man inasmuch as man was created on the sixth day of creation—so were baboons, bears, skunks, cats, and cobras!

The seraphim that praise God have six wings (Isa. 6:2) and so do the four living creatures in Rev. 4:8. Is six the number of man? On the contrary, it seems quite heavenly in these texts. The earthly tabernacle, which was a copy of heaven itself (Heb. 9:21-24), had six pieces of furniture—not seven. Thus, six is neither human nor imperfect; nor is it divine. Six is simply a number just like seven, eight, and nine.

Aside from all these thoughts, if we were to accept a translation that says "the number of man," would Revelation then be affirming that six is the number of mankind? Not at all! Revelation 13 says absolutely nothing about six. Revelation 13 is talking about 666. Six hundred and sixty-six is not six. It is not even three sixes. Three sixes are eighteen. In 666, the first six means 600, the second six means 60, and only the third six means 6. The number 666 is not one less than 7. On the contrary, 666 is 659 more than 7.

The number in question is not 6; it is 666. Nor are we told to find a mystical meaning for 666. We are commanded to count or calculate.

How to Calculate

Rev. 13:18 directs us to "calculate the number of the beast." It tells us the number is "the number of a man." In verse 17 it speaks of "the number of his name." The beast has a man's name, and that name has a number. We could properly combine all these thoughts in the following manner: calculate the number of a man's name.

In the English language, there is no such thing as a name having a number. In English, names are made up of letters of the alphabet. Numbers are made up of Arabic numerals: 1, 2, 3, etc. English letters have no numerical value; therefore, names in English have no number. To understand what Revelation is talking about, we must transport ourselves to other cultures and languages where Arabic numerals do not exist.

Actually, our journey can start close to home. We still sometimes use Roman numerals, although not nearly as often as in years gone by. Most of us struggle to read the number MDCCLXXVI. It is 1776 in Roman numerals, where the letter *I* equals 1, *V* equals 5, *X* equals 10, *L* equals 50, *C* equals one hundred, *D* equals five hundred, and *M* equals one thousand. The Romans of old used only seven letters of their Latin alphabet to express numbers. The other letters had no numerical value. They did not have Arabic numerals. In Latin, the name David has a value of 500 + 0 + 5 + 1 + 500 = 1,006. Thus, 1,006 is the number of the name David in the Roman numerals of Latin.

The Greeks, also without Arabic numerals, used individual letters of their alphabet to express values from 1 to 9, from 10 to 90 by tens, and from 100 to 900 by hundreds—a total of twenty-seven numbers to express any value from 1 to 999. They had to add three symbols to their twenty-four letter alphabet to complete the set of twenty-seven numbers. The Hebrews did a similar thing, but when they reached the end of their twenty-two letters, they simply stopped with the last letter, which had the value of 400. Thus, every word in these ancient languages could be considered to have a numerical value.

This method of calculating the numerical value of names was common among the ancients: Jews and Gentiles, Christians and pagans. For example:

> The Egyptian mystics spoke of *Mercury,* or *Thouth,* under the number 1218, because the Greek letters composing the name Thouth, when estimated according to their numerical value, together made up that number.[2]

This can be done in any language that uses letters of the alphabet to signify numerical values. Latin, Greek, and Hebrew all use letters for numerical value. Therefore, the ancients would not have to ponder what was meant by calculating the number of a name.

It is clear that in ancient languages the number of any name can easily be calculated. In addition, in any language with that system, it is obvious that *many* names can be found with the same value. There is not just one name with the numerical value of 666. A name with the value of 666 is only a part of the solution. Whatever name is found must fit into all the other circumstances predicted in Revelation.

In Which Language?

The next important question is this: In which language should we calculate? Sadly, this question is seldom asked. Commentaries offer calculations in whatever language each author desires, without giving any reason why that particular language is used.

Absurd calculations of 666 are often given using English. Some invent a system where *a* equals 1, *b* equals 2, etc. Others invent other systems. None of these systems has any value whatsoever. English letters have no numerical values. To assign them numerical values is arbitrary and fictional; it is a childish code game.

Surely the only languages to be given serious consideration are Greek, Hebrew, and Latin. These three were in existence when the Bible was written. The title on the cross was written in these three. The Bible itself was written in the first two. All three have a system of using letters to express numerical values.

A common solution proposed in Latin is *Vicarius Filii Dei,* "Vicar of the Son of God." It is said that since Daniel's fourth kingdom is the Roman-Latin empire, the language to use in the calculation is Latin. The idea is that we should expect the beast who imposes the mark to be identified by using his official language. This argument has some merit, but it likewise has problems. For example, the proposed title has questionable validity. Why? The title that Rome has used for centuries in reference to the popes is "Vicar of Christ" not "Vicar of the Son of God." There is considerable historical question as to whether the term "Vicar of the Son of God" was ever used. This solution, therefore, is doubtful. In addition to this problem, it is noteworthy that although many Christians in the first six centuries believed the fourth beast was the Roman (Latin) Empire, yet there is no record of anyone searching in Latin for a solution to 666. They all searched in Greek.

The most popular solution in Hebrew today is based on the preterist belief that the first-century Emperor Nero was the Antichrist. The numerical value of his name, Nero Caesar, is 666 in the Hebrew alphabet. Preterism says that since Revelation makes much use of Hebrew symbols and words and was written by a Jewish Christian, the solution to 666 would naturally be found in the Hebrew language. Preterism also argues that the prophecies of Revelation had to have meaning for, and be understood by, the people to whom the book was written in the first century. In opposition to these arguments stands the clear testimony of history: the idea that 666 represents Nero does not appear in any known writing prior to the nineteenth century! This fact alone contradicts a major argument in defense of the preterist position: namely, that the prophecy should be understood by the people to whom it was written. If that were so, why did it take eighteen hundred years for someone to discover that Nero's name equals 666?

When discussing the idea of Nero being the solution to 666, the well-known church historian Philip Schaff wrote:

> It seems incredible that such an easy solution of the problem should have remained unknown for eighteen centuries and been reserved for the wits of half a dozen rival rationalists in Germany.[3]

Schaff is saying that it was rationalists who first proposed Nero as a solution to 666. Rationalists believe reason, not revelation, is the source of truth; therefore, they attempt to empty the Bible of miracles and prophecy. In this case, a rationalist is satisfied that he has emptied Revelation of predictive prophecy by selecting Nero, who was not future to the book of Revelation.

Greek is the Language

In contrast to Latin and Hebrew, compelling arguments can be made for using the Greek language to arrive at the meaning of 666. In the first place, the book of Revelation was written in Greek. Students of the Bible and history have often noted that one reason the world was ready for the gospel in the first century is that a universal language, Greek, was in place. This made it much easier to spread the Scriptures everywhere. The Old Testament had already been translated from Hebrew into Greek (the Septuagint), so that it, too, was available both to Jews who no longer read Hebrew and to the population at large. Since Revelation was originally written to Greek-speaking people, a solution in Greek is by far the most natural.

Jesus told us to calculate the number of a name. The most natural thing is to make the calculation in the language that tells us to do so. The Greeks could write out numbers in two ways. They could use words equivalent to our "six hundred and sixty-six." They could also use the only system they had for expressing numerals, the letters of the alphabet: one letter for 600, one letter for 60, and one letter for 6. Using this method, like our Arabic numerals, the Greeks just needed three Greek letters to write 666. Interestingly, that is exactly the way 666 appears in many Greek manuscripts. These Greek texts read χξϛ′: 666.[4] Thus, not only is the enigma expressed in the Greek language, but many Greek manuscripts give the key for calculating the number of the name by using the numerical value of the Greek letters.

This is not the only special use of the Greek alphabet found in the book of Revelation. Like Isaiah, Revelation teaches that the Father and the Son are "the First and the Last" Isa. 44:6; 48:12; Rev. 1:11, 17; 2:8; 22:13). Deity is called "the Beginning and the End" three times in Revelation

(Rev. 1:8; 21:6; 22:13). In addition, Deity is called "the Alpha and the Omega" in four of the six Revelation texts just cited. *Alpha* (A, α) and *omega* (Ω, ω) are the first and last letters of the Greek alphabet (shown in upper and lower case).

It is the Greek alphabet that is used to express the eternality of Jesus, not the Hebrew or Latin alphabets. In Revelation, Jesus is not the *aleph* and the *tau*, the first and last letters of the Hebrew alphabet. Jesus is not the *a* and the *z*, the first and last letters of the Latin alphabet at the time of John. No, Jesus is the *alpha* and the *omega*, the first and last letters of the Greek alphabet. Revelation uses these Greek letters four times to express the eternality of the Father and the Son.

Early Christian writers who spoke of the matter unanimously used the Greek language to decipher 666. E. B. Elliott, in his very extensive and scholarly commentary on Revelation written in the middle of the nineteenth century, wrote that he was not aware of any writer in the first six centuries using anything but the Greek language in their attempts to solve 666.[5]

In summary, the strongest arguments are in favor of using the Greek language to decipher the alphabetical symbolism of 666:

1. Revelation was written in Greek.

2. 666 is written in many manuscripts using three Greek letters as digits.

3. The eternal nature of Jesus and the Father is symbolically expressed in Revelation using letters of the Greek alphabet.

4. As far as existing records indicate, writers of the first six centuries unanimously used Greek to decipher 666.

Best Solution

Inasmuch as the beasts of Revelation 13 are related to Rome, we would likewise expect "the mark or the name of the beast" and the "number of his name" to be related to Rome. Most people today assume, with little study, that the mark 666 relates to end times. However, since the Roman Empire was established over two thousand years ago, there is a vast amount of history to consider before a person even begins to think of future possibilities.

As early as the second century, Irenaeus (A.D. 130 to 202) searched seriously for Greek names with the numerical value of 666. Although Irenaeus knew that many Greek names had that value, he did not consider it useless to seek the one name that fulfilled all aspects of the prophecy. On the contrary, he stressed the need to learn the name in order to be forewarned. He realized that the name must harmonize with the rest of the prophecy. He said the prophecies could not be fulfilled until the Roman Empire was broken into ten parts:

> The number of the name of the beast, [if reckoned] according to the Greek mode of calculation by the [value of] the letters contained in it, will amount to six hundred and sixty and six . . . let them await, in the first place, the division of the kingdom into ten . . . many names can be found possessing the number mentioned . . . Then also *Lateinos* (ΛΑΤΕΙΝΟΣ) has the number six hundred and sixty-six; and it is a very probable [solution], this being the name of the last kingdom [of the four seen by Daniel]. For the Latins are they who at present bear rule: I will not, however, make any boast over this [coincidence] . . . he [John] indicates the number of the name now, that when this man comes we may avoid him.[6]

Irenaeus understood that he himself lived during the fourth kingdom predicted by Daniel. He connected this kingdom to the beasts of Revelation 13 and 17. He also recognized that there were events still in his future, such as the division of the Roman Empire into ten parts. As Rev. 17:12 says: "The ten horns which you saw are ten kings who have received no kingdom as yet." A century after John penned those words, Irenaeus understood it was still true that the ten kings had "received no kingdom as yet." He also understood an enemy of God would come sometime following the ten-fold division, and he saw that the number of this wicked one's name would equal 666.

Irenaeus lived during a part of the fulfillment of Revelation 13 but before the fulfillment of other parts. Situated in that historical context, he found it significant that the name of the kingdom then in power had the value of 666 in Greek. He did not claim that *Lateinos* was the definite solution to 666, but only a possibility. It was too early in time for him to be definitive. Today, however, with centuries of history behind us, we have the advantage over Irenaeus. From our historical perspective, many of us believe that there never has been a better solution to 666 than this one that Irenaeus suggested a mere one hundred years after John wrote Revelation.

Inasmuch as Irenaeus wrote in the Greek language, he took it for granted that his readers could check out his calculations with utmost ease; thus, he does not even mention the value of the individual letters. For those of us unacquainted with Greek, it is helpful and interesting to see the specifics that are detailed in the accompanying chart.

The numerical value is only one aspect. The name *Lateinos* fits the other aspects of Revelation 13 as well. In Chapter 10, "Why Rome?" we considered the evidence found in Daniel that the beasts of Revelation are related to Rome. The name *Lateinos* agrees with and further confirms that conclusion. Latinus (the Latin spelling) was the reputed founder of the Latin race; thus, we have the name of an individual man. Even if history cannot conclusively prove he was the father of the race, nevertheless, it is widely known that *Latin* is a designation of a people, a kingdom, individuals in that kingdom, a language, and a church. The ancient Latins lived in the central part of Italy called Latium. Latin was the language of the city of Rome from its founding, and it later became the official language of the Roman Empire.

The Latin Church

Irenaeus wrote: "The Latins are they who at present bear rule."[7] He equated those rulers with the fourth beast of

DECIPHERING "666"

Revelation says: "the number of his name . . . calculate the number" (13:17-18). Revelation was written in Greek. Each Greek letter has a numerical value. Therefore, it is simple to calculate the number of any name in Greek. The difficult part is finding a name that harmonizes with the other details predicted in Revelation 13. There is no better solution than the following one suggested by Irenaeus, who lived in the second century:

Greek Numerical System

English equivalent	Greek upper & lower case		Value
a	A	α	1
b	B	β	2
g	Γ	γ	3
d	Δ	δ	4
e	E	ε	5
		ς	6
z	Z	ζ	7
e	H	η	8
th	Θ	θ	9
i	I	ι	10
k	K	κ	20
l	Λ	λ	30
m	M	μ	40
n	N	ν	50
x	Ξ	ξ	60
o	O	ο	70
p	Π	π	80
		ϙ	90
r	P	ρ	100
s	Σ	σ,ς	200
t	T	τ	300
u	Y	υ	400
ph	Φ	φ	500
ch	X	χ	600
ps	Ψ	ψ	700
o	Ω	ω	800
		ϡ	900

The number of LATEINOS is 666.

L	Λ	=	30
a	α	=	1
t	τ	=	300
e	ε	=	5
i	ι	=	10
n	ν	=	50
o	ο	=	70
s	ς	=	200
total		=	**666**

Latinus (Greek: Lateinos)

Latinus was the reputed founder of the Latins. The Latins were the majority of the population of Rome from its foundation. Latin became the official language of the Roman Empire and later the official language of the Roman Catholic Church.

Daniel and the ten-horned beasts of Revelation 13 and 17. That much was clear to him, but Irenaeus had no way of knowing that the Latin Empire would one day develop into the Latin Church. *Latin* is a most appropriate designation for this later development of the Roman power. For over fifteen hundred years, Latin has been a distinguishing mark of the Catholic Church. *Roman* and *Latin* are two ways of identifying the same thing. *Roman* identifies the location; *Latin,* the language.

When Imperial Rome fell in A.D. 476, the empire continued in the East with Constantinople as its capital. Some designate this part of the breakup "the Eastern Roman Empire." Others more correctly call it the "Byzantine Empire." Rome was *West* and Latin; Constantinople was *East* and Greek. This division was mirrored in the churches. The eastern churches were orthodox and Greek; the western churches, catholic and Latin.

Even before the fall of Rome, Latin had become the ritual language of the Western Church regardless of the fact that much of the empire was not of Roman heritage. As the centuries went by, the peoples of Europe gradually changed from Latin to new languages: Italian, Spanish, Portuguese, French, German, and English. Despite these changes, Latin remained the language of the Catholic Church: both the official language and the language of worship. Latin continued as the language of worship until the middle of the twentieth century when the Second Vatican Council ruled that other languages could be used. Those of us born before the nineteen-sixties can well remember the time when mass was said only in Latin. The common people throughout the entire world would go to mass and not understand what the priest was saying.

Century after century, the Catholic Church worldwide was the Latin Church. As of the twenty-first century, Latin continues to be the official language of the Catholic Church, although in decline. Priests must still study Latin in preparation for the priesthood. Official documents of the Catholic

Church continue to be published in Latin. The Catholic Church considers Latin to be an instrument for the unity of the church worldwide, tying all churches to Rome.

The *Modern Catholic Dictionary* defines "Roman Catholicism" as: "The faith, worship, and practice of all Christians in communion with the Bishop of Rome, whom they acknowledge as the Vicar of Christ and the visible head of the Church founded by Christ."[8] This church is Roman because Rome rules supreme over it.

Under the Pope in Rome is the Roman Curia. The Roman Curia is "the whole ensemble of administrative and judicial offices through which the Pope directs the operations of the Catholic Church."[9] "Curia" is a Latin word that in ancient times referred to Roman councils, the Senate, and the various government offices in the Roman Empire. The Catholic Church has retained both the name and the form of government of Imperial Rome.

The special garments that today's Catholic priests wear during mass are copies of various types of clothing that were worn in the Roman Empire in the second century. Today, instead of wearing clothing typical of the nation in which the mass is being celebrated, the priests wear ancient Roman clothing.

John Paul I died suddenly, a scant thirty-three days after his election. That he was Italian was to be expected. All popes before him for the previous 455 years had been Italian. What was not at all expected following his sudden death was that the assembled cardinals would elect a non-Italian, the first Polish pope ever, John Paul II. It is well known that the majority of popes throughout history have been Italian. In the three centuries from A.D. 752 to 1046, there were 57 popes. Not only were most of them Italian, seventy-two percent of them were born in the Italian capital, Rome![10]

The Greek name *Lateinos* has a numerical value of 666. The empire that ruled when the church started was the Latin Empire. The church that gradually turned from the truth and became powerful upon the ashes of that empire was the Latin Church. Latin was the only language of worship until very recent times, and Latin remains the official language of the Catholic Church. The Latin Curia, under the (usually) Italian pope and in the ancient Latin capital remains the center of power of the church. It is the Roman Church; it is the Latin Church.

The Nature of the Mark

"He causes all, both small and great, rich and poor, free and slave, to receive a mark on their right hand or on their foreheads" (Rev. 13:16). All interpretive views agree that the beast is not a four-footed wild mammal but rather is symbolic of some great satanic power among men. The number also must be symbolic inasmuch as we are told to "calculate the number of the beast." We have to do a calculation to understand the symbol. Rev. 13:7 speaks of "one who has the mark or the name of the beast, or the number of his name." The mark, the name, or the number. Since the number is symbolic, the mark would also seem to be symbolic. There is no necessity of envisioning people literally having the number 666 stamped on their right hands or foreheads.

Behind the forehead is the brain, the mind; the hand is the action member of the body. The symbolism seems to contemplate the ability to think and the ability to do. It is a matter of belief and action. The mark is a representation of those who have yielded their minds and bodies into the service of the beast, of those who accept the teachings and obey the commands of the beast; they worship the beast.

This symbolism is very much like the symbolism used for the people of God. In Rev. 7:3, the servants of God are sealed on their foreheads, while in 22:4 God's children have His name on their foreheads. As early as Deut. 6:8, similar symbolism is recorded involving the forehead and the hand. Referring to the words of God, Moses commanded the Israelites: "You shall bind them [God's words] as a sign on your hand, and they shall be as frontlets between your eyes." This is the context Jesus quoted when proclaiming the greatest commandment of the law: loving God (Matt. 22:36-38). Loving God involves the mind and the hand; it involves what we believe and what we do. Worshipping the beast likewise involves what one believes and what one does.

Some believers are not satisfied with this symbolic interpretation and look to a more literal fulfillment. It is noteworthy that Catholics do literally "receive a mark . . . on their foreheads," not once but several times during their life. Instead of immersion in water at baptism, water is poured on the forehead and the sign of the cross is made on the forehead. At confirmation, the forehead is anointed with oil in the form of a cross. On Ash Wednesday, Catholics have ashes placed on their foreheads. The making of the "sign of the cross," which devout Catholics repeatedly practice, is begun with the right hand touching the forehead. The most remarkable of these is the importance of marking the forehead at baptism, inasmuch as this is the sacrament that makes an individual a Catholic.

"No One May Buy or Sell"

Of the lamb-like beast, Revelation says:

> He causes all, both small and great, rich and poor, free and slave, to receive a mark on their right hand or on their foreheads, and that no one may buy or sell except one who has the mark or the name of the beast, or the number of his name (13:16-17).

Present-day fascination with 666 often restricts "the mark" to the prediction of not being able to buy or sell. Yet, just one verse earlier, there is a far more drastic statement. The lamb-like beast will "cause as many as would not worship the image of the beast to be killed" (13:15). Worship the image or die.

The prophecy speaks of control over commerce and control over life, but it also has to do with one's worship. The world has seen much of this kind of persecution. However, this particular persecution has to be considered in the setting of Revelation 13, which deals with the revival of Rome as a religious power. With this setting in mind, it becomes rather obvious that the focus is upon such historical realities as the Crusades and the Inquisition. The spirit and practice of the Inquisition spanned at least the twelfth to the nineteenth century. Since we live in an age and country with religious freedom today, it may be difficult for us to imagine the centuries during which the Roman Catholic Church held sway over the souls and bodies of men.

According to Catholic authorities, the Inquisition had as its purpose:

> To discover and suppress heresy and to punish heretics . . . the relapsed heretics who were found guilty were turned over to the civil government . . . The fact that secular law prescribed death must be understood in the light of those days when heresy was anarchy and treason.[11]

Exactly. In those days, any view opposed to the teaching of Rome was treason that was worthy of death, exactly as predicted by Christ in Revelation. Furthermore, torture was freely used to elicit confessions. According to the *The Encyclopaedia Britannica,* punishments of those who refused to recant could include execution by burning or strangling, exile, short imprisonment, perpetual imprisonment, and confiscation of property.[12]

The papacy on the one hand, and the secular arm on the other, correspond very well to the second and first beasts of Revelation 13. The first beast, by connection to Daniel, surely represents the civil Roman power, while the lamblike beast, which "exercises all the authority of the first beast in his presence" (13:12), surely corresponds to the papacy headquartered in Rome.

Those who did not worship according to the dictates of Rome were subject to death. This is clear in these prophecies, just as the fulfillment is clear in all the history books telling about those times.

Economic repression was also present as was prophesied:

"No one may buy or sell except one who has the mark." The article cited in *The Encyclopaedia Britannica* speaks of the confiscation of property, and says that seizure was allowed even of property that an innocent person had inherited from someone who was not declared to be a heretic until after death. It further states: "Any contract entered into with a heretic was void in itself."[13]

Speaking of Canon 27 of the Third Lateran Council held in 1179, a Catholic authority writes:

> There is a long and very detailed decree about the restraint of heretics . . . Both the heretics and those who protect them are excommunicated; no one is to give them shelter, or allow them in his territory, or to do business with them.[14]

Here is an official law of the Catholic Church—no one was "to do business with" those whom the Catholic Church considered heretics. What a precise fulfillment of the prophecy: "No one may buy or sell except one who has the mark"! The fear of 666 is not something for the future; it is history. Give thanks to God that we did not live in those days!

Sidestepping the Obvious

Educated futurists are well aware of the basic outline, if not the details, of the historical facts alluded to in this chapter. Tim LaHaye, for example, makes numerous revealing references to the Catholic Church in his Revelation commentary. For instance, he writes:

> Both the fifth seal and Revelation 20:4 indicate that a martyrdom of true believers will exceed even that of the Dark Ages, when the Roman Catholic Church persecuted those who held to a personal faith in Jesus Christ.[15]

> When the Babylonian influence of the Church was greatest during the Dark Ages, millions of Christians were persecuted to death. This period of history is well named the "Inquisition."[16]

In his attempt to picture how terrible he thinks future

events will be, he has called up the witness of history regarding the deadly work of the Church of Rome in the Middle or Dark Ages.

When discussing Revelation 17, LaHaye argues against
the seven hills being an indication of the city of Rome, and
he claims the seventh head of the beast is "Antichrist at the
end of time."[17] In spite of his denial of this prophecy already
being fulfilled, he proceeds to fill several pages with evidence of the relationship between Revelation 17 and the
Church of Rome:

> The long history of Rome's intolerance and persecution of Chris-
> tians . . . Whenever in control of a country, Rome has not
> hesitated to put to death all who opposed her.[18]

He follows with a two-and-one-half page quote from *Halley's
Bible Handbook*, full of details of the Inquisition.

With all this evidence, it is a shame to sidestep historical
reality in favor of futuristic fiction. All a Christian needs to
do is carefully compare 2 Thessalonians 2, Daniel 7, and
Revelation 13 and 17 with the facts of history. History shows
that the prophesied Roman enemy of God arrived on the
scene centuries ago. Perhaps many miss this truth due to
the fact that today the beast does not wield nearly as much
power as it did in centuries gone by. Therefore, Christians
need to dust off their history books and investigate what
things were really like in the Middle Ages.

Why Was Revelation Written?

Revelation was written to prepare the people of God for
the spiritual battles in this present life, before Jesus returns. It was written to give us God's view of the religious
situation today and throughout history. It was written to
warn, prepare, and strengthen the church for the real battles of this present life. It was not written to entertain the
church regarding future events that the church would never
experience.

The Antichrist is not future. The little horn of Daniel 7 is not future. The beasts of Revelation 13 and 17 are not future. These are all past and present reality. They are only future to the extent they continue to exist. To push these prophecies totally into our future after the church has been raptured from this world is to act like the proverbial ostrich with its head in the sand. We need to come to grips with the historical past and the present religious reality, as unpleasant and unpopular as that might be. We need to look at the past and present through the eyes of the Lamb of God, the real author of the book of Revelation. "Blessed is he who reads and those who hear the words of this prophecy, and keep those things which are written in it; for the time is near" (Rev. 1:3).

Not Pretending To Be Prophets

"If therefore we would confine ourselves to the rules of just criticism, and not indulge lawless and extravagant fancies; if we would be content with sober and genuine interpretation, and not pretend to be prophets, nor presume to be wise above what is written; we should more consider those passages which have already been accomplished, than frame conjectures about those which remain yet to be fulfilled."

— Thomas Newton, 1704-1782
Dissertations on the Prophecies, 441-42

Section Four

From Here to Eternity

Chapter 15

The Rapture

They tell us planes will fall out of the sky. Automobiles will careen and crash. Surgeries will be halted midway. Communication systems will be in shambles. Husbands will frantically search for their wives. Why? Because all believers instantly and mysteriously had vanished. In spite of such chaos, they tell us life on earth will continue for years. They call it the Rapture.

Some believers emphasize that the word "rapture" is not found in the Bible. This is true, but this is not the real problem. In 1 Thess. 4:17, Paul says that believers "shall be caught up together with them in the clouds to meet the Lord." "Caught up." An English dictionary gives one meaning of rapture as "the carrying of a person to another place or sphere of existence."[1] If by Rapture a person simply meant that Christians will be carried up to be with Christ, then there would be little objection to this word.

The Real Problem

However, religious teachers today attach much more meaning to Rapture than the simple definition given above. Indeed, there is a whole body of doctrine wrapped up in today's word Rapture. The problem is not with the word but with this whole body of doctrine.

An important caution must be introduced before proceeding: futurist teachers have differing views on certain Bible texts. Therefore, they do not all use the same arguments to defend their doctrine of the Rapture. Although some futurist teachers may not use any given argument that follows, other teachers do. No attempt will be made to dissect and classify the differing views. What follows is simply an examination of some of the common arguments that one may hear from varying sources in favor of the Rapture doctrine.

The modern Rapture theory portrays dramatic scenes such as plane crashes and missing babies. However, there is not one verse in the Bible that hints at such a scenario. In addition, no Bible verse teaches that regular life will continue in this world after the Rapture. One of the most commonly cited texts to uphold the Rapture scenario is 1 Thess. 4:13-18; yet it is totally silent about conditions on earth after the saints are lifted up.

Another text frequently cited is Matt. 24:40: "One will be taken and the other left." Did Jesus have the modern Rapture scenario in mind when He said that? A look at the context proves otherwise. Starting only five verses earlier, Jesus said:

> Heaven and earth will pass away . . . But as the days of Noah were . . . the flood came and took them all away, so also will the coming of the Son of Man be. Then two men will be in the field: one will be taken . . . (24:35, 37, 39-40).

The context of "one will be taken and the other left" is "as the days of Noah were, so also will the coming of the Son of Man be." Jesus' coming will be like the coming of the flood in Noah's time. Did Noah mysteriously disappear? When Noah entered the ark, did the world continue with normal daily life? We all know better: "The world that then existed perished" (2 Pet. 3:6). The flood was the end of that old world. Either you were safe in the ark, or you perished under the wrath of God. That is how it will be when Jesus returns.

Did you also notice in this context *who* was taken away? It was not Noah and his family that were taken. Speaking of the wicked, Matt. 24:39 says, "And did not know until the flood came and took them all away." The wicked were taken away; Noah remained. This is the complete opposite of the modern Rapture theory.

No, Jesus did not have the modern Rapture doctrine in mind. Rather, He said that when He returns the earth will pass away, and the wicked will be taken away from the presence of the Lord.

What Jesus "Should" Have Said

If the popular Rapture theory were correct, Jesus would have used very different examples. Jesus would have said, "As the days of Enoch were . . ." or "As the days of Elijah were . . ." Righteous Enoch disappeared out of this world and the world continued on (Gen. 5:21-25). Elijah's case is even more striking. After the whirlwind took him up into heaven, fifty men went searching for him for three days (2 Kings 2:1-18). Now that has the flavor of today's Rapture doctrine! That has the flavor of the "Left Behind" series. There is only one problem. Jesus never said, "As the days of Elijah were"! Jesus said, "As the days of Noah were."

Jesus never said, "As the days of Enoch were." However, He did say, "Likewise as it was also in the days of Lot . . . it rained fire and brimstone from heaven and destroyed them all. Even so will it be in the day when the Son of Man is revealed" (Luke 17:28-30).

The comparisons that Jesus made are with Lot and Noah. Both involved the immediate destruction of the wicked, while the righteous were saved. Both eliminated any possibility of the wicked having a second chance to hear God's word and repent. Both were the end. The case of Sodom, of course, was not the end of the world; but it certainly was the end of Sodom and Gomorrah. Those cities have never been found. Those people never lived long

What Will Jesus' Coming Be Like?

Not like this:

Elijah went up to heaven, and fifty men searched for three days but did not find him. Normal life continued. (2 Kings 2:11-17)

Woodcut by Gustave Doré, 1865.

But like this:

"As the days of Noah were ... they were eating and drinking ... and did not know until the flood came and took them [the wicked] all away, so also will the coming of the Son of Man be."

Painting courtesy of Gospel Services, Inc.

Jesus said so. (Matt. 24:37-39)

enough to wonder what happened to Lot. There were no chariot wrecks or search parties. God simply blotted them off the face of the earth with fire and brimstone. Jesus said His coming would be like that.

"Come as a Thief"

Some futurist teachers uphold the secret Rapture theory with the statement that Jesus will come as a thief. Yes, the Bible says that, but what does it mean? Figures of speech can be tricky. Both Jesus and Satan are likened to lions. A red flag goes up: interpret with caution. Jesus is called both a lion and a lamb. Another red flag. We dare not wring every possible meaning out of any figure of speech. To do so is to make the Bible a plaything for our every imagination.

How do thieves come? Consider two ideas. A thief may come and go secretly without being detected at the moment. On the other hand, a thief may come openly, but suddenly without warning. Which of these two ideas does the Bible teach regarding Jesus' coming?

Out of six New Testament texts that use this figure, only one does not state which meaning is intended. In the other five, the idea is always a thief coming without warning. Secrecy is never an issue, except to deny it. Example:

> If the master of the house had known what hour the thief would come, he would have watched and not allowed his house to be broken into. Therefore you also be ready, for the Son of Man is coming at an hour you do not expect (Luke 12:39-40).

The message is clear: Jesus will come when you least expect Him, just like a thief. Be ready at all times. Notice 2 Pet. 3:10:

> The day of the Lord will come as a thief in the night, in which the heavens will pass away with a great noise, and the elements will melt with fervent heat; both the earth and the works that are in it will be burned up.

"Thief . . . great noise . . . earth . . . burned up." Hardly secret. It is the end of the world!

No Bible text hints that "come as a thief" contains the idea of secrecy. No Bible text hints that Jesus' coming will be hidden from the eyes and understanding of the masses. When Jesus comes, there will be no secrecy and no second chances. Eternity will have arrived. Everyone will know it.

"Shout . . . Voice . . . Trumpet"

The only text that speaks directly of being "caught up" (raptured) makes it clear that it is anything but a covert operation:

> For the Lord Himself will descend from heaven with a shout, with the voice of an archangel, and with the trumpet of God. And the dead in Christ will rise first. Then we who are alive and remain shall be caught up (1 Thess. 4:16-17).

Shout! Voice of an archangel! Trumpet of God! Jesus coming certainly will not be secret.

In fact, Jesus specifically warned us not to believe those people who claim His return is a private, secret, hidden affair.

> Therefore if they say to you, "Look, He is in the desert!" do not go out; or "Look, He is in the inner rooms!" do not believe it. For as the lightning comes from the east and flashes to the west, so also will the coming of the Son of Man be (Matt. 24:26-27).

If someone tries to explain to you that Jesus has already come again, do not believe it. If he tries to convince you that Jesus came in 1914, do not believe him. If he tries to convince you that in the future Jesus will secretly rapture away the believers and the world will not know what happened, do not believe him. When Jesus returns, no TV newsperson will have to broadcast His arrival. When Jesus returns, no self-appointed prophet will have to explain it to anybody. It will be like the lightning from the east to the west. All will see for themselves. Everyone will know.

Two Second Comings?

Today's Rapture theory says that Jesus will return to earth two more times: once before and once after the seven years of Tribulation. Futurists most commonly call these two future events the Rapture and the Second Coming. Some explain it as *two phases* to Jesus' second coming. None, however, seem willing to openly admit what futurism really believes in: a second coming and a third coming.

Various arguments are used to sustain the concept of two future comings. For example, it is said that two comings are required because the Word says Jesus will come "for the saints," and it also says He will come "with the saints." Their explanation is that "for the saints" refers to the time He comes to take Christians to heaven, while "with the saints" refers to seven years later when He returns to earth with those same saints.

Although no text uses the exact expression "for the saints" in relationship to Jesus' coming, the concept is clearly taught in many texts. All believers have the hope that Jesus will return to receive us unto Himself (John 14:3).

On the other hand, 1 Thess. 3:13 talks about "the coming of our Lord Jesus Christ *with* all His saints" (italics mine). Jude 14 also says, "Behold, the Lord comes *with* ten thousands of His saints" (italics mine). The problem is to understand what coming with His saints means. Does it mean that Jesus first will come to get His saints and seven years later bring them back with him, or is there some other explanation?

With the souls of the dead saints. Some believers find in 1 Thess. 4:14 the explanation of Jesus coming with the saints: "Even so God will bring with Him those who sleep in Jesus." They believe Jesus will come to earth bringing with him the souls of the departed saints in order to unite those souls with their bodies in the resurrection.

Others, however, object to this view of "bring." The Thessalonians text does not say, "Jesus will bring with Him to earth." It says, "God will bring with Him." "Bring" depends on the viewpoint involved. Jesus, not the Father, returns to earth. The Father in heaven will bring the resurrected saints with Jesus from earth to heaven. This is just like John 14:3: "And if I go and prepare a place for you, I will come again and receive you to Myself; that where I am, there you may be also." Both expressions—"bring" and "receive"—are from the viewpoint of heaven.

"With the holy angels." This may be a better explanation of Jesus coming with the saints. In 2 Thess. 1:7, Paul speaks of "when the Lord Jesus is revealed from heaven with His mighty angels." Mark 8:38 says, "When He comes in the glory of His Father with the holy angels." Clearly, Jesus will come with the angels, and the angels are holy.

For the benefit of the average person, I seldom appeal to the original Greek. In this case, however, it is especially helpful for English readers. A language such as Spanish requires no Greek explanation here, because the Spanish closely follows the Greek. The Greek word *hagios* is always translated into Spanish as *santo(s)*. However, in English it is sometimes translated "saint(s)" and sometimes "holy." In other words, the two English words "saint" and "holy" come from the same Greek word.

Angels are holy. Thus, they are saints (same word in the Greek). Therefore, when Scripture says that Jesus will come *with* the saints—the holy ones—Mark 8:38 clarifies that this may well refer to His holy angels.

It is debatable whether Jesus will come with the souls of the dead saints. It is not debatable whether Jesus will come "with the holy angels." Whichever view a person prefers, Jesus' coming "for" and "with" the saints in no way necessitates two comings. "For" and "with" easily harmonize with *just one* future second coming of Christ.

No verse of Scripture says Jesus will come a third time bringing "with" Him human saints whom he came "for" some seven years earlier. In Heb. 9:28 the Bible clearly says of Jesus: "He will appear a second time." No verse says he will appear a third time.

Two Resurrections?

According to the Rapture theory, there will be several future resurrections of bodies from the grave. Futurism claims 1 Thess. 4:16 teaches that Christians will be raised long before the wicked are raised. Paul indeed wrote that "the dead in Christ will rise first." "First" before what?

If I tell you, "I am going to the mall first," without any other information, you have no clue about where I will go next. However, add some context to it, such as, "Are you going to the post office?" "Yes, but I am going to the mall first." Now "first" has meaning.

The same is true with Paul's text. Do not try to guess what is second unless you look at the context: "The dead in Christ will rise first. Then we who are alive and remain shall be caught up together with them in the clouds." Paul is not talking about dead saints and dead sinners when he writes ". . . first. Then . . ." He is talking about dead saints and live saints. He is saying that before the live saints are caught up in the clouds, the dead saints will be raised first. Nothing whatsoever is said about two resurrections.

Jesus did speak of two future bodily resurrections—but not in reference to time. He spoke of the destiny of each group: Some participate in "the resurrection of life," while others experience "the resurrection of condemnation." However, these two resurrections will take place at the same time:

> The *hour* is coming in which *all* who are in the graves will hear His voice and come forth—those who have done good, to the resurrection of life, and those who have done evil, to the resurrection of condemnation (John 5:28-29; italics mine).

Rev. 20:5-6 is the only text in Scripture that says, "the first resurrection." Keep in mind, also, that neither Revelation 20 nor any other text of Scripture speaks of a "second resurrection"; therefore, great care must be exercised in determining the identity of the "first." Revelation is highly figurative. Who takes the dragon, the key, the chain, or the seal literally? Thus, it is quite possible that the first resurrection is likewise figurative or spiritual.

In the futurist scheme of things, the "first resurrection" of Revelation 20 is actually *not* their first resurrection. According to futurism's own teaching, the "first resurrection" of Revelation 20 becomes the third resurrection, taking place seven years after the first resurrection. Obviously, they must find some way to explain such a contradiction. Tim LaHaye explains it as three phases of the first resurrection:

> It is important to understand that just as there are two phases to Christ's second coming—(1) the Rapture of the Church and (2) the Glorious Appearing—so there are three phases to the resurrection of believers: (1) the Church, (2) seven years later the Old Testament saints, and finally (3) the Tribulation saints . . .
>
> Church Age Saints — Phase 1: The saints of the church age will be resurrected in the first phase of the first resurrection, as outlined in 1 Thessalonians 4:13-18. This passage described the Rapture . . .
>
> Old Testament Saints — Phase 2: . . . the resurrection of Israel after the Tribulation. In Daniel 12 . . . Israel will be resurrected before the Glorious Appearing . . .
>
> Tribulation Saints — Phase 3: . . . the end of the Tribulation period, at which time, when Christ comes in His glory to set up His millennial kingdom, the Tribulation saints will be resurrected . . . Rev. 20:4.[2]

Here is a summary of Tim LaHaye's explanation of the two phases of Christ's second coming related to the three phases of the first resurrection:

1. The first phase of the first resurrection takes place at the first phase of the second coming.

2. The second phase of the first resurrection takes place between the first and second phases of the second coming.

3. The third phase of the first resurrection takes place at the second phase of the second coming.

Are you confused? Of course! Why not call Jesus' future

coming "the second phase of His first coming"? How about Columbus? He came to the New World in 1492, 1493, 1498, and 1502. So Columbus' first coming was in 1492. The first phase of his second coming was in 1493. The second phase of his second coming was in 1498. The third phase of his second coming was in 1502. Would anyone accept a history book with such distorted nonsense?

Making "first" mean "second" or "third" is simply not the type of literal interpretation that futurism claims as its foundation. Since futurism puts the third-first resurrection of Revelation 20 seven years after the first-first resurrection of the Rapture, it cannot complain that other views do not interpret the text literally. Futurism invents three phases of the first resurrection, which is nowhere spoken of in Scripture.

Rather than accepting human invention, let us examine the Holy Spirit's explanation of a resurrection that certainly is the first resurrection in the life of every child of God:

> Buried with Him in baptism, in which you also were *raised* with Him through faith in the working of God . . . If then you were *raised* with Christ, seek those things which are above, where Christ is (Col. 2:12; 3:1; italics mine).

"Raised"—past tense. (See also Romans 6.) Just as conversion is a new birth, so it is also a death, burial, and resurrection. For the Christian, this is the first resurrection.

"The Day of the Lord"

The Rapture theory holds that "the day of the Lord" (or "day of Christ") is neither the Second Coming nor the Third Coming. Rather, according to some futurist teachers, it is the time between the Second and Third. According to others, it extends from the Rapture to the end of the Millennium. As in many other matters, futurism leans heavily on Old Testament usage to uphold its claims. In the New Testament, however, how did the apostle Peter use the term "day of the Lord"?

> But the day of the Lord will come as a thief in the night, in
> which the heavens will pass away with a great noise, and the
> elements will melt with fervent heat; both the earth and the
> works that are in it will be burned up (2 Pet. 3:10).

Clearly, "the day of the Lord" to Peter was the end of the
world. Follow Peter's arguments throughout chapter 3. In
verses 3 and 4, he warns of scoffers who will mock the belief
in Jesus' return by saying, "Where is the promise of His
coming?" Peter replies by arguing that these people willfully
forget about the flood [in Noah's day] at which time the old
world perished. Then Peter affirms that the present earth is
reserved for fire in "the day of judgment" (3:7). Peter further
explains, "The Lord is not slack concerning His promise"
(3:9). Which promise? In the context (3:4), it is "the promise
of His coming."

Peter continues (3:10): "But the day of the Lord will come
as a thief in the night, in which the heavens will pass away
with a great noise." Since this is so, we should be prepared
for "the coming of the day of God, because of which the
heavens will be dissolved, being on fire, and the elements
will melt with fervent heat" (3:12). You see, Peter builds his
argument about the coming of the Lord by discussing "the
day of judgment," "the day of the Lord," and "the day of
God," which are all terms that refer to the end of the world.
Peter the apostle does not disconnect the day of the Lord
from the coming of the Lord. Rather, the way he uses the
terms shows that the "day of the Lord" is that day in which
the Lord comes to judge and destroy this world.

"The Last Day"

The expression "the last day" appears six times in Scripture, all in the Gospel of John. Four times in the sixth chapter Jesus says of the believer, "I will raise him up at the last
day" (John 6:40, 44, 54, and with slight variation in 6:39). In
11:24, Martha affirms her belief in this truth: "I know that
he [Lazarus] will rise again in the resurrection at the last

day." The resurrection of the righteous clearly will take place at the last day.

According to the modern Rapture doctrine, the resurrection of the righteous does not take place at the last day, but rather 1,007 years *before* the last day. This is because futurism says that after the resurrection of the righteous (the Rapture) comes the seven years of Tribulation and the Millennium. Then, after those 1,007 years, there will be a resurrection and judgment of the wicked.

However, the remaining "last day" verse in John also denies this scenario. Again Jesus is speaking—this time not of the righteous, but of the wicked. He says, "He who rejects Me, and does not receive My words, has that which judges him—the word that I have spoken will judge him in the last day" (John 12:48). Thus, Jesus taught that both the resurrection of the righteous and the judgment of the wicked would take place in the last day. There is no room for 1,007 years between the two events.

The parable of the tares (Matt. 13:24-30, 36-43) teaches the same truth. Verse 38 explains "the field is the world," not the church. This parable is not a contradiction of Jesus' teaching on church discipline. Rather, it is a parable about the entire world. It is a parable about good and bad people living together until the end: "Let both grow together until the harvest . . . the harvest is the end of the age" (13:30, 39). "And at the time of harvest I will say to the reapers, 'First gather together the tares and bind them in bundles to burn them, but gather the wheat into my barn'" (13:30). Saint and sinner are in this world together until the end. Who is taken out first according to this parable? The popular Rapture theory says, "First gather the wheat." However, Jesus said, "First gather together the tares."

We cannot possibly understand it all before it happens, nor can we possibly detail ahead of time the exact sequence and timing of all the events to take place. Clearly, however, the parable of the tares teaches that the righteous and the wicked will live together until the end of the world:

The servants said to him, "Do you want us then to go and gather them up?" But he said, "No, lest while you gather up the tares you also uproot the wheat with them. Let both grow together until the harvest" (Matt. 13:28-30).

The scenario of crashing planes, surgical operations halted midway, and communication systems in shambles is the exact scenario Jesus said he wanted to avoid. The modern futurists want to root up the wheat out of the world; the servants in the parable wanted to root up the tares out of the world. The same principle applies in both cases. The master said, "No," because when you root up one you will root up the other. *Let both grow together until the harvest*! Only then will they be separated. In the parable of the tares, Jesus taught that neither the righteous nor the wicked will be raptured away from the world before God is ready to end it all. Both will grow together until the harvest. That will be the end. That will be the last day.

The Beginning or the End?

According to the modern Rapture theory, Jesus' next coming will just be the beginning. According to this theory, most of the book of Revelation and large amounts of both Old and New Testament prophecies cannot be fulfilled until after the Rapture. Futurism says the Rapture is just the beginning of at least 1,007 years of world history.

A careful look at Scripture, however, presents a very different picture. Jesus' next coming (there is only one more) will be the end of this world, the end of history, the end of time, the end of life as we know it, the end of the wicked living unpunished, the end of tears for God's saints, the end of the battle between God and Satan, the end of the Antichrist, and the end of opportunities to get right with God.

On the other hand, His return will be the beginning—the beginning of eternity. "Prepare to meet your God"! "Watch and pray"!

Chapter 16

The Millennium Is Not . . .

The very thought of a thousand-year reign of Christ excites the imagination. Usually this period is termed the Millennium, which comes from the Latin word meaning one thousand years. This widely discussed period of a thousand years is named only six times in Scripture. Moreover, all six times are in the same text: Rev. 20:1-7. With such scant mention in the Bible, students should be very careful in reaching a conclusion regarding the meaning of this period of time.

What Revelation 20:1-7 Does *Not* Say

Before examining what Revelation 20 *does* say, it can be quite enlightening to notice what it does *not* say:

1. It does *not* say where Christ is during this period, whether in heaven or on earth.

2. It does *not* say where the martyrs are during this period.

3. Although it does mention the first resurrection and the second death, it does *not* mention the second resurrection.

4. It does *not* say Satan is powerless during the thousand years.

5. It does *not* say the thousand years is a period of great peace with no persecution.

6. It does *not* mention the Jews, Jerusalem, or any temple.

7. It does *not* say everyone on earth is in subjection to Christ during the thousand years.

8. It does *not* offer a second opportunity for salvation.

9. It does *not* say the reign is a physical, earthly one, like David's reign.

There is so much that Revelation 20 does not say, one may wonder where all the ideas come from that are taught about the Millennium. While some of the ideas come from assuming a literal fulfillment of selected parts of this prophecy, a good share of the ideas come from the Old Testament. Without question, we must study the rest of Scripture to understand Revelation 20. We must look into both the Old and the New Testaments. In such a study we must remember that the New Testament supersedes the Old. We must also allow easy, clear texts to help us understand the more difficult ones.

No One Interprets It All Literally

The claim is made that the thousand years of Revelation 20, along with various other elements of verses 1 to 7, must be understood literally. However, upon examination, these verses definitely contain various symbols. That being the case, we must give serious consideration to the possibility that the thousand years itself should be understood symbolically or spiritually.

No one believes the dragon/serpent is literal. In fact, the book itself specifically and clearly says otherwise. In both Rev. 20:2 and 12:9, the inspired writer says that the dragon, the serpent of old, is Satan, the Devil.

No one believes the beast mentioned in 20:4 is a literal four-legged animal. The reference, of course, is to chapter 13, which in turn is based on Daniel 7. Dan. 7:23 says that the fourth beast would be "a fourth kingdom on earth." Most interpreters agree that the beast represents Rome, although they disagree on the details. Even those who do not apply it to Rome believe the beast is a symbol of some anti-Christian power.

Then there are the chain, the key, and the seal. Does anyone believe they are literal? Is not Satan a spirit being, albeit an evil spirit? Can a physical chain bind a spirit? Would a literal, physical seal be any deterrent to him?

The entire book of Revelation is a highly symbolical book. Jesus himself explains that the seven lampstands are the seven churches, and the seven stars are the angels of the seven churches (1:20). Whether one understands these angels as heavenly beings or earthly messengers, Jesus confirms what is seen in other Bible prophecies—namely, that stars in prophecy often represent outstanding individuals. There is nothing unusual about this; in our everyday English, for example, we speak of movie stars and Olympic stars.

Symbols continue throughout Revelation to the very last chapter, where Jesus calls himself "the Bright and Morning Star" (22:16). Then verse 17 speaks of "the bride," a reference to Christ's church. With all this figurative language throughout the book and specifically in chapter 20, there is no inherent necessity that other elements in the chapter be interpreted literally.

"Thousand" in the Bible

English dictionaries give these definitions for thousand: "a very large number"[1] and "a great number or amount."[2] This use is very common in our daily language. Mom says, "I told you a thousand times to clean up your room." Then there are the Thousand Islands in the Saint Lawrence River, which include more than 1,500 islands. We all use thousand to simply express a big amount, whether known or unknown, whether close to one thousand or far from it.

There are several prophecies in Daniel and Revelation that include numerical values: 3½, 42, 62, 69, 1,260, 1,290, and 1,335. In these cases, the numbers are definite and specific. The number 1,000, on the other hand, is a round number, frequently used to express an indefinitely large amount, whether in English or Spanish or Russian—or in the Bible.

In Deut. 1:11 Moses expresses to Israel: "May the LORD God of your fathers make you a thousand times more numerous than you are." Israel at that time consisted of 600,000 men of war, not counting women and children. A very conservative estimate of the entire nation would be two million. A thousand times two million is two billion! Was Moses literally wishing they would number exactly two billion, or was he simply using thousand like we often do?

Another example is found in Ps. 50:10: "Every beast of the forest is Mine," says God, "and the cattle on a thousand hills." How about the cattle on the rest of the hills? Would anyone dare limit God's ownership to an exact one thousand count? Surely not.

Consider also Psalm 90:4:

> For a thousand years in Your sight
> Are like yesterday when it is past,
> And like a watch in the night.

If we take this verse literally, it contradicts itself. "Yesterday" is a period of twenty-four hours. Inasmuch as the ancient Israelites divided each night into three watches, a "watch in the night" would be about four hours. If twenty-four hours is equal to one thousand years, then a four-hour watch would be equal to about 167 years, but the verse says the watch is equal to a thousand years. Who could accept any attempt at a literal calculation of this verse? Such a calculation is self-contradictory, and it misses the whole point. It is just like the self-contradiction involved when people suggest calculations based on 2 Pet. 3:8: "With the Lord one day is as a thousand years, and a thousand years as one day." In this case, the time references are expressed in opposite directions—one day is a thousand years, and a thousand years is one day. Each literal calculation nullifies the other. Therefore, no calculations can be based on this verse. The verse has no mathematical meaning. In both Psalms 90 and 2 Peter 3, a thousand is obviously just a very large, unspecified, and indefinite amount. The meaning in both verses is simply that God is not bound by time as we humans are.

In short, the Bible often uses a thousand as an indefinitely large number, just as we do in everyday English. There is no reason why the same cannot be true in Revelation 20.

Other Scripture Must Be Studied

From all of the above, it is very clear that Rev. 20:1-7 cannot possibly be understood alone. It raises too many questions. Everyone's explanation, whatever their view, is based more on other Scriptures than on Revelation 20 itself.

There are at least two major views on the matter. Both views connect the Millennium to all the Old Testament kingdom prophecies. The most popular view in evangelical churches today, the dispensational-futurist view, says that Jesus did not fulfill these prophecies at His first coming. It says that because of the Jews' rejection, Jesus failed to set up the kingdom and had to postpone its arrival. This view proclaims a literal, future, thousand-year reign in which all the Old Testament prophecies will be literally fulfilled via an earthly kingdom centering around Israel, Jerusalem, and a rebuilt temple.

There is another view that has been held by many believers throughout the ages. This view agrees that the thousand years is the fulfillment of the Old Testament prophecies of the kingdom. However, this view says that these prophecies are not something yet to be fulfilled in our future. It says that Jesus was not a failure—He accomplished the work He came to do on earth. It says that God set up His kingdom on schedule in the first century. It says the kingdom of God is not a physical kingdom nor a Jewish kingdom. It says the kingdom is spiritual; it is for Jew and Gentile alike, and it is here now. It says that the expression "thousand years" is a general term expressing an indefinitely long period of time. This view is sometimes referred to as amillennialism, a term simply expressing a rejection of the idea of a future literal thousand-year kingdom.

It is clear that a person's understanding of the Millennium in Revelation 20 is very much determined by his understanding of other kingdom prophecies and their fulfillment. Too often students limit their concepts of the kingdom to the information they gain from the Old Testament. However, a knowledge of New Testament teaching on the kingdom is vital before delving into something as difficult as Revelation 20. Among other things, it is essential to examine what Jesus had to say about the kingdom. That is the theme of Chapter 17, "Jesus Revealed the Nature of the Kingdom." In addition to a study of the kingdom itself, other teachings of Jesus must be taken into consideration. One important topic is what He taught about resurrection.

Two Future Resurrections?
What Did Jesus Say?

A superficial glance at Revelation 20 would appear to uphold the idea that there will be two future resurrections separated by a thousand years. It seems to say that there will be a resurrection of the righteous before the thousand years, followed by a resurrection of the wicked after the thousand years.

However, as already seen in Chapter 15, "The Rapture," such a concept does not harmonize with Jesus' teaching on the subject. In the parable of the tares (Matt. 13), Jesus clearly taught that saints and sinners must live together in this world until the end: "Let both grow together until the harvest." He further clarified, "First gather together the tares." There is no way to harmonize this parable with the concept of taking the wheat out first, allowing the tares to continue in the world for years. Likewise, Jesus taught that at the last day, the righteous will be raised from the dead and the wicked will be judged. It will be the end. There is no room in Jesus' last-day teaching for a thousand years to follow the resurrection of the righteous.

Recognition of What Jesus Taught

In a widely distributed and translated prophecy magazine, *Midnight Call*, Norbert Lieth makes some amazing statements concerning Jesus' resurrection teaching. In an article about the Rapture based on 1 Thess. 4:13-18, Mr. Lieth discusses the circumstances surrounding the origin of Paul's first epistle to the Thessalonians:

> Until then, the doctrine of the first resurrection had been a mystery. It wasn't taught in The Old Testament, nor in the Gospels.
> The first letter to the Thessalonians was written in about A.D. 50, and the first letter to the Corinthians about 6 years later. Only in them was the mystery of the Rapture revealed (1st Corinthians 15:51-53).
> Until then, it was believed that the resurrection of all the dead would take place on the last day (Daniel 12:2 and 13, John 5:25-29 and 11:24).[3]

I do not know all Mr. Lieth had in mind when he wrote this. However, taking it at face value, the following can be seen: By comparing the first two paragraphs, it is clear that when Mr. Lieth says "the first resurrection" he is speaking of the Rapture. This, of course, is one of the basic doctrines of futurism. Therefore, in the first paragraph just quoted, Mr. Lieth is stating that the Rapture "wasn't taught in the Old Testament, *nor in the Gospels*" (italics mine). This means that Jesus did not teach the Rapture.

According to the *Midnight Call*, the Rapture was a new doctrine revealed about twenty years after Jesus' ascension. There is no inherent problem with that—the Spirit was leading the apostles into all truth (John 16:12-13). The problem is that the supposed new revelation *contradicts* the clear teachings of Jesus. Mr. Lieth supports his affirmation that "it was believed . . ." by referring to the book of Daniel and to remarks of Jesus and Martha recorded in the Gospel of John. Perhaps Mr. Lieth meant to imply that Jesus knew the mystery of the Rapture but that He did not reveal it while on earth. Nevertheless, Mr. Lieth still is saying that Jesus did not teach the Rapture. When all three paragraphs are examined together, it can be seen that Mr. Lieth is saying the Rapture doctrine is substantially different from Jesus' teaching about *all the dead* being resurrected on the last day.

Mr. Lieth understands what Jesus taught: The resurrection of all the dead will take place at the same time. What he and many others fail to see is that the doctrine of two future resurrections, separated by a Millennium, is not only different from Jesus' teaching—it opposes and contradicts this clear teaching of our Lord, the very one who will be in charge of the resurrection of all the dead. If the Rapture is true, then Jesus' words in John 6:40 are contradicted: He said, "Everyone who sees the Son and believes in Him may have everlasting life; and I will raise him up at the last day." If believers will already be raised in the Rapture, how can Jesus raise them again in the last day? Jesus' teaching simply leaves no room for a future, literal, thousand-year kingdom to follow the resurrection.

Nor does 1 Thess. 4:13-18 offer any new revelation regarding two different resurrections. This text only speaks of one resurrection. This text does not say that the world continues after the resurrection; neither does it mention a thousand-year reign. This text mentions only one resurrection and agrees perfectly with what Jesus taught while here on earth. For further study regarding the resurrection as taught in 1 Thessalonians 4, review Chapter 15, "The Rapture," especially the section entitled "Two Resurrections?"

The Kingdom in Revelation

As indicated previously, any interpretation of Revelation 20 is strongly influenced by one's understanding of the nature and timing of the kingdom of God as taught in the rest of Scripture. Certainly one book to be studied is Revelation itself, inasmuch as it is the only book in the entire Bible that mentions a thousand-year reign. What do the other portions of Revelation tell us about the nature and timing of the kingdom of God?

In the opening verses of Revelation John says: "I, John, both your brother and *companion in the tribulation and kingdom* and patience of Jesus Christ" (1:9, italics mine). John was already in the tribulation! John was already in the kingdom! This clear statement at the very beginning of the book, before John received any of the prophetic visions, must have a strong bearing on the way we interpret any prophecies relating to either tribulation or kingdom. John declares that he and his brethren were already "in the tribulation and kingdom and patience of Jesus Christ."

In 1:5-6 John also speaks of "Jesus Christ . . . who loved us and washed us from our sins in His own blood, and has made us kings and priests to His God and Father." Some Greek manuscripts here read "kings" while others read "kingdom." There is little difference in the ultimate meaning. Revelation 20 declares: "They shall be priests of God and of Christ, and shall reign with Him a thousand years" (20:6). "Priests" and "reign" in chapter 20 is practically a repeat of "kingdom and priests" or "kings and priests" in chapter 1. Moreover, 1:6 reads, "Has made us." That is past tense. It expresses an accomplished fact, a present reality. We are reigning now! The "thousand years" is here now!

In Rev. 2:11 Jesus promises: "He who overcomes shall not be hurt by the second death." Avoiding the second death is thus a blessing for all faithful Christians. Therefore, Revelation 20 is not stating a new truth nor a truth reserved for a special group of Christians when it affirms: "Blessed and holy is he who has part in the first resurrection. Over such the second death has no power" (20:6). This is true of all Christians.

Rev. 1:5 also says: "Jesus Christ . . . the ruler over the kings of the earth." Jesus is ruler now! We all know what type of ruler He is: a king. Jesus is king now! In 3:21 Jesus says of himself: "I also overcame and sat down with My Father on His throne." Jesus is on the throne now! During the seventh trumpet (11:15), there are "loud voices in heaven, saying, 'The kingdoms of this world have become the kingdoms of our Lord and of His Christ, and He shall reign forever and ever!'" Whatever historical date is placed on the fulfillment of the seventh trumpet, it must be noticed that Jesus' reign is "forever and ever." It is eternal, as Dan. 2:44 had prophesied.

Relationship between Chapters 12 and 20

Among the texts in Revelation that speak of the kingdom, chapter 12 is one of the most important. The interpretation of the woman, the dragon, the male child, and the war in heaven is not without difficulties. Nevertheless, consider these truths expressed in verses 10 and 11:

> Then I heard a loud voice saying in heaven, "Now salvation, and strength, and the kingdom of our God, and the power of His Christ have come, for the accuser of our brethren, who accused them before our God day and night, has been cast down. And they overcame him by the blood of the Lamb and by the word of their testimony, and they did not love their lives to the death."

First, note that salvation and the kingdom arrive at the same time—when Satan is cast down out of heaven. What is the *earliest* possible point in history for the arrival of salvation and the kingdom of God? Verse 11 says Satan was overcome "by the blood of the Lamb." So all of this must necessarily have taken place after Christ died on Calvary.

A more difficult question arises: What is the *latest* possible point in history for the casting down of Satan and the arrival of salvation and the kingdom? Verses 13 and 14 say

Arrival of Kingdom as Seen in Revelation 12

Futurist view, contrary to Rev. 12, places arrival of kingdom AFTER "3½ years":

Kingdom postponed

(Present church age parenthesis)

Seven-year Tribulation

Rapture

Second Coming

Satan cast out

A.D. 30

① ③ ② Kingdom arrives – Millennium | Eternity
(OUT OF SEQUENCE)

3½ years

Rev. 12:9-14 reveals the following sequence:

① Satan is cast out of heaven by the blood of Jesus.

② That is when salvation and the kingdom arrive.

③ Then, the persecuted woman flees to the wilderness for 3½ years.

Futurist and historical views agree:

1260 days = "time, times, and half a time" = 3½ years,

1 day = 1 year for 70-week prophecy using Ezek. 4:6 key,

BUT

only the historical view applies this key to the 3½ years.

Historical view, agreeing with Rev. 12, places arrival of kingdom BEFORE "3½ years":

① Satan cast out

② Salvation & Kingdom arrived

③ 3½ years = 1260 prophetic days/years

Woman & offspring persecuted by Satan

Present Church – Kingdom – Millenium age

A.D. 30

Second Coming

Eternity

The kingdom arrived with salvation in A.D. 30.

that after Satan was cast to the earth, he persecuted the woman. Then the woman fled into the wilderness where she remained for "a time and times and half a time." Therefore, the casting out of Satan and the arrival of salvation and the kingdom all had to take place *before* the persecution of the woman for "a time and times and half a time."

It is easy to agree with most students of Revelation, whatever their views on other matters may be, that "a time and times and half a time" in 12:14 is equivalent to the 1,260 days in 12:6. The calculation is simply this: if "time" equals one year, and "times" two years, then "time and times and half a time" equals 3½ years, which is also 42 months (see Rev. 11:2-3). If we round off all months to 30 days, 42 months equals exactly 1,260 days. Most believers who have considered the matter conclude that the three expressions refer to the same length of time. What is not so clear is whether these expressions refer to 1,260 literal days (3½ years), or if they should be given a figurative day-for-a-year interpretation that would result in 1,260 years. Either way, the persecution of the woman takes place following the casting out of Satan, the arrival of salvation, and the arrival of the kingdom: "When the dragon saw that he had been cast to the earth, he persecuted the woman" (12:13).

The prevailing futurist view is that this 3½ years refers to the second half of a future seven-year Tribulation, which is followed by the arrival of the Millennium of Revelation 20. However, such an interpretation does not agree with all the information in Revelation 12. Revelation 12:9-10 says that when Satan is cast out of heaven, a loud voice in heaven declares: "Now salvation . . . and the kingdom of our God . . . have come." The persecution of the woman for 3½ years comes after Satan is cast down and *after* the arrival of the kingdom. Futurism teaches that the 3½ years takes place *before* the arrival of the millennial kingdom, but Revelation 12 places 3½ years of persecuting the woman *after* the arrival of God's kingdom.

Chapter 12 points to two events as being simultaneous

with the casting down of Satan: the arrival of salvation, and the arrival of the kingdom. "Now salvation . . . and the kingdom of our God . . . have come." If the kingdom is not here yet, then salvation is not here yet. However, salvation is here! Toward the end of his life Paul declared (in past tense), "the salvation of God has been sent to the Gentiles" (Acts 28:28). That salvation, of course is through the gospel: "I am not ashamed of the gospel of Christ, for it is the power of God to salvation for everyone who believes" (Rom. 1:16). According to Revelation 12, since salvation is here now, the kingdom is here now. The two arrived together.

That the kingdom is here now agrees exactly with what John affirmed at the very beginning of the book: "I, John, both your brother and companion in the tribulation and kingdom" (Rev. 1:9). John in A.D. 95 or 96 declared that he was already in the kingdom. Revelation 12 declares that the kingdom of God arrived at the same time salvation arrived. Revelation 20, therefore, cannot be predicting a yet future, literal thousand-year kingdom. Revelation 20 needs to be interpreted in harmony with the rest of the book of Revelation, as well as the rest of the New Testament.

The Millennium is *Not* . . .

Most of the beliefs that anyone has about the Millennium are not based on Revelation 20, which is the only text that specifically mentions the thousand-year period. Beliefs about the nature of this thousand-year period are derived from other sources.

Based on other Scriptures, we have seen that:

1. The thousand years is *not* a yet future arrival of Jesus' kingdom in which He is supposed to fulfill what He failed to fulfill the first time He came.

2. The thousand years is *not* a period of time between the resurrection of the righteous and the resurrection of the wicked.

3. The thousand years is *not* some time yet future when Jesus for the first time will sit on His throne and reign as King.

4. The thousand years is *not* a period of time that will arrive two thousand years after salvation arrived in the world.

What is the Millennium?

What then is the "thousand years" of Revelation 20? Yes, this thousand-year reign refers to Christ's kingdom. Yes, it refers to God's kingdom as predicted in Daniel 2. The truth so often missed is that this kingdom was set up when the fourth empire, Rome, was in power, according to the time Daniel predicted. Since the first century, God's kingdom on earth has been a reality, just as John declared at the beginning of Revelation: "I, John, both your brother and companion in the tribulation and kingdom" (1:9). John and his brethren were already in the kingdom of God.

With these truths in mind, many Christians interpret the "thousand years" as a symbolic term referring to the entire gospel age or church age. In the Bible, just as in modern English, thousand often means a great number. The kingdom has already existed for almost two thousand years, which surely is a great number of years. The thousand years can thus be understood as extending from Christ's first coming to His second coming. The most plausible interpretations are those that are in agreement with sound Scriptural doctrine; they see the millennium as taking place during the present gospel-church age. They proclaim Jesus as King now and teach that God's kingdom is here now.

What kind of kingdom did Jesus come to establish on earth? Chapter 17, "Jesus Revealed the Nature of the Kingdom," offers considerable insight into this important question. Rev. 20:4 says, "they lived and reigned with Christ for a thousand years." The thousand years has to do with the reign of Christ; it has to do with Christ's kingdom. Therefore, whatever we can learn about the nature of Jesus' kingdom will help us understand what the thousand years is about. Let us listen to the King to see what He had to say about it.

Chapter 17

Jesus Revealed the Nature of the Kingdom

The Jews of Jesus' day believed that their prophets had foretold a physical and nationalistic kingdom. We can hardly blame them. On the surface many of the prophecies appear to predict glorious days for the physical nation of Israel. Even Jesus' apostles viewed the kingdom in this light.

It is not surprising that the twelve apostles did not understand the true nature of the predicted kingdom. They did not even understand that Jesus had to die on the cross to take away the sin of the world! What is more basic to the gospel than that? Yet, they missed it. Their prophets certainly had foretold Jesus' suffering for sin. In addition, Jesus himself plainly told them ahead of time. Yet, they still missed it. When Jesus died, the disciples did not praise God for the great sacrifice of the Lamb of God. No, indeed. They thought it was all over. It is no wonder, then, that they had no idea of the true nature of the kingdom of God.

A true Christian needs to accept God's own interpretation of His prophecies: "No prophecy of Scripture is of any private interpretation" (2 Pet. 1:20). Therefore, we must study the

Gospels. We must hear King Jesus. We must interpret Old Testament kingdom prophecies in the light of New Testament revelations.

The Sermon on the Kingdom

Yes, we usually call it the Sermon on the Mount. However, where the sermon was delivered is immaterial. The content is what matters.

This outstanding sermon begins with the famous Beatitudes. What are they? They are blessings related to the kingdom of God. The sermon opens with these words: "Blessed are the poor in spirit," Jesus said, "for theirs is the kingdom of heaven" (Matt. 5:3). Those who are humble, those who recognize their spiritual poverty—the kingdom belongs to them.

As the Beatitudes close, they dwell on the theme of persecution: "Blessed are those who are persecuted for righteousness' sake," the Master said, "for theirs is the kingdom of heaven" (5:10). This is not a blessing on those who kill the enemies of God; it is a blessing on those who are persecuted. Persecution implies suffering without retaliating. The kingdom of heaven is for those who stand up for righteousness at any cost—those who are willing to suffer for what they believe.

The kingdom of heaven requires holiness of life: "Unless your righteousness exceeds the righteousness of the scribes and Pharisees, you will by no means enter the kingdom of heaven" (5:20). The scribes and Pharisees were the religious leaders of the Jews. According to Jesus' statement, these Jewish leaders would not be in the kingdom of heaven. This means God's kingdom is not based on nationality or mere religion. The kingdom is only for those who are truly righteous in the eyes of God.

Again, in 6:33, Jesus taught that godliness is interconnected with the kingdom: "Seek first the kingdom of God and His righteousness." In the context, there is a contrast between the material and the spiritual. Jesus called on His followers to make righteousness their top priority, more important than food and clothes. Yes, God promises to take care of the material, but that is on the condition that we put the spiritual first. God's kingdom is about spiritual concerns.

Entrance into the kingdom of heaven depends upon one's relationship to Jesus: "Not everyone who says to Me, 'Lord, Lord,' shall enter the kingdom of heaven, but he who does the will of My Father in heaven" (7:21). This verse is often quoted to point out that merely calling on Jesus' name is not enough to enter the kingdom; one must also be obedient. True. Yet, the expression, "not everyone who says to Me, 'Lord, Lord,'" contains the underlying implication that a person certainly must recognize Jesus as Lord (King) in order to enter the kingdom. Such recognition is not the total requirement, but it is a requirement. As Jesus clarified elsewhere: "No one comes to the Father except through Me" (John 14:6). Neither Jews nor Gentiles can enter God's kingdom without making Jesus the Lord of their life.

This sermon is a spiritual message about a spiritual kingdom. It contains nothing of a political nature, nothing of a nationalistic nature, nothing about an earthly kingdom like David's.

"The Kingdom of Heaven is Like . . ."

To help His disciples better understand the true nature of God's kingdom, Jesus told many parables. Matthew 13 records seven of them: the sower, the tares, the mustard seed, the leaven, the hidden treasure, the pearl of great price, and the dragnet. All but the first begin with "the kingdom of heaven is like . . ." Nor is the first really different. When Jesus explains it, He says it has to do with hearing "the word of the kingdom" (13:19). When His disciples asked Him why He spoke in parables, Jesus replied, "Because it has been given to you to know the mysteries of the kingdom of heaven" (13:11).

There were no mysteries related to David's kingdom. However, Jesus' kingdom has mysteries precisely because it

is not a temporal, nationalistic kingdom. These mysteries
have to do with the spiritual nature of the kingdom. They
tell that the kingdom is enlarged by planting the Word of
God in people's hearts. It is hearts that are captured, not
bodies. Some will accept the message of the kingdom while
others will reject it. Some will first accept and afterward
reject the Word of God because of persecution and "the cares
of this world" (13:22). The parables warn that the Devil also
sows seed and that his followers will live in the midst of "the
sons of the kingdom" until "the end of the age" (13:38-39).
Then, the angels will "separate the wicked from among the
just" (13:49).

We rightly connect all these ideas to the gospel message
of salvation. Moreover, Jesus connected the gospel to the
kingdom of heaven. Mark 1:14 states that Jesus began his
ministry "preaching the gospel of the kingdom of God." The
gospel and the kingdom are not two separate entities—one
is the message, the other is the organization. They are in-
separable elements in God's plans for the salvation of sinners.

Aside from Matthew 13, there are many other parables of
the kingdom recorded in the Gospels. For example, in Matthew 22 Jesus taught, "The kingdom of heaven is like a
certain king who arranged a marriage for his son, and sent
out his servants to call those who were invited to the wed-
ding" (22:2-3). Entrance into the kingdom of heaven is by
way of invitation. An appeal is made. No one is forced in. No
one enters automatically, whatever his nationality may be.
Each individual—male or female, young or old, American or
African, rich or poor, Jew or Gentile—makes a personal
decision to accept or reject the invitation to enter the kingdom.

Not Necessarily Jewish

Even before Jesus began His ministry, John the Baptist
preached truths that had an important bearing on the nature of the kingdom. John made an amazing declaration to

the Jews: "Do not think to say to yourselves, 'We have Abraham as our father.' For I say to you that God is able to raise up children to Abraham from these stones" (Matt. 3:9).

God had made man out of dust. God had made woman out of a rib. God had made a son for Abraham in the womb of a woman past menopause. Therefore, it would be no problem for God to make more children for Abraham out of stones. Indeed, spiritually speaking, that is what God did.

In his first epistle, the apostle Peter wrote to those who had been "redeemed . . . with the precious blood of Christ . . . having been born again." He explained to them: "You also, as living stones, are being built up a spiritual house . . . you are . . . a holy nation . . . who once were not a people but are now the people of God" (1 Pet. 1:18-19, 23; 2:5, 9-10). Those who are redeemed by the blood of Jesus are the people of God today. They are God's holy nation, redeemed by the blood of the Lamb. The Holy Spirit has declared: "For as many of you as were baptized into Christ have put on Christ . . . And if you are Christ's, then you are Abraham's seed, and heirs according to the promise" (Gal. 3:27, 29). God takes stonyhearted Gentiles, as well as stonyhearted physical Jews, and converts them into sons of Abraham when they are baptized into Christ. Christians today are the heirs of the promises God made to Abraham. Christians today are the true descendents of Abraham: "If you are Christ's, then you are Abraham's seed."

Less than a week before the mobs cried out for His crucifixion, Jesus spoke of this dramatic change in God's dealing with the human race (Matt. 21:33-46). In this text He told about a landowner who placed vinedressers in charge of his vineyard. In due time, the owner sent servants to collect the fruits, but the vinedressers dealt cruelly with them, wounding some, killing others. Finally, the owner sent his own son, and the vinedressers killed him. It does not require much Bible understanding to discern that the owner represents God, the servants represent the Old Testament prophets, and the son represents Jesus. And the vinedressers? Who could they be but the Jewish nation in general, or the Jews' religious leaders in particular? "Now when the chief priests and Pharisees heard His parables, they perceived that He was speaking of them" (21:45).

Jesus told the chief priests, elders, and Pharisees—the Jewish clergy—"The kingdom of God will be taken from you and given to a nation bearing the fruits of it" (Matt. 21:43). Jesus simply told them, paraphrased in popular language, "If you don't want it, I'll find someone else who does." The rejection of the promised kingdom by the Jewish leaders would in no way change God's plans. In fact, such texts as Isa. 53:3 and Ps. 118:22 show God had anticipated their rejection. Daniel had prophesied: "In the days of these kings the God of heaven will set up a kingdom which shall never be destroyed" (2:44). No conditions were given for setting up the kingdom. The coming kingdom would not depend upon Israel's positive response; others more worthy could take their place. "The God of heaven *will* . . ." (italics mine). The New Testament confirms that the God of heaven *did* set up His kingdom and that it *was* given to a new holy nation.

Before giving the parable of the vineyard, Jesus had already told the religious leaders of Israel:

> Assuredly, I say to you that tax collectors and harlots enter the kingdom of God before you. For John came to you in the way of righteousness, and you did not believe him; but tax collectors and harlots believed him (Matt. 21:31-32).

Once again, we see that the kingdom of God has to do with righteousness and faith. It is altogether a spiritual matter. Neither color of skin, nor nationality—not even Jewish-ness—has anything to do with being a part of God's king-dom. It was, and still is, a matter of the heart and spirit.

Refused to Be an Earthly King

If Jesus had come to set up a physical kingdom, there was no better time than after the feeding of the five thou-sand. The Jews were so stirred up that "they were about to come and take Him by force to make Him king" (John 6:15). Far from seizing the opportunity, Jesus "departed again to the mountain by Himself alone." When the crowds found Him the next day, Jesus preached a powerful sermon, contrasting the physical with the spiritual:

> Jesus answered them and said, "Most assuredly, I say to you, you seek Me, not because you saw the signs, but because you ate of the loaves and were filled. Do not labor for the food which perishes, but for the food which endures to everlasting life . . . I am the living bread which came down from heaven. If anyone eats of this bread, he will live forever; and the bread that I shall give is My flesh, which I shall give for the life of the world . . . Whoever eats My flesh and drinks My blood has eternal life . . . It is the Spirit who gives life; the flesh profits nothing. The words that I speak to you are spirit, and they are life" (John 6:26-27, 51, 54, 63).

The result? "From that time many of His disciples went back and walked with Him no more" (6:66). From what time? From the time Jesus refused to become their physical king. From the time Jesus probed deep into their minds and hearts to uncover their true inner materialistic hearts. From the time Jesus scorned politics with its earthly concerns, choosing rather to preach to them about eternal life. From the time Jesus refused to become a king like David and Solomon over physical Israel. From that time, many disciples—disillusioned—turned their backs on Jesus precisely because Jesus refused to establish the literal, physical kingdom of Israel they thought the prophets had promised.

Disciples Not Soldiers

At the time of the triumphal entry, the fervor and expectation of the Jews was raised once again. The crowds shouted:

> Hosanna to the Son of David!
> "Blessed is He who comes in the name of the LORD!" . . .
> Blessed is the kingdom of our father David
> That comes in the name of the Lord . . .

Two Kingdoms Contrasted

The OLD Way	The NEW Way
From his youth up, with God's blessing and help, David slaughtered his enemies, starting with Goliath.	Jesus said that <u>if</u> His kingdom were of this world, His servants would fight (just like David); but Jesus' kingdom is not for warriors; it is for peacemakers.

David's Kingdom OLD Testament	Jesus' Kingdom NEW Testament
1. Enter via natural birth	1. Enter via spiritual birth
2. Open basically to one nation	2. Open to all nations
3. For a small territory	3. For the whole world
4. David could not build temple	4. Christians are the temple
5. Denounce civil rulers	5. Denounce religious error
6. Capital punishment	6. Withdraw fellowship
7. Denounce wicked nations	7. Preach to wicked nations
8. War against enemies	8. Evangelize enemies
9. Physical weapons	9. God's Word: sword of Spirit

Jesus said:
"My kingdom is not of this world."

"Blessed is the King who comes in the name of the LORD!"
(Matt. 21:9; Mark 11:10; Luke 19:38)

They proclaimed the King, the son of David, and the king-dom of David as all coming right then. They believed Jesus was fulfilling the Old Testament kingdom prophecies.

The Jews knew the close relationship between David and Jesus—between David's kingdom and Jesus' kingdom. This relationship concerned ancestry as well as God's direct involvement. However, they did not know that the *nature* of the two kings and the *nature* of the two kingdoms would be very different.

The week of the triumphal entry was one filled with rapid and dramatic change. Near the end of the week, Jesus stood before the Roman governor, Pontius Pilate. Pilate asked Jesus: "Are You the King of the Jews?" Jesus offered a powerful and definitive reply: "My kingdom is not of this world." He further clarified the relationship between His kingdom and the current political situation by saying: "If My kingdom were of this world, My servants would fight, so that I should not be delivered to the Jews; but now My kingdom is not from here" (John 18:33, 36).

Jesus' kingship and kingdom were fundamentally differ-ent from David's. David *did* fight that he might "not be delivered" to the Philistines (remember Goliath?). David also fought that he might not be delivered to the Amalekites, the Jebusites, the Moabites, the Syrians, the Ammonites, and the Edomites. David had his "mighty men of valor fit for war" (1 Chron. 12:25). Like many other Old Testament heroes, David was a man of violence, blood, and war. He fought for a physical kingdom, conquered Jerusalem, and greatly extended his earthly dominion.

Jesus, in dramatic contrast, refused to take up arms either to save his own life from the Jews or to rescue Jerusa-lem from the Romans. His kingship and kingdom were not only different from David's but also from that of Rome. "My kingdom is not of this world." Jesus pointedly declared that

His kingdom was not one that expands and takes control by force of arms. Babylon, Persia, Greece, and Rome, represented in the great-image dream of Daniel 2, all came into power and stayed in power by force of arms. Not so with God's kingdom, which was to start as a stone that was "cut out without hands" (2:34).

If Jesus, the Son of David, were to set up a kingdom like David's, He would have fought and thrown the Romans out of the Promised Land. No matter what the kingdom prophecies seem to be saying in their Old Testament context, they must be interpreted in the light of Jesus' declaration to the Roman governor: "My kingdom is not of this world. *If* My kingdom were of this world, My servants would fight" (italics mine). Jesus' kingdom does not have soldiers; it is neither defended nor extended by force of physical arms. Jesus' kingdom is a spiritual kingdom.

Pilate clearly understood Jesus' words, for Pilate then declared to the mob, "I find no fault in Him" (John 18:38). If Jesus were claiming to be king of a temporal kingdom, that would have been treason against Caesar and Rome—sufficient cause to put Jesus to death. When Pilate said, "I find no fault in Him," Pilate clearly confessed his own understanding of the spiritual nature of Jesus' kingdom.

The mob cried out, "Crucify Him!" Pilate tried every way he could think of to release Jesus, "but the Jews cried out, saying, 'If you let this Man go, you are not Caesar's friend. Whoever makes himself a king speaks against Caesar'" (John 19:12). The chief priests cried, "We have no king but Caesar!" (19:15). With that, Pilate ceased his efforts to free Jesus and gave orders that He be crucified as they wished.

We say the Jews did not understand. However, there was something they most assuredly did understand. The Jews could see that Jesus was not going to set up an earthly kingdom like David's earthly kingdom! They could see that Jesus wanted no part in attempting to oust the Romans from Jewish soil. They could see that Jesus was neither a Zealot, nor a patriot, nor a subversive.

It is unthinkable that the Jews in Jesus' day would yell, "We have no king but Caesar!" That was an absolute, bold-faced lie! The only reason they would yell such a fabrication is that they were desperate to get rid of this "man" who preached at them rather than becoming the political king they expected and thought He should be. They hated Caesar. Nonetheless, they hated Jesus even more than they hated Caesar: Jesus failed to take up their cause to rid the land of Caesar. Jesus refused to set up a physical kingdom like David's. Jesus did not comply with their literal understanding of the Old Testament kingdom prophecies.

Keys of Kingdom Promised to Peter

It is widely known that before His death, Jesus promised "the keys of the kingdom of heaven" to Simon Peter. However, it is not so widely understood what these keys were. Obviously, he who holds keys controls entry. In this case, it is entry into the kingdom. Anyone who wants to enter the kingdom of God must seek the keys from the apostle Peter.

These keys are mentioned only in Matt. 16:19. The context beginning with verse 13 reveals that the prime topic of consideration was the identity of Jesus. The populace had many views, but Peter had it right when he said, "You are the Christ, the Son of the living God" (16:16). In reply, Jesus referred to both the church and the kingdom:

> Blessed are you, Simon Bar-Jonah, for flesh and blood has not revealed this to you, but My Father who is in heaven. And I also say to you that you are Peter, and on this rock I will build My church, and the gates of Hades shall not prevail against it. And I will give you the keys of the kingdom of heaven, and whatever you bind on earth will be bound in heaven, and whatever you loose on earth will be loosed in heaven (Matt. 16:17-19).

There is no indication here that Jesus was changing

subjects; He certainly appears to use "My church" and "the kingdom of heaven" as two terms referring to the same entity.

In addition, Jesus connected Peter's use of the keys to "whatever you bind on earth . . . and whatever you loose on earth." Peter would be using the keys to bind and loose *on earth*. Therefore, he was to use the keys during his lifetime. Two chapters later, Jesus tells all the apostles, "whatever you bind on earth will be bound in heaven" (18:18). It was not only Peter who would be binding and loosing but also the other apostles.

· The idea of binding is spelled out in Matt. 23:2, 4: "The scribes and the Pharisees . . . bind heavy burdens, hard to bear." The binding here is obviously what religious teachers tell their followers they must do. Jesus told the apostles, "Whatever you bind on earth will be bound in heaven." The apostles' word would be divinely authoritative.

While all the apostles would be involved in binding and loosing, only Peter would be given the keys of the kingdom. Keys open doors. Once open, others can enter. Christ chose Peter to open the doors of the kingdom. Peter would be the first one to tell the people of Israel what was required of them to enter the kingdom of God on earth.

Since Jesus never fails, His promises amount to prophecies. His promise to give Peter the keys of the kingdom is an important kingdom prophecy. We cannot understand the truth about God's promised kingdom without taking into consideration these words of Jesus. Jesus' prophecy says that Peter would open the way into the kingdom and that he would make binding decrees regarding the kingdom. At the same moment, Jesus referred to His church— and all believers understand the importance of Peter in the establishment of the church on the day of Pentecost in A.D. 30. Even futurism applies this prophecy of the keys to Peter's earthly ministry in the church beginning on the day of Pentecost. By doing so, futurism inadvertently confesses that the church is the kingdom and that the kingdom of God began on the day of Pentecost in the year A.D. 30!

The Importance of Pentecost

Religious people often speak longingly of a return to Pentecost. They usually are referring either to speaking in tongues or to the conversion of great multitudes. However, neither of these should be the major issue for us today when evaluating the importance of that particular Jewish Pentecost.

It was the year 30, less than two months after Jesus' death and resurrection and only ten days after His ascension. Before Jesus left for heaven, He had given His apostles a very important command: "Not to depart from Jerusalem, but to wait" (Acts 1:4). In Mark 9:1, Jesus had prophesied that the kingdom of God would come with *power* during the lifetime of His listeners. Later, following His resurrection, He told the apostles: "I send the Promise of My Father upon you; but tarry in the city of Jerusalem until you are endued with power from on high" (Luke 24:49). Before His ascension, He further clarified the matter: "You shall receive power when the Holy Spirit has come upon you" (Acts 1:8). The kingdom would come with power in their lifetime, and the Holy Spirit would provide that power.

All this happened exactly ten days after His ascension, on the day of Pentecost, when the twelve apostles were baptized in the Holy Spirit (Acts 2). Speaking in tongues, of itself, was not the important thing. Rather, the tongues were proof of the important thing—that Peter was not preaching his own ideas, but that he was infallibly inspired by the Holy Spirit to interpret the Old Testament prophecies, to explain the meaning of the cross and the empty tomb, and to offer to the Jews the divine means of entering the kingdom of God!

Since Jesus had promised Peter the keys of the kingdom, it is no coincidence that Peter was the leading spokesman on the day of Pentecost. Keys open doors. Jesus chose Peter to inaugurate the kingdom of heaven and to inform people how they could enter. Jesus had said Hades would not prevail against His plans to build His church. One of Peter's main points in his sermon was that Jesus victoriously escaped Hades; He had risen; He had ascended. The risen Lord had sent the Holy Spirit from heaven with power. The same Jesus whom they crucified was now seated at the right hand of God as Lord and Christ.

The multitudes, stricken in their innermost being, cried out wanting to know what they could do to gain God's favor on their sinful lives. Peter then used the keys of the kingdom to open wide the doors of Jesus' church. Administering the keys to unlock the doors of God's promised kingdom, Peter said: "Repent, and let every one of you be baptized in the name of Jesus Christ for the remission of sins; and you shall receive the gift of the Holy Spirit" (Acts 2:38).

A Second Birth Required

Most believers have no difficulty in recognizing that particular day of Pentecost as the moment in which the Lord's church began. But we should equally recognize that Peter's statement is a variation and divine explanation of what Jesus had told Nicodemus: "Unless one is born of water and the Spirit, he cannot enter the kingdom of God" (John 3:5). Notice the parallelism between "born of water and the Spirit" on the one hand, and "repent...be baptized...receive...the Holy Spirit" on the other. Entering the kingdom and entering the church are one and the same. A new birth is required.

What is the nature of God's kingdom? Listen to the King:

> The disciples came to Jesus, saying, "Who then is greatest in the kingdom of heaven?" Then Jesus called a little child to Him, set him in the midst of them, and said, "Assuredly, I say to you, unless you are converted and become as little children, you will by no means enter the kingdom of heaven" (Matt. 18:1-3).

Physical birth cannot do the job. Greatness, as men measure it, will not help. Rather, it is a matter of being converted and becoming like little children; that is what the kingdom of heaven is all about.

Jesus told the Pharisee Nicodemus that birth as a Jew, by itself, would never provide entrance into the kingdom of God. Jesus explained: "Unless one is born again, he cannot see the kingdom of God . . . unless one is born of water and the Spirit, he cannot enter the kingdom of God" (John 3:3, 5). Jewishness would never do it. Religiousness would never do it. Theological education would never do it. An emotional experience would never do it. Simply accepting Jesus into the heart would never do it. Praying the sinner's prayer at the conclusion of a tract would never do it. No amount of man-made religion would ever do it. "Unless one is born of water and the Spirit, he cannot enter the kingdom of God." God's kingdom is totally a spiritual matter. Entrance into the kingdom is dependent upon a second birth—it has nothing to do with physical birth. God's kingdom was not established for one physical nation. Men, women, and youth of every nation on the face of the earth are offered the privilege of becoming members of God's eternal kingdom if they become like little children and are born of the water and the Spirit. The King has spoken.

Not Just a Question of Prophecy

Daniel had prophesied that God's kingdom would be set up during the reign of the Roman Empire (Daniel 2). It was while Rome was in power that John the Baptist announced the imminent arrival of the kingdom of God, calling on Israel to repent and look to their Messiah. Jesus made the same proclamation, and He promised the kingdom would arrive with power during the lifetime of those listening (Mark 9:1).

That power came with the outpouring of the Holy Spirit on the day of Pentecost A.D. 30. The power of the kingdom was the power to save men from sin, even from the sin of crucifying their Messiah. It was *not* the power of the sword. It was *not* the power of a theocratic world government. It was and is the power of a message of love touching men's hearts and changing them from the inside out. It was and is a power to enable souls to be born again.

The "kingdom question" is not just an academic question of unimportant prophecy. The kingdom question is a question of the heart, of the soul. It does not concern a mere thousand-year earthly kingdom. It is a heavenly kingdom "which shall never be destroyed . . . and it shall stand forever" (Dan. 2:44). The kingdom question is not a question of end-times-yet-to-be-fulfilled prophecy. It is a question of accepting or rejecting the kingdom that Jesus has already established. Consider carefully that Jesus pointed to the establishment of His kingdom to take place in the first century. No one claims that an earthly-physical kingdom of God began in the first century; everyone knows that Jesus' church was established in the first century. The conclusion is inescapable: the church is the kingdom.

Futurism recognizes that a spiritual kingdom was set up in the first century. After quoting John 18:36, "My kingdom is not of this world," Tim LaHaye says: "He came the first time to establish a spiritual kingdom, to which one gains entrance by being born again."[1] Precisely! Surely, this spiritual kingdom has to be the kingdom that Daniel predicted would be set up in the time of the Roman Empire. Surely, this spiritual kingdom has to be the kingdom that Jesus promised would be set up during the lifetime of His apostles. How can we escape the conclusion that the church of Jesus Christ is the kingdom of heaven that both Daniel and Jesus predicted?

The church of Jesus is the kingdom of God—this is a profound truth with powerful implications. Who has ever heard it said, "One kingdom is as good as another"? In the spiritual realm, who would dare say, "Belong to the kingdom of your choice"? As surely as Jesus is the King of only one kingdom, He is the Head of only one church. Paul told the saints in Colosse that God "has delivered us from the power of darkness and conveyed us into the kingdom of the Son of

His love" (Col. 1:13). Paul told the Ephesian brethren that Jesus now is "far above all principality . . . and head over all things to the church" (Eph. 1:21-22). We cannot have the King without His kingdom. We cannot have the Head without His church.

Paul also informed us that Jesus "loved the church and gave Himself for her" (Eph. 5:25). Jesus loves His kingdom, His church. Do we? One of the saddest things about futurism today is that it places Jesus' church in a parenthesis or gap. Futurism thereby teaches that God's eternal plans are all related to Israel, whereas the church is merely a space filler until God's prophetic clock starts ticking again.

Is the matter of the kingdom of God just a side issue of prophecy? What did King Jesus say? Speaking of the difference between material and spiritual concerns, the King said, "But seek first the kingdom of God and His righteousness, and all these things shall be added to you" (Matt. 6:33). Seek first the kingdom of God. That means to place the church of Jesus Christ first in our lives. Ahead of jobs. Ahead of family and friends. Ahead of empty pleasure. Ahead of political agendas. We cannot possibly "seek first the kingdom of God" until we allow King Jesus to have the final word on the nature of that kingdom. We cannot possibly "seek first the kingdom of God" until we awaken to the fact that His kingdom is already in existence. The King invites us to be subjects of His kingdom today.

Beware of simplistic salvation!

"If anyone takes away from the words of the book of this prophecy, God shall take away his part from the Book of Life, from the holy city, and from the things which are written in this book."

– Rev. 22:19

How much New Testament teaching on salvation can we ignore and still have our names in the Book of Life?

Chapter 18

The "Salvation Prayer"

"If you accept God's message of salvation, his Holy Spirit will come in unto you and make you spiritually born anew . . . You can become a child of God by praying to him right now as I lead you."[1] This concept, frequently repeated by LaHaye and Jenkins, is an expression of a widely-proclaimed, popular road to salvation. The invitation is often similar to the following advertisement entitled "The Pathway to Heaven":

Follow these Steps:
1. You need to be saved.
2. You cannot save yourself. [Eph. 2:8-9 quoted]
3. God loves us enough to provide salvation. [John 3:16 quoted]
4. By faith believe Jesus and accept Him. [Acts 16:31; Rom. 10:9 quoted]
If you would like to invite Jesus into your life, repeat this prayer . . . [prayer given]
If you said this prayer, we would like to know. Please contact our office at . . .[2]

Here is an example of such a prayer written at the end of a tract by the American Tract Society:

Dear God, I know I am a sinner and unable to save myself. But I do believe You love me, and that You sent Your Son, Jesus, to die on the cross for my sins. Right here and now, I ask You to forgive my every sin and give me the gift of eternal life. Thank You, dear God, for hearing and answering my prayer, and for giving me eternal life as You promised You would. Amen.[3]

The authors of the "Left Behind" series believe that salvation is obtained by making a decision to "receive Christ" in prayer. As LaHaye expresses it elsewhere: "If there is any question in your mind as to whether you have ever invited Jesus Christ into your life, may I urge you to get down on your knees right now and ask Him to save you."[4] The variations are many, but the essence is the same: "Accept Christ . . . Believe and pray this prayer."

The Issue is Not . . .

Before examining the "salvation prayer" and considering the alternative for that prayer, we must clearly understand what is *not* at issue here—as far as Bible believers are concerned.

Jesus' blood is not the issue here. There are religions and even churches that teach a bloodless salvation, that is, if they teach any personal salvation at all. However, virtually all of us who accept the Bible as the inspired Word of God are in full agreement that "without shedding of blood there is no remission" (Heb. 9:22). This is not the issue in this chapter. We all agree "Christ died for our sins according to the Scriptures" (1 Cor. 15:3). We agree Jesus is the only Savior.

Grace is not the issue here. Those who accept tradition on a par with the Bible might not think much about grace. However, the majority of us who accept the Bible as the only authoritative source of divine doctrine agree that apart from the grace of God there is no salvation. Man cannot save himself: "'There is none righteous, no, not one' . . . for all have sinned . . . being justified freely by His grace" (Rom.

3:10, 23-24). We agree "the wages of sin is death, but the gift of God is eternal life in Christ Jesus our Lord" (Rom. 6:23). In other words, the second death—the lake of eternal fire—is what we all deserve; it is what we all earn. Salvation, on the other hand, cannot be earned by anyone; no one deserves it; it is a gift of God. Grace is not an issue in this chapter. To express these first two items another way: God's part in man's salvation is not the issue here.

Faith is not the issue here. Who would argue with one of the best-known verses in the Bible? "For God so loved the world that He gave His only begotten Son, that whoever believes in Him should not perish but have everlasting life" (John 3:16). Heb. 11:6 tells us "without faith it is impossible to please Him [God]." The gospel of Jesus Christ is "the power of God to salvation for everyone who believes, for the Jew first and also for the Greek" (Rom. 1:16). Paul, by the Spirit, wrote to the brothers and sisters in Ephesus about Christ, grace, and faith:

> That in the ages to come He might show the exceeding riches of His grace in His kindness toward us in Christ Jesus. For by grace you have been saved through faith, and that not of your-selves; it is the gift of God, not of works, lest anyone should boast (Eph. 2:7-9).

We are saved "by grace . . . through faith" because of what Jesus has done for us. Aside from Jesus, His blood, grace, and faith there is no salvation. None of these is an issue in this chapter.

What is the Issue?

The issue in this chapter is not about Jesus' part in our salvation; the issue is about our part. What is required of us in order that God's grace and Jesus' blood may be applied to our lives? We all agree that sinners must believe—they must have faith. However, is faith by itself sufficient? Does simply believing that Jesus is my Savior thereby make Him my Savior? Is salvation based solely on what the mind accepts as truth? Can I obtain salvation by simply inviting Jesus into my heart? There is really no issue in the "Left Behind" series that is more important than this one.

The issue in this chapter is whether faith *alone* is a sufficient response on the part of the sinner to obtain salvation. Does salvation come the moment one believes? Does all faith save? If not, what kind or degree of faith saves? Have we heard everything that is essential to salvation when we read, "Believe on the Lord Jesus Christ, and you will be saved" (Acts 16:31)?

The issue in this chapter is identifying the moment a person is changed from being unsaved to being saved. Exactly when and how is a person born again? At what point in a person's life can he or she say, "Now I am a Christian"? What is the precise moment a person's past sins are forgiven, giving that person a clean slate upon which to begin a new life in Christ? At what point in a person's life does God declare that person to be justified, redeemed, and forgiven? This is the issue.

The "Faith Only" Doctrine

The most popular teaching on salvation among Bible believers today is that we are saved by faith alone. It is common to read a tract or view a preacher on TV stating that a person cannot be saved by religion, church membership, a good life, baptism, the Ten Commandments, or love for one's neighbor. Rather, we are told it is simply a matter of believing, accepting Jesus' sacrifice for our sins, and inviting Jesus into our hearts. In his Revelation commentary, Tim LaHaye says: "The steps of salvation here are clear: (1) 'whoever hears my word' and (2) 'believes him who sent me.' That means trusting in Jesus . . . The one who trusts has everlasting life."[5] LaHaye continues to explain that believing and trusting have to do with receiving everlasting life and accepting Jesus. All this follows his item (2). He offers no item (3). Thus, LaHaye teaches there are only two steps to salvation: hear and believe.

Today's faith-only concept owes much of its impetus to Martin Luther. As Luther studied the Bible, especially the book of Romans, he became increasingly aware of the false doctrines and practices by which Roman Catholics attempted to earn their salvation by works. These works included such doctrines and practices as indulgences, veneration of relics, the sacraments, masses for the dead, pilgrimages, purgatory, penance, and intercessions by "saints," especially "the virgin." Luther clearly saw in the Word of God, which had been virtually closed for centuries, that we cannot save ourselves. He saw that salvation is by grace and can be obtained through faith in the redemptive work of Jesus on the cross.

However, Luther took this newfound truth to the opposite extreme. As is often the case in such circumstances, the pendulum swung from one extreme to the other. Luther concluded that we are saved not only by faith but by faith alone. So convinced was he of this new idea that he dared to add the word "alone" to the text of the Bible. With no evidence whatsoever from Greek manuscripts, he dared to alter the Word of God. Rom. 3:28 reads: "Therefore we conclude that a man is justified by faith apart from the deeds of the law." Luther changed it to read, "justified by faith alone." Some modern versions, such as *The Bible in Today's English Version,* have followed Luther's example. Furthermore, Luther belittled the book of James as an "epistle of straw" because it declares: "You see then that a man is justified by works, and *not* by faith only" (James 2:24, italics mine). He could not agree with the only text in the entire Bible that uses the phrase "faith only"!

It is true that Luther saw more to faith than a persuasion of the existence of God, more than mental agreement with the teaching of Scripture. For Luther faith was something more than a simplistic faith that involved the mind without translating into a changed life. For him, faith included more than the intellectual element. Today's popular religion so often waters down Luther's concept until what is taught and practiced is not what he had in mind at all. The sad reality is that many believers have latched onto Luther's "only" while lacking the depth of Luther's faith. Luther did mankind a great disservice by *adding* "only" to Romans and *subtracting* the epistle of James from authoritative Scripture. The fact that he found it necessary to openly revise the Bible is sufficient evidence to demonstrate that something was lacking in Luther's understanding.

Even if James is an "epistle of straw" and is removed from the Bible, the Bible still teaches that we must *do* something to be saved. In fact, the Master declared faith itself to be a work. When the people asked, "What shall we do, that we may work the works of God?" Jesus replied, "This is the work of God, that you believe in Him whom He sent" (John 6:28-29). Furthermore, Jesus declared: "Not everyone who says to Me, 'Lord, Lord,' shall enter the kingdom of heaven, but he who does the will of My Father in heaven" (Matt. 7:21). Calling on Jesus is not enough for salvation. Jesus says we must also do God's will. Are Jesus' words also straw? God forbid! Did Jesus teach faith? Absolutely! Did he teach faith only? Absolutely not! Did Paul teach faith? Absolutely! Did he teach faith only? Absolutely not! Paul's epistle to the Romans begins and ends with a reference to "obedience to the faith" (1:5; 16:26).

"Only" Perverts Divine Truth

Grace: Our need of the grace of God as well as our need of faith were discussed earlier. Both truths are abundantly clear in Scripture. Without grace there is no salvation; without faith there is no salvation. However, when "only" is added to these statements, confusion results. Often the dual statement is made that we are saved by grace alone and by faith alone. This is a self-contradiction. If we are saved by grace alone, faith is not required. If we are saved by faith alone, grace is not needed. It is an abuse of language to say we are saved by both and then add "alone" to each one.

Jesus' death: It is one thing to say that we are saved by

Jesus' death. It is a very different thing to say that we are saved only by Jesus' death. In 1 Cor. 15:3 Paul affirms, "Christ died for our sins." However, verse 17 shows we cannot add "only" to verse 3. Verse 17, written by inspiration, says: "If Christ is not risen, your faith is futile; you are still in your sins!" Yes, Jesus died for our sins. However, His death saves no one without His resurrection. A dead savior is no savior at all. We dare not add "only" to God's holy Word.

Qualifications of a bishop: It is one thing to say that a bishop in the Lord's church must be "the husband of one wife" (1 Tim. 3:2). It is a very different thing to say that this is the only requirement. This Timothy text gives eighteen requirements for a man to become a bishop. To say that any of these requirements is the only requirement is to deny the other seventeen. To agree with even 15 of the 18 is still a denial of the remaining three. We dare not treat the Word of God this way. The Bible is not a cafeteria from which to pick and choose. We must take the full menu.

Faith: It is one thing to say we are saved by faith. It is a very different thing to say we are saved only by faith. Paul by the Spirit informs us: "Though I have all faith, so that I could remove mountains, but have not love, I am nothing" (1 Cor. 13:2). Faith minus love equals nothing. A few verses later Paul concludes: "Now abide faith, hope, love, these three; but the greatest of these is love" (13:13). Love is greater than faith. The apostle John wrote: "Everyone who loves is born of God and knows God. He who does not love does not know God" (1 John 4:7-8). Faith without love is empty; it will save no one.

What does the Word mean when it says we are not saved by works? Romans 4 can help us understand: "For if Abraham was justified by works, he has something to boast about, but not before God . . . Now to him who works, the wages are not counted as grace but as debt" (4:2, 4). In these verses, Paul is talking about earning salvation. He speaks of works as deserving wages. The message of the early chapters of Romans is that we are all sinners, that no one deserves salvation, that salvation is a gift of God, that we cannot earn salvation, and that salvation comes through faith in the work of Christ on the cross. Yet even our faith does not *merit* salvation, otherwise there would be no need for God's grace. Faith saves simply because God has so decreed, not because by having faith we *deserve* to enter heaven. Neither does our obedience help us to *earn* salvation. We are saved by grace. Nothing we believe or do can merit, deserve, or earn eternal life.

When Paul spoke of faith in the epistle to the Romans, did he mean faith alone? Did he mean we could disobey God as long as we believe in His Son? Did he mean that mental assent is all God cares about? Did he mean that nothing matters except what we believe in our heart? In Rom. 6:17, Paul speaks of the transformation that had taken place in the lives of the brethren in Rome: "God be thanked that though you were slaves of sin, yet you *obeyed* from the heart that form of *doctrine* to which you were delivered" (italics mine). Then in 10:9-10 he asserts: "If you *confess with your mouth* the Lord Jesus and believe in your heart that God has raised Him from the dead, you will be saved. For with the heart one believes unto righteousness, and *with the mouth* confession is made *unto salvation*" (italics mine). The faith that saves is not limited to the mind. One text refers to obeying doctrine, the other to expressing faith "with the mouth . . . unto salvation." Romans is a great book about salvation by faith; it never was a book about salvation by faith alone. "Only" and "alone" pervert God's Word by exalting selected truths while minimizing others.

Nobody Accepts "Faith Only"

The above discussion, by itself, misses the real issue. The reality is that nobody believes that salvation is by faith alone. The idea may be mouthed, defended, and preached. The idea may be sincerely believed. Yet, the faith-only doctrine and practice demonstrate that the term "faith only" is a misnomer. Even those who teach the doctrine will make such confusing statements as: "Salvation is received by faith alone, but saving faith does not remain alone."

Those who teach salvation by faith alone readily agree that not all faith saves. That is why they often speak of "saving faith." A case of faulty faith is seen in certain influential persons referred to by John: "even among the rulers many believed in Him, but because of the Pharisees they did not confess Him, lest they should be put out of the synagogue" (John 12:42). They "believed in Him, but . . ." To describe this deficient faith, one might suggest that their faith was not strong enough. Another might explain that they did not mix their faith with action. Yet another might express the view that they had mental faith but lacked trust. Some would clarify that there are different *kinds* of faith, others that there are different *degrees* of faith, others that we must consider what must be *added* to faith, others that we must take into account what is *included* in saving faith.

Whichever way a person desires to express it, there is general agreement among all Bible believers that we need more than simplistic faith, more than intellectual acceptance of the truth of the Bible, and more than acknowledgement that Jesus died for our sins. Faith that produces no change of life is insufficient; faith that is never expressed is lacking something; faith that does not motivate to action does not meet God's requirements. The following specifics may help to clarify these concepts.

Repentance: Even though it is often not expressed, many of those who hold the faith-only doctrine agree that there can be no salvation without repentance. They agree with this even though repentance is not mentioned in most of the Scriptures that teach salvation by faith. The explanation is made that repentance is a part of saving faith or that faith and repentance are opposite sides of the same coin. It is assumed that we must repent because Jesus commands it in Scriptures such as Luke 13:3: "Unless you repent you will all likewise perish." This assumption is quite right. We absolutely must look at other verses besides the ones that speak of faith.

However, once other verses are included and repentance is accepted as a requirement for forgiveness of sins, salvation is no longer by faith only—mentally believing is insufficient. A person's faith must be real enough and strong enough to produce a change in behavior. Anything less raises questions about what the person actually believes. Of course, repentance must be based in and motivated by faith; it must be an expression of faith. In whatever way a person wants to explain the relationship between faith and repentance, one without the other is unacceptable to God. Even if a person wants to explain that saving faith includes repentance, he has made "saving faith" more than faith alone.

Calling on the Lord: The faith-only view is frequently upheld by quoting Rom. 10:13: "Whoever calls on the name of the LORD shall be saved." Amen. We must recognize that Jesus is Lord. We must look to Him for salvation. Calling upon the Lord is putting our faith into action. Paul followed that statement with a series of rhetorical questions on this very issue:

> How then shall they call on Him in whom they have not believed? And how shall they believe in Him of whom they have not heard? And how shall they hear without a preacher? And how shall they preach unless they are sent? (Rom. 10:14-15).

Five steps are involved here to produce salvation: sending, preaching, hearing, believing, and calling. When a person hears, he can believe or disbelieve. When a person believes, he can call or not call. This is not faith only. Even Tim LaHaye confirms this point when he writes: "These are the individuals who demonstrated their sincere faith by calling on the name of the Lord for salvation . . . only those who call on the name of the Lord will be saved."[6] He says calling is a demonstration of faith. Amen. Only those who demonstrate their faith will be saved. Amen. Faith alone does not save. No one really believes it does.

The Salvation Prayer: Why do sermons end with an invitation to "pray this prayer with me"? Why do so many tracts end with the sinner's prayer? In the first book of the "Left Behind" series, the authors do not wait until the final chapter as is often done in books. Throughout the book, they make it clear that the way to "receive Christ" is through prayer. However, if salvation is by faith only, why the prayer? Could it be that even though preachers mouth the faith-only words, yet in their innermost being they realize that we all need to act on our faith? Could it be that deep inside, their common sense, or even "Scriptural sense," tells them that there must be some kind of visible response, that salvation cannot be a totally private affair, and that people must *do something?* An unexpressed faith is insufficient faith.

Jesus agrees that sinners need to do something. However, Jesus did *not* say, "He who believes and says the sinner's prayer will be saved." Never! Jesus said, "He who believes and is baptized will be saved" (Mark 16:16). Men have substituted the sinner's prayer for sinner's baptism! In Acts 2, read the account of the first time after Jesus' death, resurrection, and ascension that the gospel in its fullness was preached. Peter did not invite the people to come forward to pray with him. Not at all! Nevertheless, Peter, like present-day preachers, did expect a visible response from his hearers. There is nothing wrong with that. However, the visible response the inspired apostle called for was this: "Let every one of you be baptized in the name of Jesus Christ for the remission of sins; and you shall receive the gift of the Holy Spirit" (Acts 2:38). "Then those who gladly received his word were baptized; and that day about three thousand souls were added to them" (2:41).

Why Baptism?

Baptism is not arbitrary. God did not pick just anything. The symbolism in baptism is most impressive. The physical act of immersion in water portrays a death, burial, and resurrection. The significance is twofold. Baptism pictures the death, burial, and resurrection of Christ Jesus who is the only one who can forgive our sins. Baptism also pictures what is happening spiritually to the person at the moment of baptism. A person who has died to sin buries the "old man" of sin in the watery grave, then rises from the water to walk in a new life.

Just as Jesus taught that "he who believes and is baptized will be saved" (Mark 16:16), so He likewise taught that one must be "born of water and the Spirit" (John 3:5). It does not take much thought to realize that being born again on the one hand, and going from death to life on the other hand, are two similar figures that vividly refer to the same process. In the one case, conversion is pictured as a new birth. In the other case, conversion is pictured as a death, burial, and resurrection. In both cases, conversion is declared to be the start of a new life.

This spiritual reality, of course, is invisible. It is a matter of faith in God's Word. The same is true of Jesus' death for our sins. His death was visible to those present; however, the purpose of Jesus' death could not be seen with the physical eye. It is a matter of faith that He died for our sins. Likewise, baptism in water can be seen by those present, but it is a matter of faith that immersion in water is the moment sins are forgiven and new life begins.

The apostle Paul saw no contradiction between 1) faith being the basis of salvation and 2) baptism being the moment salvation arrives with a new life. In the same Roman epistle that teaches salvation by faith, Paul wrote:

> How shall we who *died* to sin live any longer in it? Or do you not know that as many of us as were baptized into Christ Jesus were baptized into His *death?* Therefore we were *buried with Him* through baptism into *death,* that just as Christ was *raised from the dead* by the glory of the Father, even so we also should walk in *newness of life* . . . knowing this, that our old man was *crucified with Him* (Rom. 6:2-4, 6, italics mine).

Baptized into His death. Jesus died for our sins. He shed His blood on the cross for our sins. How do we contact His blood and death? Paul says we are "baptized into His death." We contact His death in the water. Keep in mind that Jesus was buried when He was dead. As obvious and simplistic as that might sound, the same must be true with us. We must die to sin—the old man must be crucified—before we are buried. The faith-only doctrine teaches that baptism is one of the first acts of obedience *after* a person has been born again. However, burial is not for those who are alive; burial is for those who are dead.

Paul described the relationship between faith and baptism in Col. 2:12-13: *"Buried* with Him *in baptism,* in which you also were *raised* with Him *through faith* in the working of God . . . having forgiven you all trespasses" (italics mine). A sinner is dead in sin (Eph. 2:1). The dead person must be buried. Once buried in the watery grave, the person is "raised with Him through faith in the working of God." Biblical baptism is not a meritorious work on our part; the text says that God is the one who does the work. Our part is to have faith in His work. God promises to forgive our trespasses at baptism when we do it through faith. If one is baptized simply to become a church member, the action is not based on faith in God's working through baptism; therefore, it is meaningless. Since an infant is incapable of faith, its baptism is likewise meaningless. Many people who believe they are saved without baptism go ahead and get baptized simply to obey Jesus' command. However, such an action empties baptism of its true meaning; the person has no faith in the working of God to forgive trespasses at the moment of baptism. Biblical baptism is an act of faith in the saving power of Jesus' death on the part of a lost sinner who at that moment is united with Jesus' death.

Not only is baptism not a meritorious work, it is not a work at all on the part of the person being baptized. Speaking of the physical aspect, when we are baptized we do nothing; we yield our bodies to someone else to do the work.

Buried with Christ Jesus in Baptism

Baptism: the point of contact with the death of Christ

"Baptized into Christ . . .
   baptized into His death . . .
      buried with Him through baptism into death . . .
         as Christ was raised . . .
            so we also should walk in newness of life . . .
               we have been united together in the likeness of His death . . .
                  our old man was crucified with Him,
                     that the body of sin might be done away . . .
                        we shall also live with Him."
                           – Rom. 6:3-8

Persons depicted are models; photograph used for illustrative purposes only.

Photograph © by CrossDaily.com (Mary Bustraan). Used by permission.

Baptism: an act of faith

"Buried with Him in baptism, in which you also were raised with Him through faith in the working of God, who raised Him from the dead."
– Col. 2:12

Baptism: a symbol with a two-fold reality of death, burial, and resurrection

Jesus Christ:
- He died for our sins
- His body was buried
- He rose and lives

Repentant Believers:
- We die to sin
- Our sinful self is buried
- We rise to a new life

At the same time, spiritually we yield our souls to Jesus, confessing we cannot save ourselves—only He can do it. When we are baptized according to Scripture, we are confessing that we merit nothing, admitting our inability to save ourselves, and confessing our need to be saved by Christ.

Far from being a meritorious work, baptism is an act of deep faith. That must be why so many stumble over it. Just as many worldly persons have a hard time accepting a blood sacrifice as the means of forgiving sin; likewise, many religious persons have a hard time accepting water as having any relationship to salvation. The former want to be saved without blood, the latter without water. Nevertheless, Scripture teaches that in baptism we are buried with Jesus; we are "baptized into His death," thus contacting His blood. At the moment of baptism, we are "born of water and the Spirit" (John 3:5). Decades after Jesus spoke these words, the apostle John wrote by inspiration: "And there are three that bear witness on earth: the Spirit, the water, and the blood; and these three agree as one" (1 John 5:8). God united blood and water.

Really Calling on the Name of the Lord

What does it mean—biblically—to call on the name of the Lord? After Jesus' ascension into heaven, what examples do we have in the New Testament of people calling upon the name of the Lord?

The first case is found in Acts 2 just ten days after Jesus returned to heaven. Peter, having been baptized in the Holy Spirit, preached the gospel as an accomplished fact for the first time in history. In his sermon he quoted a text from Joel:

> And it shall come to pass
> That whoever calls on the name of the LORD
> Shall be saved (Acts 2:21).

As Peter preached, his listeners became so convicted in their hearts, believing all that Peter was saying, that they cried out "to Peter and the rest of the apostles, 'Men and brethren, what shall we do?'" (Acts 2:37). Did Peter say, "There is nothing you can do; Jesus did it all"? No, he did not. Did Peter say, "Receive Jesus into your heart"? No, he did not. Did Peter say, "Pray this prayer with me"? No, he did not.

What did Peter say? "Repent, and let every one of you be baptized in the name of Jesus Christ for the remission of sins; and you shall receive the gift of the Holy Spirit" (Acts 2:38). What did the people do? "Then those who gladly received his word were baptized; and that day about three thousand souls were added to them" (2:41). Peter first told the people to call on the name of the Lord to be saved. Then he told those who believed to repent and be baptized to be saved. Therefore, faith, repentance, and baptism must be the real way to call on the name of the Lord for salvation.

If there is any doubt, Acts 22:16 should clear it up. This is the second case where the Scriptures specifically tell us what people did to call on the name of the Lord for salvation. Acts 22 contains one of three accounts of Paul's conversion; the others are in Acts 9 and 26. When Paul (then called Saul) encountered Jesus on the road to Damascus, "He, trembling and astonished, said, 'Lord, what do You want me to do?' Then the Lord said to him, 'Arise and go into the city, and you will be told what you must do'" (9:6). "Do" is not a bad word. Paul directly asked the Savior a "do" question. Jesus told him where to find out what he should do. Notice that Jesus neither saved Paul in that moment, nor did Jesus tell him how to be saved. Rather, Jesus told Paul where to go to get the right answer to his vital question.

According to Acts 9:8-12, Paul went to Damascus and fasted and prayed for three days, receiving a further vision. When Ananias arrived, he answered the "do" question. What did he tell Paul to do? "Arise and be baptized, and wash away your sins, calling on the name of the Lord" (Acts 22:16). Paul had already come to faith back on the road to Damascus. Paul must have already been deep in repentance asking God for forgiveness during those three days. Now Paul was told what to do to be saved. Paul did not say a little two-minute prayer asking Jesus to come into his life. He had been praying for three days! If a prayer was ever the moment for receiving salvation in Christ, certainly Paul was already more than saved before Ananias ever arrived. However, just as Paul was not saved by seeing Jesus nor by his vision in Damascus, neither was he saved by three days of prayer and fasting. Ananias had come to tell Paul that it was time to stop praying; it was time to "be baptized, and wash away your sins, calling on the name of the Lord." In baptism one calls on the name of the Lord for salvation.

Baptism is not a meritorious sacrament nor a work of righteousness by which someone earns salvation. On the contrary, it is a humble, obedient act of allowing oneself to be lowered into a watery grave. In baptism a repentant believer is calling upon the Lord for salvation through Jesus' grace, mercy, love, and blood. The two cases in Acts are the only two examples in Scripture that explain exactly what calling on the name of the Lord for salvation is. There is no example of just praying a prayer to invite Jesus into one's heart. If a person truly believes in Jesus and truly believes what Jesus says, that person will seek and accept salvation on Jesus' terms, not on a popular preacher's terms. We must not only believe the gospel, we must obey it. No heartfelt salvation prayer can exempt a sinner from the "flaming fire taking vengeance on those who do not know God, and on those who *do not obey the gospel* of our Lord Jesus Christ" (2 Thess. 1:8). The italics are mine, but the words are the Holy Spirit's.

How important is it to understand all of this? Listen to what the Savior himself said: "Not everyone who says to Me, 'Lord, Lord,' shall enter the kingdom of heaven, but he who does the will of My Father in heaven" (Matt. 7:21). This is in a context where Jesus says: "Narrow is the gate and difficult is the way which leads to life, and there are few who find it" (7:14). This is in a context where Jesus says: "Beware of false prophets" (7:15). This is in a context where Jesus says: "Everyone who hears these sayings of Mine, and does not do them, will be like a foolish man who built his house on the sand" (7:26). Calling out vocally or mentally to the Lord Jesus is not enough. Jesus said so! Inviting Jesus into one's heart is not enough. Jesus said: "He who does the will of My Father." Therefore, when Scripture says, "Whoever calls on the name of the Lord shall be saved," it must be understood in a deeper and more meaningful sense than simply asking Jesus to save us.

Our Way or God's Way?

From the beginning of time, men have approached God in their own way. Before Cain murdered his brother, he had a direct confrontation with God. He brought his own offering to God in his own way. "And the LORD respected Abel and his offering, but He did not respect Cain and his offering" (Gen. 4:4-5). We do not know the details, but Cain and Abel certainly knew. What we do know is that Cain brought an offering to the Lord that the Lord did not accept. Thus, from the very beginning of the Bible, we are warned against approaching God on our own terms. We must approach God on His terms or not at all.

That is what Naaman had to learn. Naaman was a commander of the Syrian army. However, he had leprosy and greatly desired to be healed. He was willing to travel to be healed. He was willing to pay big money to be healed. Nevertheless, he was not willing to humble himself to be healed. Although he knew he had no power to heal himself, and although he had faith that a prophet of a foreign God could heal him, yet he had his own preconceived idea as to how the healing should take place. He was so set on his own idea and so averse to humbling himself that he actually went into a rage over the healing offered. He headed for home, unhealed.

The healing offered to Naaman was simple: "Go and wash in the Jordan seven times, and your flesh shall be restored" (2 Kings 5:10). Naaman had two problems with this instruction. First, because of nationalistic pride, he considered the rivers of his homeland far superior to those in the land of the enemy Israel. Second, he wanted to be treated with respect. The prophet of God, Elisha, had not even come out of his house to greet the commander. Rather, Elisha had sent a messenger who told Naaman to dip seven times in the Jordan. None of this fit Naaman's preconceived concept of how it would happen: "I said to myself, 'He [Elisha] will surely come out to me, and stand and call on the name of the LORD his God, and wave his hand over the place, and heal the leprosy'" (5:11).

Fortunately for Naaman, he had some loving servants who cared enough for their master that they dared to challenge his unreasonable behavior. They said, "My father, if the prophet had told you to do something great, would you not have done it? How much more then, when he says to you, 'Wash, and be clean'?" (5:13). To his credit, Naaman listened to his reasonable servants, dropped his preconceived prejudices, humbled himself, and went and dipped in the Jordan seven times. He was healed!

There is an amazing parallel between Naaman's case and the situation in modern times regarding salvation. Many people today realize they are lost sinners, they cannot cure themselves, and the "prophet of Israel," Jesus, is the only one with power to transform their lives. However, like Naaman, these people have their own preconceived ideas of how they can be saved. When they are told they need to dip in water to have their sins washed away, they get upset and say that water certainly can have nothing to do with salvation. On the other hand, when a preacher invites them to the front of the auditorium and places his hand on them to pray with them for salvation, they like the idea and feel very confident that God has taken away their sins.

A grave problem is that forgiveness of sins cannot be physically seen like cleansing from leprosy. Therefore, people can easily be deceived into thinking that, inasmuch as a great preacher of God prayed the sinner's prayer with them, surely their sins have been forgiven. They are even deceived into *feeling* forgiven. However, feelings do not prove reality; rather feelings are a reaction to our perception of reality. The patriarch Jacob went into real grief when he believed false evidence that Joseph had been slain (Gen. 37:28-35). No one would suggest that Jacob's grief was proof of Joseph's death. Likewise, a feeling of forgiveness is no proof of forgiveness. Forgiveness occurs in God's mind; it is God who dictates when we are saved. Therefore, we need the humility that Naaman had when his servants talked with him. We need to listen while a servant of God reads the Word of God to us. We need to humble ourselves and come to Jesus on His terms, not on our own terms, nor on a famous preacher's terms.

Naaman's stubborn rebellion was prefaced with these words: "Indeed, I said to myself . . ." or, as it says in the old King James Version: "Behold, I thought . . ." This pinpoints the problem. "I said to myself; I thought." We have our own preconceived ideas. We think we know what God should do. However, as God declared through Isaiah many, many years ago:

> "For My thoughts are not your thoughts,
> Nor are your ways My ways," says the LORD.
> "For as the heavens are higher than the earth,
> So are My ways higher than your ways,
> And My thoughts than your thoughts" (Isa. 55:8-9).

Central to our whole relationship with the Creator is the molding of our thoughts to His thoughts.

Was Naaman cleansed by meritorious works? Not at all. He was cleansed when he humbled himself and had enough faith in God to do it God's way. God's preconditions are simply a test of man's faith and humility. Scripture says of the Savior: "Though He was a Son, yet He learned obedience by the things which He suffered" (Heb. 5:8). Did you catch that? Our dear Savior who died on the cross for our sins was, in that very act, learning obedience. Do we dare think we can avail ourselves of His saving sacrifice without learning obedience in our own lives? As a matter of fact, the sacred text continues: "And having been perfected, He became the author of eternal salvation to all who *obey* Him" (italics mine). Baptism is not a human work to earn salvation. On the contrary, Scriptural baptism is the result of having a faith strong enough to humbly obey Jesus. Scriptural baptism is the result of repenting for doing things our way instead of God's way.

Today's popular sinner's prayer is a reenactment of the way Naaman thought he ought to be healed. Repentance and baptism are a reenactment of the way Naaman actually was healed. The "salvation prayer" is man's substitute for believer's baptism. Jesus never said, "He who believes and prays will be saved." However, He did say, "He who believes and is baptized will be saved." We all have to decide if we will put our faith in the modern preacher and novelist or in the eternal Son of God.

Faith that is strong enough to lead to humble obedience is not only a condition for receiving initial forgiveness, but also a condition for remaining in Christ. Listen to the Holy Spirit speaking through Paul: "Therefore, my beloved, as you have always obeyed, not as in my presence only, but now much more in my absence, work out your own salvation with fear and trembling" (Phil. 2:12). Is salvation by faith? Absolutely! Can anyone earn salvation? Absolutely not! Nevertheless, salvation is neither gained nor retained by a faith devoid of humility, repentance, obedience, and love. It is the Savior himself who said: "Not everyone who says to Me, 'Lord, Lord,' shall enter the kingdom of heaven, but he who does the will of My Father in heaven . . . Beware of false prophets" (Matt. 7:21, 15).

Prophecy: the Great Miracle

"Lying oracles have been in the world; but all the wit and malice of men and devils cannot produce any such prophecies as are recorded in Scripture . . . You have the greatest and most striking of miracles in the series of Scripture-prophecies accomplished . . . and if the Scripture-prophecies are accomplished, the Scripture must be the word of God."   – Thomas Newton, 636-37

"We have the prophetic word confirmed, which you do well to heed as a light that shines in a dark place."
(2 Pet. 1:19)

"For if the word spoken through angels proved steadfast, and every transgression and disobedience received a just reward, how shall we escape if we neglect so great a salvation."   (Heb. 2:2-3)

**Fulfillment of prophecy in the past
is our reason to believe what
God says about our future.**

Chapter 19

Nobody Left Behind

"Don't take life too seriously. Don't worry about the consequences of how you behave, especially consequences after this life. Live life to the fullest. Do what makes you feel good. Follow your dreams. When you die, it's all over." Sound familiar? It is the voice of the *choice* philosophy, which is not limited to those who choose to murder unborn babies. The right of choice is the underlying philosophy of all who want to be subject to no one but themselves and their own desires. This is the view of evolutionists, who believe that the human race is an accident of blind chance and that there is nothing beyond death except the decay of the body in the grave. Paul expressed this materialist view of life in these terms: "If the dead do not rise, 'Let us eat and drink, for tomorrow we die!'" (1 Cor. 15:32).

Religious people, on the other hand, usually believe in life after death. We believe in the soul and spirit of human beings. We believe death is a portal to the afterlife. Nevertheless, religious people, too, are often motivated to live according to our desires. We easily suppress thoughts about eternal consequences. We frequently have an underlying feeling that somehow in the end everything will turn out fine. This mentality is even part of some religious doctrines—those that offer a second chance after this life.

Reincarnation

Among Eastern religions, the most popular second-chance doctrine is reincarnation. In recent times, many Westerners have grown weary of their own heritage, and they increasingly look to the East for philosophical and religious ideas. Having rejected the Bible, many persons easily accept the theory of reincarnation. "Your present life is only the current event in a long chain of incarnations in this world," say believers in reincarnation.

Whether people realize it or not, the underlying attraction of reincarnation is that it eliminates the fear of the judgment of God after death. It eliminates the sobering realization that one day we must all come face to face with our Creator to give an account of ourselves. Reincarnation teaches that the process of gradual purification and enlightenment takes place by utilizing as many lives on earth as necessary until a person is finally absorbed into what they call Nirvana.

In reality, only the Creator of the world can possibly have the knowledge of what transpires after death. What has He said? "It is appointed for men to die once, but after this the judgment" (Heb. 9:27). Since we only die once, we have only one life to live in this world. What comes after our one life and one death? The judgment of God.

Purgatory

Turning from pagan to "Christian" beliefs, we find that many people are of the opinion that although they are not bad enough to go to hell, neither are they good enough to go to heaven. Certainly, they think, there must be another option. The Church of Rome officially offers that third option: purgatory.

Rome says that purgatory is a place for the dead who were neither very bad nor very good. It says those who die with unforgiven *mortal* (serious) sin go to hell, while those who live as "saints" go to heaven. Most Catholics supposedly end up in purgatory, which gets its name from the verb *purge*, to purify or cleanse. Their belief is that temporary suffering in purgatory's fires purge souls of guilt for their *venial* (not so serious) sins. However, Rome also teaches that those still living can aid the dead in purgatory by way of prayers, alms, fasting, indulgences, and masses conducted on their behalf. Catholics believe that such good deeds done on the earth can reduce the amount of suffering those in purgatory must endure. However, since the amount of suffering required and the amount of suffering alleviated are never clearly defined, loved ones continue these activities for as long as their concern motivates them. At the end of the world, so the belief goes, purgatory comes to an end, and those who have had their sins purged through suffering are welcomed into eternal heaven.

Although no one likes the idea of suffering in purgatory, the doctrine is comforting because it offers an escape from eternal hell. "Well, yes," a believer in this doctrine says to himself, "I will suffer in purgatory for a while, but there is suffering in this life, too. The important thing is that I will escape eternal suffering." Consciously or unconsciously, one who believes in the existence of purgatory does not have to be too preoccupied with his or her life on earth because, in the end, everything will turn out all right.

The Bible nowhere mentions purgatory. On the contrary, Jesus' account of a rich man and Lazarus proves this theory to be false. The rich man died and was in torment; Lazarus died and was at peace. Then the text explains:

> Between us and you there is a great gulf fixed, so that those who want to pass from here to you cannot, nor can those from there pass to us (Luke 16:26).

At death, there is a place of torment and a place of bliss.

Between the two is an impassible gulf. All Scripture agrees with this. God's Word speaks of only two alternatives that occur at death or when Jesus comes: a person is lost or saved, a person goes to torment or rest:

> Wide is the gate and broad is the way that leads to destruction, and there are many who go in by it. Because narrow is the gate and difficult is the way which leads to life, and there are few who find it (Matt. 7:13-14).

Scripture knows of no in-between place for those who are neither very evil nor very good. According to the Word of the Creator, there is no second chance after death; rather, at death a person's destiny is sealed for torment or bliss—eternally.

Protestant Purgatory

Strange as it may seem, evangelical futurism also offers a second chance for salvation—not after death but after Jesus' return. According to the Rapture doctrine, those who are left behind have a second chance to receive Christ. The hope that futurism offers is escape from the Great Tribulation. However, at the same time, futurism leaves the door of salvation wide open for those who are left behind. With this in view, the Great Tribulation is rather like a shortened Protestant purgatory—if you do not accept Jesus before the Rapture, you can still be saved, but you will have to pass through a lot of terrible suffering in the process.

Such teaching allows a person who doubts the truth of the Rapture doctrine to decide: "I will wait to see what happens. If the Rapture takes place, I will know that futurism is true, and then I will have my chance to get right with God. Yes, I will have to suffer some, but it will be in exciting times and everything will come out all right in the end." Listen to Tim LaHaye admit this problem: "I have heard unthinking people make such statements as, 'I am going to wait until the Tribulation to receive Christ.'"[1] Well, why not? Are such people really unthinking, or are they waiting for proof that futurism's Rapture doctrine is true? It would seem the Rapture doctrine is giving them comfort in postponing a decision to get right with God.

Futurism's offer of hope for a second chance after the Rapture is more than just a passing, minor issue. Listen to Mark Hitchcock:

> The Rapture may turn out to be the greatest evangelistic event of all time. Millions of people who have heard about the Rapture but never received Christ will suddenly realize that everything they'd been told was true.[2]

It is not just the Rapture that is viewed as a great evangelistic event offering a second chance; so is the Tribulation:

> In fact, the salvation of the lost seems to be one of the chief purposes of the tribulation period . . . God will use the horror of the tribulation period to bring millions of sinners to faith in His Son. There will be great revival . . . there will certainly be some who have been given a second opportunity.[3]

Tim LaHaye agrees:

> There is to be a great soul harvest, maybe a billion or more people, coming to Christ.[4]

> Revelation 7:9 indicates that during the first part of Tribulation the greatest soul harvest in all history will take place. In fact, it is this writer's belief that more people will accept Christ during the early months of the Tribulation, before the Antichrist really has a chance to consolidate his one-world government and set up his one-world religion of self-worship (Rev. 13:5-7), than have been converted in the nearly two thousand years of the Church Age.[5]

Did you catch what he is saying? He is saying that in less than seven years ("the early months of the Tribulation"), there will be more people converted to Christ than have been converted in the past two thousand years! He is saying that once Jesus removes His church from the earth via the Rapture, His work will really be able to go forward!

Second Chances

Will Jesus' return for His church be a great evangelistic opportunity, or will it be the *end* of all opportunity? Will Jesus' return usher in exciting days for this world, or will Jesus' return bring the *end* of this world? Will the Rapture and the Great Tribulation be God's final call to me, or is the gospel in the Bible already His final call to me? These are not just interesting prophecy questions. These are questions of life and death—eternal life and the second death. We cannot depend upon prophecy novels to give us the answers. We must turn to the Word of God.

Of course, many people receive a second chance in *this life* to yield their lives to Christ. Indeed, most people have numerous opportunities. Thus, the term "second chance" by itself does not express the issue. The issue is whether there is another chance to give one's life to Christ after death or after Christ's return. In the case of reincarnation and purgatory, at issue is the idea that death does not place a seal on our final destiny. In the case of the "Left Behind" scenario, at issue is the idea that Jesus' return does not place a seal on our final destiny.

The proposition of this book, *Nobody Left Behind,* is that while all the second-chance doctrines offer people a false hope, the truth according to the Bible is that when Jesus returns, the world will end, physical life will be no more, opportunity to get right with God will be no more, and time will be no more—no seven years, no thousand years, no time at all. Eternity will have arrived. The proposition of *Nobody Left Behind* is that Jesus will come again only one second time.

The concept behind the term "nobody left behind" must be understood. It does not mean that everyone in the world will be raptured. Neither does it mean that when the church is raptured, the wicked will be annihilated. Rather, "nobody left behind" is just one way of expressing the truth that nobody will be left on this earth after the momentous events connected with Jesus' return. He is coming to judge both the living and the dead. He is coming to receive some into eternal life and cast others into eternal damnation. Everyone will face Him. All opportunity for conversion will be terminated. This life, this world, time itself will be no more. There will be no last-minute opportunities to get right with God.

Futurism's Timetable Not in Scripture

The futurist view is far more than a teaching that Jesus is coming again. Futurism presents a complex timetable of events and places the fulfillment of most biblical prophecy into our future. It declares two more comings of Jesus, several resurrections, separate bodies of saved individuals, several judgments, and two rebuilt Jewish temples.

Futurism notices Bible texts that express different aspects of Jesus' second coming. It claims the differences can only be harmonized by theorizing two future comings. However, no Scripture teaches two future comings; neither do different aspects require two comings. For example, the Word teaches that Jesus' return will be both a joyous event and an event to fear. This in no way indicates two comings; rather, it indicates there will be two classes of people on earth when He comes. For the saved, it will be a time of joy; for the lost, it will be a time of doom.

In addition to pitting one text against another, futurism reads ideas that are not there into many texts, and it connects texts that have no relationship to one another. The truth is that the timetable presented by futurism can nowhere be found in Scripture. Consider the following admission by Hal Lindsey, the most influential futurist writer before the "Left Behind" series was written:

Gundry [a post-tribulationist] objects to this scenario. He

makes a big point of the fact that the Scriptures nowhere mention a resurrection of the Church prior to the Tribulation. But then the Scriptures nowhere specifically mention the resurrection of the Church at the middle or end of the Tribulation either.[6]

Lindsey admits Gundry's "big point," adds to it, then reaches this conclusion: Scripture nowhere specifically mentions a resurrection of the church (Rapture) prior to, in the middle of, or at the end of the Tribulation! This is amazing! In spite of all the sermons preached, books written, and charts published, futurism's end-time timetable does not exist in Scripture—neither in the relationship between the Rapture and the Tribulation, as admitted here, nor in many other vital points discussed earlier in *Nobody Left Behind*. To express it in the kindest terms possible, the futurist timetable is a man-made unproven theory. It is an invented timetable utilizing many prophecies that have already been powerfully fulfilled, as has already been demonstrated in *Nobody Left Behind*. With the fall of the futurist timetable, the theory of two future comings of Christ also falls. No Scripture offers their timetable or any reference to two future comings.

The End is the End

Jesus did not say, "As it was in the days of Enoch or Elijah . . ." Jesus said, "As it was in the days Noah . . . as it was also in the days of Lot . . ." (Luke 17:26, 28). When Enoch was raptured to heaven, the world *did* continue. When Elijah was raptured to heaven, the world *did* continue. However, when Lot escaped from Sodom, all those left behind were burned alive. When Noah escaped into the ark, all those left outside the ark drowned. Jesus never compared His return to the days of Enoch or Elijah but rather to the days of Lot and Noah.

There is no verse of Scripture that even hints at normal life on this planet after Jesus returns, whether His return is called the Rapture or the Second Coming. The plane crashes, babies disappearing, etc. are all fables, nowhere hinted at in Scripture. Rather Scripture teaches that when Jesus returns, it will be the end.

JESUS IS COMING . . .

Once we recognize that Scripture teaches only one second coming, we are ready to examine the many texts that speak of this momentous event. This does not mean that Scripture gives us a detailed account or that we will be able to construct a timetable of all the elements involved. We must beware of the temptation to expound on what we do not know. "The secret things belong to the LORD our God, but those things which are revealed belong to us" (Deut. 29:29).

Many texts deal with events related to Jesus' return. However, in order to help clarify the issue, in this study only texts that directly mention His return will be quoted. In nearly all instances, some form of the verb "come" is used. The aim is to gain an insight into what events and characteristics the Scriptures connect to Jesus' second coming. In A.D. 30, as Jesus ascended,

> a cloud received Him out of their sight. And while they looked steadfastly toward heaven as He went up, behold, two men stood by them in white apparel, who also said, "Men of Galilee, why do you stand gazing up into heaven? This same Jesus, who was taken up from you into heaven, will so come in like manner as you saw Him go into heaven" (Acts 1: 9-11).

Years after Jesus' ascension, the Holy Spirit declared:

> We should live soberly, righteously, and godly in the present age, looking for the blessed hope and glorious appearing of our great God and Savior Jesus Christ (Titus 2:12-13).

> Christ was offered once to bear the sins of many. To those who eagerly wait for Him He will appear a second time, apart from sin, for salvation (Heb. 9:28).

Jesus is coming a second time! Let us now see what His coming will be like.

. . . Coming Visibly to All

Jesus' coming will be observed by all:

> Behold, He is coming with clouds, and every eye will see Him, even they who pierced Him. And all the tribes of the earth will mourn because of Him. Even so, Amen (Rev. 1:7).

Even the wicked will understand what is happening; therefore, they will mourn. In fact, Jesus himself categorized any news report of His coming as a proof that He has not yet come. Any explanation that He has come is automatically proof that He has not come. When He does come, everyone will know it; no one will need explanations. Listen to the Master:

> Then if anyone says to you, "Look, here is the Christ!" or "There!" do not believe it . . . if they say to you, "Look, He is in the desert!" do not go out; or "Look, He is in the inner rooms!" do not believe it. For as the lightning comes from the east and flashes to the west, so also will the coming of the Son of Man be . . . then all the tribes of the earth will mourn, and they will see the Son of Man coming on the clouds of heaven (Matt. 24:23, 26-27, 30).

. . . Coming in Glory and Power

Continuing with the previous text, Jesus says His second coming will be with power and glory. It will be in great contrast to His first coming, when He came humbly as a carpenter to be abused by His own people:

> They will see the Son of Man coming on the clouds of heaven with power and great glory (Matt. 24:30).

> The Son of Man . . . when He comes in the glory of His Father with the holy angels (Mark 8:38).

For the Son of Man will come in the glory of His Father with His angels (Matt. 16:27).

. . . Coming to Raise the Dead

Since by man came death, by Man also came the resurrection of the dead. For as in Adam all die, even so in Christ all shall be made alive. But each one in his own order: Christ the firstfruits, afterward those who are Christ's at His coming. Then comes the end, when He delivers the kingdom to God the Father (1 Cor. 15:21-24).

For this we say to you by the word of the Lord, that we who are alive and remain until the coming of the Lord will by no means precede those who are asleep. For the Lord Himself will descend from heaven with a shout, with the voice of an archangel, and with the trumpet of God. And the dead in Christ will rise first. Then we who are alive and remain shall be caught up together with them in the clouds to meet the Lord in the air. And thus we shall always be with the Lord (1 Thess. 4:15-17).

Whether good or evil, we all die because of Adam. In like manner, we all shall be raised from the dead because of Christ. Those who are alive when Jesus returns will have no advantage over those who are dead. In fact, the dead saints will be raised before anyone is caught up to be with the Lord.

. . . Coming to Judge the World

Jesus' coming will bring blessing and cursing, hope and dread, promise and punishment. It will be wonderful and terrible. How will it be both at the same time? Because He is coming to judge and reward us all according to the lives we have lived:

For the Son of Man will come in the glory of His Father with His angels, and then He will reward each according to his works (Matt. 16: 27).

An outstanding account of Jesus' return to judge all

mankind is found in Matthew 25:

> When the Son of Man comes in His glory, and all the holy an-
> gels with Him, then He will sit on the throne of His glory. All
> the nations will be gathered before Him, and He will separate
> them one from another, as a shepherd divides his sheep from
> the goats . . . Then the King will say to those on His right hand,
> "Come, you blessed of My Father, inherit the kingdom prepared
> for you from the foundation of the world . . . inasmuch as you
> did it to one of the least of these My brethren, you did it to Me."
> Then He will also say to those on the left hand, "Depart from
> Me, you cursed, into the everlasting fire prepared for the devil
> and his angels" (Matt. 25:31-32, 34, 40-41).

Jesus is coming with glory and with the angels. It will be judgment day! He will sit on a throne with all the nations gathered before Him, and He will separate them into two groups. Jesus indicates that one basis for judgment will be how we have treated His brethren. Other Scriptures teach that these are spiritual brethren and not physical ones. During His ministry, Jesus made it abundantly clear that physical relationship to Him did not result in special favors, whether it be for His mother or brothers:

> And a multitude was sitting around Him; and they said to Him,
> "Look, Your mother and Your brothers are outside seeking
> You." But He answered them, saying, "Who is My mother, or
> My brothers?" And He looked around in a circle at those who
> sat about Him, and said, "Here are My mother and My broth-
> ers! For whoever does the will of God is My brother and My sis-
> ter and mother" (Mark 3:32-35).

Our judgment and eternal destiny are based in part on our behavior toward Jesus' brothers, sisters, and mothers—those who do the will of God. Jesus further says that He will come to judge us according to what we have done with what He has entrusted unto us:

> For the kingdom of heaven is like a man traveling to a far

country, who called his own servants and delivered his goods to them . . . After a long time the lord of those servants came and settled accounts with them (Matt. 25:14, 19).

Behold, the Lord comes with ten thousands of His saints, to execute judgment on all, to convict all who are ungodly among them of all their ungodly deeds which they have committed in an ungodly way, and of all the harsh things which ungodly sinners have spoken against Him (Jude 14-15).

Judgment involves a divine decision that results in exoneration or punishment. Therefore, the texts cited speak of both results. The texts in the following two sections are closely related to judgment but focus more on the results than on the judgment itself.

. . . Coming to Punish the Wicked

In Paul's second epistle to the Thessalonians, he presents many truths related to the coming of the Lord, including the punishment of the wicked in general and the punishment of the man of sin in particular:

When the Lord Jesus is revealed from heaven with His mighty angels, in flaming fire taking vengeance on those who do not know God, and on those who do not obey the gospel of our Lord Jesus Christ. These shall be punished with everlasting destruction from the presence of the Lord and from the glory of His power, when He comes, in that Day, to be glorified in His saints and to be admired among all those who believe . . . Now, brethren, concerning the coming of our Lord Jesus Christ and our gathering together to Him . . . Let no one deceive you by any means; for that Day will not come unless the falling away comes first, and the man of sin is revealed . . . whom the Lord will consume with the breath of His mouth and destroy with the brightness of His coming (2 Thess. 1:7 to 2:8).

One of the clearest things in prophecy is Paul's teaching in 2 Thessalonians 2. Read it again for yourself to see if the following is a true paraphrase of the text partially quoted above: Jesus is coming to eternally punish the wicked at the same time He glorifies His saints. His coming would not be immediate, because the apostasy and man of sin had to come first. In fact, when Jesus does come, the man of sin will be destroyed.

. . . Coming to Receive the Saved into Heaven

The Holy Spirit says in Eph. 4:4 that Christians have "one hope." That blessed hope is a heavenly hope connected to Jesus' return:

> They will see the Son of Man coming on the clouds of heaven with power and great glory. And He will send His angels with a great sound of a trumpet, and they will gather together His elect from the four winds, from one end of heaven to the other (Matt. 24:30-31).

> Let not your heart be troubled; you believe in God, believe also in Me. In My Father's house are many mansions; if it were not so, I would have told you. I go to prepare a place for you. And if I go and prepare a place for you, I will come again and receive you to Myself; that where I am, there you may be also (John 14:1-3).

> For our citizenship is in heaven, from which we also eagerly wait for the Savior, the Lord Jesus Christ, who will transform our lowly body that it may be conformed to His glorious body, according to the working by which He is able even to subdue all things to Himself (Phil. 3:20-21).

. . . Coming to Destroy the Earth

> Heaven and earth will pass away, but My words will by no means pass away. But of that day and hour no one knows, not even the angels of heaven, but My Father only. But as the days of Noah were, so also will the coming of the Son of Man be. For as in the days before the flood, they were eating and drinking, marrying and giving in marriage, until the day that Noah entered the ark, and did not know until the flood came and took

them all away, so also will the coming of the Son of Man be (Matt. 24:35-39).

The Son of Man himself uttered these exciting words. Here are some of the vital truths He expressed:
1. This earth will one day be destroyed.
2. No one knows when it will happen.
3. It will be similar to the days of Noah.
4. It will take place when Jesus comes again.
5. Life on the earth will be normal up to that time.
6. The end will come unexpectedly.
7. The wicked will be taken away without a second chance.

Many years after Jesus' ascension, the inspired apostle Peter wrote about the same events:

> Scoffers will come in the last days, walking according to their own lusts, and saying, "Where is the promise of His coming?" . . . This they willfully forget . . . the world that then existed perished, being flooded with water. But the heavens and the earth which are now preserved by the same word, are reserved for fire until the day of judgment and perdition of ungodly men . . . The day of the Lord will come as a thief in the night, in which the heavens will pass away with a great noise, and the elements will melt with fervent heat; both the earth and the works that are in it will be burned up . . . Nevertheless we, according to His promise, look for new heavens and a new earth in which righteousness dwells (2 Pet. 3:3-7, 10, 13).

Peter's inspired words help us understand many things related to Jesus' second coming:
1. Unbelievers, living in lust, ridicule Jesus' next coming.
2. They also willfully ignore the evidence of a worldwide flood.
3. The world that existed in Noah's time perished.
4. The same God who once destroyed the earth with a flood is preparing to destroy it a second time with fire.
5. The destruction of the earth will *not* be man's doing. It will happen "by the same word" that flooded the world in

Noah's time; it will be "the day of the Lord."

6. No one knows when it will happen.

7. The end will come unexpectedly like the coming of a thief.

8. Not only the earth but also the heavens will be dissolved.

9. It will be a time of judgment and perdition for the wicked; no second chance is mentioned.

10. It will be the beginning of new heavens and a new earth for the righteous.

Both Jesus and Peter declare important parallels between the flood of Noah and the coming of Jesus. Both happen unexpectedly. Both bring an end to the world then in existence. Both eliminate any possibility of a second chance.

As man's knowledge increases, so does his ability to inflict pain and death. Is the day soon coming when someone will "push the button" to destroy civilization? Is man headed for inevitable self-destruction?

Not at all! Man did not create himself; nor will he destroy himself. No third world war or any human action will bring this world to an end. Not even overpopulation or global warming. The end of this world will not be "the day of man." It will be "the day of the Lord," the day of "the coming of the Son of Man"! Lest someone thinks the text sounds like it might be talking about a man-made nuclear war, note that the heavens will also pass away. The Judge of all is going to end both the earth and the heavens by His own power when He is ready to do it. He does not require our help. What He requires is that we be ready to meet Him.

. . . Coming to Usher in Eternity

A portion of the text in Matthew 25 concerning judgment was quoted previously. This chapter also tells us that His coming and the judgment usher in eternity. Jesus comes, He judges the nations, and all of us enter into eternity.

When the Son of Man comes in His glory, and all the holy angels with Him, then He will sit on the throne of His glory. All the nations will be gathered before Him, and He will separate them ... And these will go away into everlasting punishment, but the righteous into eternal life (Matt. 25:31-32, 46).

... Coming Without Warning

Jesus is coming like a thief. This does not mean He is coming secretly. This concept in Scripture is always explained as coming without advance warning, coming unexpectedly:

Blessed are those servants whom the master, when he comes, will find watching ... if he should come in the second watch, or come in the third watch, and find them so, blessed are those servants. But know this, that if the master of the house had known what hour the thief would come, he would have watched and not allowed his house to be broken into. Therefore you also be ready, for the Son of Man is coming at an hour you do not expect (Luke 12:37-40).

Jesus warns us to be ready and to watch. We do not watch by searching the sky for Him. We do not watch by looking for signs. We watch by paying close attention to the spiritual battle we are fighting. After agonizing in prayer for a while in the Garden of Gethsemane, Jesus found the disciples sleeping. He asked,

What? Could you not watch with Me one hour? Watch and pray, lest you enter into temptation. The spirit indeed is willing, but the flesh is weak (Matt. 26:40-41).

When the authorities arrived to arrest Jesus, Peter bravely unsheathed and wielded his sword. However, within hours he demonstrated how weak his flesh was. When questioned by a simple servant girl about his relationship to Jesus, Peter denied even knowing Him.

Like Samson and many of us, Peter was strong for the physical battle but turned coward during the spiritual battle. Jesus had even forewarned Peter that this would happen, but Peter was self-confident. For this reason, he did not bother to watch in prayer in order to resist the coming temptation. We do not watch for Jesus' coming by looking heavenward with physical eyes. Nor do we watch by drawing the sword against the enemies of God. Rather, we watch by being alert to personal spiritual dangers. We watch by being true to Jesus in every situation, by being spiritually ready for His return.

. . . Coming to Shut the Door

When Noah and his family entered the ark, "the Lord shut him in" (Gen. 7:16). Just as God shut the door then, so the door to heaven will be shut when Jesus comes:

> The kingdom of heaven shall be likened to ten virgins who took their lamps and went out to meet the bridegroom . . . at midnight a cry was heard: "Behold, the bridegroom is coming" . . . And the foolish said . . . "Our lamps are going out" . . . while they went to buy, the bridegroom came . . . and the door was shut. Afterward the other virgins came also, saying, "Lord, Lord, open to us!" But he answered and said, "Assuredly, I say to you, I do not know you." Watch therefore, for you know neither the day nor the hour in which the Son of Man is coming (Matt. 25:1, 6, 8, 10-13).

The door was shut. The issue is *not* if we are prepared for the next terrorist attack. It is *not* if we are prepared for the collapse of civilization due to overpollution, overpopulation, and overproduction. The issue is whether we are prepared to meet our God (Amos 4:12). The issue is whether we are prepared for Jesus' coming and prepared for our own death, whichever may happen first. The issue is whether we are prepared for the judgment and for eternity.

The message of the parable of the ten virgins is not so much to *get* ready as it is to *stay* ready. The problem of the five foolish virgins was that "the bridegroom was delayed" (Matt. 25:5). The five foolish virgins had sufficient oil for the short haul. However, they were not prepared for the long haul. They did not have what it took to keep on keeping on. The message of the ten virgins is not to get ready for Jesus' coming in the year 2004 only to slack off when He fails to come. The message is to get ready and always stay ready no matter how much longer He delays His coming.

The message of this parable is also that "the door was shut." When Jesus returns, it is all over—no last-hour repentance, no last-minute plea, and no time to reflect and change. "The door was shut" has a ring of finality about it. When Jesus comes, time ends and eternity begins. No chance for reincarnation, no chance for purgatory, no chance to become a Tribulation saint, no chance for anything. It will be judgment time. Dead or alive we will all stand before the Judge for Him to declare our eternal destiny. Our opportunities to choose will suddenly and irrevocably cease. The door will be shut.

Are You Ready?

One day a couple of Christian ladies indicated they were not much interested in prophecy. Rather, they were interested in the practical aspects of the Christian life. Is prophecy practical or not? Several replies can be given to this question. Among other things, prophecy is practical because it motivates us to live holy lives in preparation for eternity. Listen to the inspired apostle:

> Scoffers will come in the last days, walking according to their own lusts, and saying, "Where is the promise of His coming?" . . . But the day of the Lord will come as a thief in the night, in which the heavens will pass away with a great noise . . . since all these things will be dissolved, what manner of persons ought you to be in holy conduct and godliness (2 Pet. 3:3-4, 10-11).

Those who scoff at the unfulfilled prediction of Jesus' return do so to ease their consciences while they live in lust. On the other hand, those who heed prophecies of the end are motivated to live holy lives. This sounds very practical in the midst of our pleasure-loving society.

JESUS IS COMING . . .

   . . . Coming Visibly to All
      . . . Coming in Glory and Power
         . . . Coming to Raise the Dead
            . . . Coming to Judge the World
               . . . Coming to Punish the Wicked
                  . . . Coming to Receive the Saved into Heaven
                     . . . Coming to Destroy the Earth
                        . . . Coming to Usher in Eternity
                           . . . Coming Without Warning
                              . . . Coming to Shut the Door

Are You Ready?

Here is an old proverb by an unknown author that has touched many souls:

Only one life, 'twill soon be past;
Only what's done for Christ will last.

Only one life. Only one death. Only one return of Christ. Only one opportunity to get right with God—now, in this life, before death or before Jesus returns.

The Holy Spirit says:
"Today, if you will hear His voice,
Do not harden your hearts" (Heb. 3:7-8).

Today, while there is time. "You also be ready, for the Son of Man is coming at an hour you do not expect" (Matt. 24:44). When He comes, time will be no more.

Notes

Chapter 2—Introducing the Issues

1. Tim LaHaye, *Revelation Unveiled* (Grand Rapids: Zondervan, 1999), 132-140.
2. Ibid., 331.
3. Ibid., 211.
4. Hal Lindsey, *The Late Great Planet Earth* (New York: Bantam Books, 1973), 83.
5. LaHaye, *Revelation,* 215-216.
6. Ibid., 148.
7. Ibid., 151-57.
8. Tim LaHaye and Jerry Jenkins, *Left Behind, A Novel of the Earth's Last Days,* #1 of the "Left Behind" series (Wheaton, Ill.: Tyndale House, 1995), 215.

Chapter 3—Prophecy: Literal or Figurative?

1. Tim LaHaye, *Revelation Unveiled* (Grand Rapids: Zondervan, 1999), 331.
2. Ibid., pages given in text.
3. Ibid., 17.
4. *Funk & Wagnalls Standard Dictionary,* "star."
5. LaHaye, *Revelation,* 265.

Chapter 4—Which Tribulation?

1. Word counts in this chapter are based on the New King James Version. Other versions may vary.
2. Hal Lindsey, *The Rapture: Truth or Consequences* (New York: Bantam Books, 1985), 36-37.
3. John F. Walvoord, *Every Prophecy of the Bible* (Colorado Springs: Chariot Victor Publishing, 1999), 544.
4. *Webster's Seventh New Collegiate Dictionary,* "tribulation."
5. Ralph Kinney Bennett, "The Global War on Christians," *Reader's Digest* (August, 1997): 51.

Chapter 7—"Not One Stone upon Another"

1. Flavius Josephus, *A History of the Jewish Wars* (trans. William Whiston), 6.2.4.
2. Ibid., 6.6.2.
3. Ibid., 7.1.1.
4. Ibid., 5.9.4.
5. Thomas Newton, *Dissertations on the Prophecies,* revised by W. S. Dobson (Philadelphia: J. J. Woodward, 1838), 384.

Chapter 8—Three Great Tribulations

1. Chrysostom, *Homilies on the Gospel of St. Matthew,* in vol. 10, *The Nicene and Post-Nicene Fathers: First Series,* 76.1.8-9.
2. Flavius Josephus, *A History of the Jewish Wars* (trans. William Whiston), 5.1.3.
3. Ibid., preface.4.
4. Philip Schaff, *Ante-Nicene Christianity,* vol. 2 of *History of the Christian Church,* second edition (Edinburgh: T. & T. Clark, 1884), 64-68 (II.24.2, 6, 8).

Chapter 9—Did God Stop the Prophetic Clock?

1. Hal Lindsey, *The Rapture: Truth or Consequences* (New York: Bantam Books, paperback edition, 1985), 3-4.
2. Ibid., 184.
3. Ibid., 1-2.
4. Tim LaHaye, *Revelation Unveiled* (Grand Rapids: Zondervan, 1999), 140.
5. Tim LaHaye and Jerry Jenkins, *Tribulation Force,* "Left Behind" #2 (Wheaton, Ill.: Tyndale House, 1996), 29.

Chapter 10—Why Rome?

1. Hippolytus, *Treatise on Christ and Antichrist,* in vol. 5, *The Ante-Nicene Fathers,* par. 28.
2. Thomas Newton, *Dissertations on the Prophecies,* revised by W. S. Dobson (Philadelphia: J. J. Woodward, 1838), 192.
3. Irenaeus, *Against Heresies,* in vol. 1, *The Ante-Nicene Fathers,* 5.26.1.
4. Hippolytus, *Treatise,* par. 28.

Chapter 12—Man of Sin–the History

1. Thomas Newton, *Dissertations on the Prophecies,* revised by W. S. Dobson (Philadelphia: J. J. Woodward, 1838), 400.
2. Irenaeus, *Against Heresies,* in vol. 1, *The Ante-Nicene Fathers,* 5.25.3.
3. Ibid., 5.26.1.
4. Tertullian, *On the Resurrection of the Flesh,* in vol. 3, *The Ante-Nicene Fathers,* chap. 24.
5. Hippolytus, *Treatise on Christ and Antichrist,* in vol. 5, *The Ante-Nicene Fathers,* par. 28.
6. Cyril, *Lecture 15,* in vol. 7, *The Nicene and Post-Nicene Fathers: Second Series,* par. 9.
7. Ibid., par. 12.
8. Ibid., par. 15.
9. Chrysostom, *Homilies on Second Thessalonians, Homily 4: 2 Thess. 2:6-9,* in vol. 13, *The Nicene and Post-Nicene Fathers: First Series,* par. 1.
10. Ibid., par. 2.
11. Jerome, *Letter #60 to Heliodorus,* in vol. 6, *The Nicene and Post-Nicene Fathers: Second Series,* par. 16-17.

12. Jerome, *Letter #123 to Ageruchia,* in vol. 6, *The Nicene and Post-Nicene Fathers: Second Series,* par. 16-17.
13. Augustine, *City of God,* in vol. 2, *The Nicene and Post-Nicene Fathers: First Series,* 20.19.1-3.
14. Gary DeMar, *Last Days Madness, Obsession of the Modern Church* (Atlanta: American Vision, 1994), 207-8.
15. Ibid., 330.
16. Dave Hunt, *Global Peace and the Rise of Antichrist* (Eugene, Ore.: Harvest House Publishers, 1990), 108.
17. Ibid., 136.
18. Tim LaHaye, *Revelation Unveiled* (Grand Rapids: Zondervan, 1999), 269.
19. Tim LaHaye and Jerry Jenkins, *Tribulation Force,* "Left Behind" #2 (Wheaton, Ill.: Tyndale House, 1996), 401.
20. Ibid., 53.

Chapter 14—666: the Mark of the Beast

1. *The American Heritage Dictionary of the English Language,* "dozen."
2. E. B. Elliott, *Horae Apocalypticae,* fifth edition, vol. 3 (London: Seeley, Jackson, and Halliday, 1862), 242.
3. Philip Schaff, *History of the Christian Church,* third edition, vol. 1 (reprint, Grand Rapids: Eerdmans, 1966), 847.
4. Albert Barnes, *Notes on the New Testament, Revelation* (reprint, Grand Rapids: Baker, 1949), 335.
5. E. B. Elliott, *Horae Apocalypticae,* vol. 3, 246.
6. Irenaeus, *Against Heresies,* in vol. 1, *The Ante-Nicene Fathers,* 5.30.1-4.
7. Ibid., 5.30.3.
8. John A. Hardon, *Modern Catholic Dictionary* (Garden City, N. Y.: Doubleday, 1980), 472.
9. Ibid., 141.
10. Felician A. Foy, editor, *1980 Catholic Almanac* (Huntington, Ind.: Our Sunday Visitor, 1979), 170-71.
11. Hardon, *Catholic Dictionary,* 280.
12. "Inquisition," *The Encyclopaedia Britannica,* Handy Volume Issue, eleventh edition, vol. XIV (New York: The Encyclopaedia Britannica Company, 1910), 587-596.
13. Ibid.
14. Mgr. Philip Hughes, *The Church in Crisis: A History of the General Councils: 325-1870,* with the *Imprimatur* of Cardinal Spellman (Internet: available on various Catholic sites, 1960, for example: http://65.108.168.229/Lateran%201179.htm), Chapter 11, "The Third General Council of the Lateran, 1179."
15. Tim LaHaye, *Revelation Unveiled* (Grand Rapids: Zondervan, 1999), 226.
16. Ibid., 236.

17. Ibid., 262.
18. Ibid., 272.

Chapter 15—The Rapture

1. *Webster's Encyclopedic Unabridged Dictionary of the English Language,* "rapture."
2. Tim LaHaye, *Revelation Unveiled* (Grand Rapids: Zondervan, 1999), 325-26.

Chapter 16—The Millennium Is Not . . .

1. *Webster's Seventh New Collegiate Dictionary,* "thousand."
2. *Webster's Encyclopedic Unabridged Dictionary of the English Language,* "thousand."
3. Norbert Lieth, "A Sure Answer to an Uncertain Question," *Midnight Call* (January, 1999): 30.

Chapter 17—Jesus Revealed the Nature of the Kingdom

1. Tim LaHaye, *Revelation Unveiled* (Grand Rapids: Zondervan, 1999), 265.

Chapter 18—The "Salvation Prayer"

1. Tim LaHaye and Jerry Jenkins, *Left Behind, A Novel of the Earth's Last Days,* #1 of the "Left Behind" series (Wheaton, Ill.: Tyndale House, 1995), 215.
2. *Disciple's Directory, 2000,* Kenneth and Nancy Dorothy, Publishers (Wilmington, Mass.: Disciple's Directory, Inc., 2000), 76.
3. Arthur DeMoss, *Power for Living, How to be Sure . . .,* a small tract (Garland, Tex.: American Tract Society, 1998).
4. Tim LaHaye, *Revelation Unveiled* (Grand Rapids: Zondervan, 1999), 359.
5. Ibid., 353-54.
6. Ibid., 266.

Chapter 19—Nobody Left Behind

1. Tim LaHaye, *Revelation Unveiled* (Grand Rapids: Zondervan, 1999), 226.
2. Mark Hitchcock, *101 Answers to the Most Asked Questions about the End Times* (Sisters, Ore.: Multnomah, 2001), 108.
3. Ibid., 110-11.
4. Tim LaHaye and Jerry Jenkins, *Tribulation Force,* "Left Behind" #2 (Wheaton, Ill.: Tyndale House, 1996), 30.
5. LaHaye, *Revelation,* 153.
6. Hal Lindsey, *The Rapture: Truth or Consequences* (New York: Bantam Books, 1985), 192-93.

Bibliography

Ancient Christian writings:

———— of Hippolytus, Irenaeus, and Tertullian are available in *The Ante-Nicene Fathers*. Edited by Alexander Roberts and James Donaldson. Reprint, Peabody, Mass.: Hendrickson, 1994. First published 1885.

———— of Augustine and Chrysostom are available in *The Nicene and Post-Nicene Fathers: First Series*. Edited by Philip Schaff. Reprint, Peabody, Mass.: Hendrickson, 1994. First published 1885.

———— of Cyril and Jerome are available in *The Nicene and Post-Nicene Fathers: Second Series*. Edited by Philip Schaff and Henry Wace. Reprint, Peabody, Mass.: Hendrickson, 1994. First published 1885.

- - - - - - - - - - -

Barnes, Albert. *Notes on the New Testament, Revelation*. Reprint, Grand Rapids: Baker, 1983. First published 1851.

————. *Notes on the Old Testament, Daniel*. 2 vols. Reprint, Grand Rapids: Baker, 1983. First published 1851.

Biederwolf, William Edward. *The Millennium Bible*. Reprint, Grand Rapids: Baker, 1964. First published 1924.

Boatman, Russell. *The End Time*. Joplin, Mo.: College Press, 1980.

DeMar, Gary. *Last Days Madness, Obsession of the Modern Church*. Atlanta: American Vision, 1994.

Elliott, E. B. *Horae Apocalypticae*. 5th ed. 4 vols. London: Seeley, Jackson, and Halliday, 1862.

Foy, Felician A., ed. *1980 Catholic Almanac*. Huntington, Ind.: Our Sunday Visitor, 1979.

Gregg, Steve, ed. *Revelation, Four Views: A Parallel Commentary*. Nashville: Thomas Nelson, 1997.

Halley, Henry H. *Halley's Bible Handbook*. 24th ed. Grand Rapids: Zondervan, 1965.

Hardon, John A. *Modern Catholic Dictionary*. Garden City, N.Y.: Doubleday, 1980.

Hinds, John T. *A Commentary on the Book of Revelation*. Nashville: Gospel Advocate, 1966. First published 1937.

Hitchcock, Mark. *101 Answers to the Most Asked Questions about the End Times*. Sisters, Ore.: Multnomah, 2001.

Hughes, Mgr. Philip. *The Church in Crisis: A History of the General Councils: 325-1870.* Chapter 11, "The Third General Council of the Lateran, 1179." 1960. Available online at http://65.108.168.229/Lateran%201179.htm

Hunt, Dave. *Global Peace and the Rise of Antichrist.* Eugene, Ore.: Harvest House, 1990.

Johnson, B. W. *A Vision of the Ages.* 6th ed. Dallas: Eugene S. Smith, publisher, n.d. First published 1881.

Josephus, Flavius. *A History of the Jewish Wars.* Translated by William Whiston, Reprint, Peabody, Mass.: Hendrickson, 1987. First published 1737.

LaHaye, Tim. *Revelation Unveiled.* Grand Rapids: Zondervan, 1999.

LaHaye, Tim and Jenkins, Jerry. *Left Behind, A Novel of the Earth's Last Days,* #1 of the "Left Behind" series. Wheaton, Ill.: Tyndale House, 1995.

———. *Tribulation Force,* #2 of the "Left Behind" series. Wheaton, Ill.: Tyndale House, 1996.

Lindsey, Hal. *The Late Great Planet Earth.* Bantam edition. New York: Bantam Books, 1973.

———. *The Rapture: Truth or Consequences.* Bantam paperback edition. New York: Bantam Books, 1985.

Miller, Fred P. *Revelation: A Panorama of the Gospel Age.* Revised edition. Clermont, Fla.: Moellerhaus Books, 1993.

Newton, Thomas. *Dissertations on the Prophecies,* revised by W. S. Dobson. Reprint, Philadelphia: J. J. Woodward, 1838.

Ryrie, Charles C. *The Basis of the Premillennial Faith.* Neptune, N.J.: Loizeaux Brothers, 1953.

Schaff, Philip. *History of the Christian Church.* 8 vols. Reprint, Peabody, Mass.: Hendrickson, 1985. First published 1858.

Tomlinson, Lee G. *The Wonder Book of the Bible.* Joplin, Mo: College Press, 1963.

Walvoord, John F. *Every Prophecy of the Bible.* Colorado Springs: Chariot Victor Publishing, 1999.

Woodrow, Ralph. *Great Prophecies of the Bible.* Riverside, Calif.: Ralph Woodrow Evangelistic Association, 1989.

Scripture Index

Subject Index

S